ACCESS ADVENTURE

The UK's best trails and outdoor activities by wheelchair and on foot

DEBBIE NORTH

CONWAY
LONDON · OXFORD · NEW YORK · NEW DELHI · SYDNEY

CONWAY
Bloomsbury Publishing Plc
50 Bedford Square, London, WC1B 3DP, UK
Bloomsbury Publishing Ireland Limited,
29 Earlsfort Terrace, Dublin 2, D02 AY28, Ireland

BLOOMSBURY, CONWAY and the Conway logo are trademarks of Bloomsbury Publishing Plc

First published in Great Britain 2026

Copyright © Debbie North, 2026

Debbi North has asserted her right under the Copyright, Designs and Patents Act, 1988, to be identified as Author of this work

For legal purposes the photo credits on p. 223 constitute an extension of this copyright page

This book is a guide for when you spend time outdoors. Undertaking any activity outdoors carries with it some risks that cannot be entirely eliminated. For example, you might get lost on a route or caught in bad weather. Before you spend time outdoors, we therefore advise that you always take the necessary precautions, such as checking weather forecasts and ensuring that you have all the equipment you need. Any walking routes that are described in this book should not be relied upon as a sole means of navigation, so we recommend that you refer to an Ordnance Survey map or authoritative equivalent.

This book may also reference businesses and venues. Whilst every effort is made by the author and the publisher to ensure the accuracy of the business and venue information contained in our books before they go to print, changes to such information can occur during the production and lifetime of a publication. Therefore, we also advise that you check with businesses or venues for the latest information before setting out.

All internet addresses given in this book were correct at the time of going to press. Bloomsbury Publishing Plc does not have any control over, or responsibility for, any third-party websites referred to or in this book. The author and the publisher regret any inconvenience caused if some facts have changed or sites have ceased to exist, but can accept no responsibility for any such changes.

All rights reserved. No part of this publication may be: i) reproduced or transmitted in any form, electronic or mechanical, including photocopying, recording or by means of any information storage or retrieval system without prior permission in writing from the publishers; or ii) used or reproduced in any way for the training, development or operation of artificial intelligence (AI) technologies, including generative AI technologies. The rights holders expressly reserve this publication from the text and data mining exception as per Article 4(3) of the Digital Single Market Directive (EU) 2019/790

Bloomsbury Publishing Plc does not have any control over, or responsibility for, any third-party websites referred to or in this book. All internet addresses given in this book were correct at the time of going to press. The author and publisher regret any inconvenience caused if addresses have changed or sites have ceased to exist, but can accept no responsibility for any such changes

A catalogue record for this book is available from the British Library

ISBN: PB: 978-1-8448-6724-0; eBook: 978-1-8448-6721-9; ePDF: 978-1-8448-6723-3; audio: 978-1-8448-6722-6

2 4 6 8 10 9 7 5 3 1

Designed by Nicola Liddiard
Printed and bound in China by RR Donnelley Asia Printing Solutions Limited

To find out more about our authors and books visit www.bloomsbury.com and sign up for our newsletters
For product safety related questions contact productsafety@bloomsbury.com

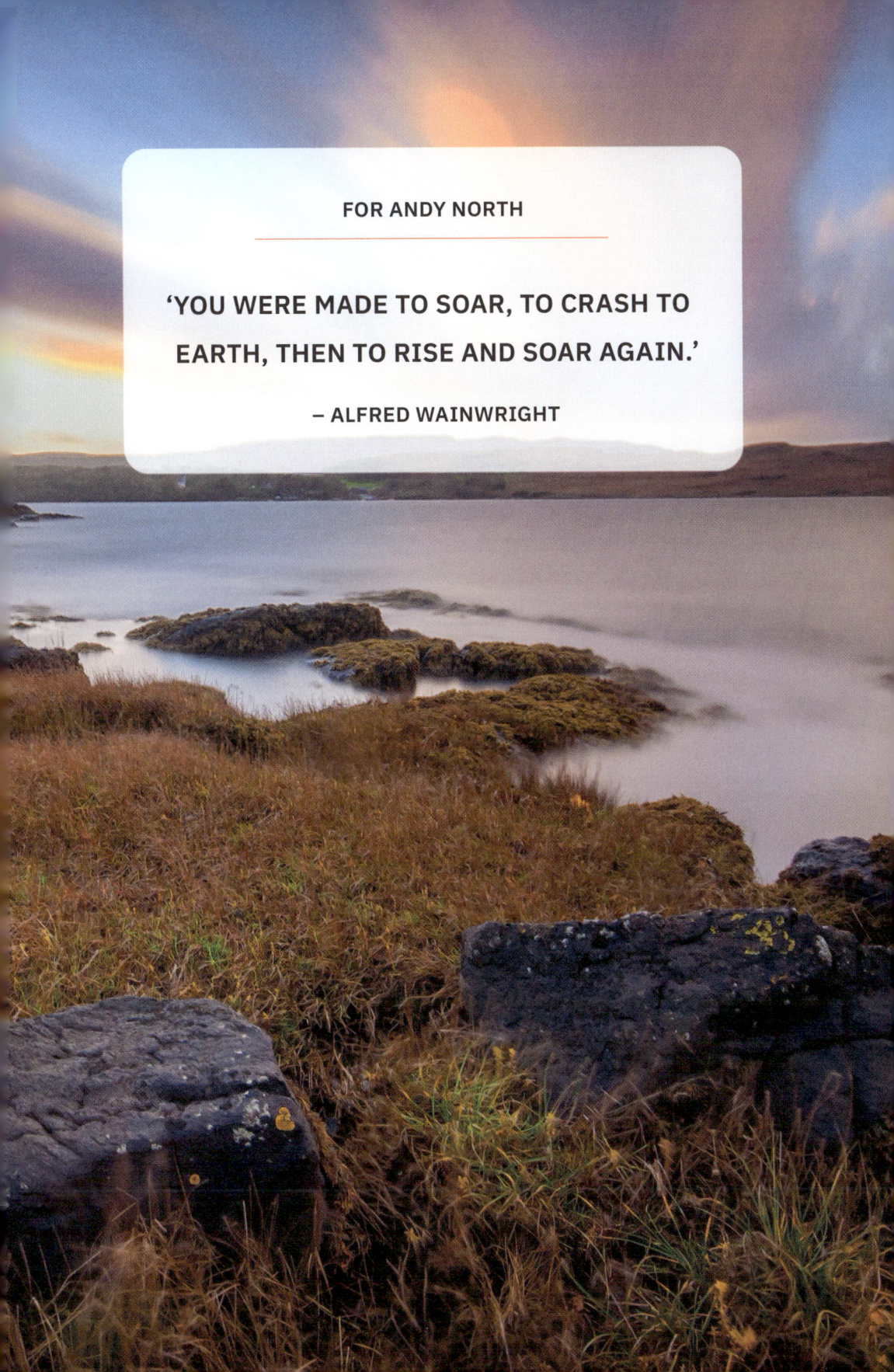

FOR ANDY NORTH

'YOU WERE MADE TO SOAR, TO CRASH TO EARTH, THEN TO RISE AND SOAR AGAIN.'

— ALFRED WAINWRIGHT

CONTENTS

Acknowledgements 6
About the author 7
Note from the author 7
Introduction 8
Miles without Stiles Grades 9

The *Watercut*, Mallerstang, Cumbria | DEBBIE NORTH 10
Sutton Bank, North York Moors National Park | SARA TOWERS 16
Threlkeld to Keswick, Lake District National Park | ARRON HART 24
Orrest Head, Lake District National Park | DAWN AND ALAN TOWART 30
Coniston to Tarn Hows Circular, Lake District National Park |
    ALEX STANIFORTH 36
Newborough National Nature Reserve and Forest, Anglesey |
    MIKE PALMER 42
Beacon Fell, Craig-y-nos Country Park, Bannau Brycheiniog
    National Park | KAREN HARRIS 50
The Wye Valley, Redbrook, Gloucester | BETHANY HANDLEY 58
Hergest Ridge, Herefordshire | MARIKA KOVACS 64
Leigh Woods, Abbots Leigh, Somerset | DEE CRUTE 70
Kings Wood, St Austell, Cornwall | PAT SMITH 77
River Otter Estuary, Budleigh Salterton, Devon | ISAAC KENYON 84
Ashdown Forest, East Sussex | ANITA KERWIN-NYE 90
Heartwood Forest, nr St Albans, Hertfordshire | EMMA HARRISON 96

Sutton Park, Sutton Coldfield, West Midlands | DARREN HARRIS 104

Stansted Park, Stoughton, West Sussex | STEPHANIE JANE QUINTRELL 112

Folkestone Warren, Kent | GINI MITCHELL 120

Millennium Quay, Portsmouth, Hampshire | PAULINE NIXON 126

Folkestone Coastal Path, Kent | TINA, CAS AND FREDDIE BUSH 134

Holmwood Common, Dorking, Surrey | GENNY BROWN 142

UFO Trail, Rendlesham Forest nr Woodbridge, Suffolk |
    NATASHA SONES 148

Sutton Hoo, Woodbridge, Suffolk | OZZY AND VICTORIA RAYNOR 156

Lady Canning's Plantation, Ringinglow, South Yorkshire |
    MAXWELL AYAMBA 164

Cullen to Portknockie, Moray | GEORGINA JACKSON 171

The Kelpies **to the Falkirk Wheel** | CHRIS BUTTERFIELD 177

Edinbane, Isle of Skye | SARAH LISTER 184

Beacon Fell, Goosnargh, Lancashire | SARAH DORNAN 190

Gisburn Forest, Ribble Valley, Lancashire | DECLAN FRASER-HIGGINS 198

Sprotbrough, Doncaster, South Yorkshire | ANDI WHITE 204

Nateby Fell, Yorkshire Dales National Park | ADAM MEDLOCK 212

Useful websites 220

Index 221

Photo credits 224

ACKNOWLEDGEMENTS

This book is the sum of countless footsteps and the kindness of many.

To everyone I met along my journey around the UK – thank you for welcoming me into your world, for sharing your favourite walks, and for entrusting me with your stories. Each tale and trail has left its mark on these pages and on me.

To all those who accompanied me on my tours, your companionship turned solitary paths into shared adventures. To those who stepped in when I found myself floundering, your generosity and patience steadied my way more than you know.

To my family – for enduring my long absences from family life, and my constant planning of 'just one more' adventure – thank you for letting me follow the pull of the path.

Special thanks to my late husband, Andy, who taught me the love of the written word and for encouraging me to seek out adventure.

This book is not simply my story. It is a tapestry woven from the voices, footsteps and kindness of all who joined me along the way.

THE ROLLING BEAUTY OF NATEBY FELL

ABOUT THE AUTHOR

Debbie North is a dedicated advocate for outdoor accessibility who, after being diagnosed with spinal degeneration in 2011, refused to let her condition stop her passion for fell walking. Alongside her late husband, Andy, she tackled challenging terrain using an all-terrain wheelchair, completing the iconic Coast to Coast Walk across the UK. Their journey inspired many and highlighted the possibilities for people with limited mobility to enjoy the outdoors.

Following Andy's passing, Debbie founded Access the Dales, a charity that provides all-terrain wheelchairs at key locations across Yorkshire and Lancashire, breaking down barriers to outdoor access. She is also a sought-after motivational speaker, consultant and writer, contributing to publications like Countryfile Magazine and appearing on national TV. As an ambassador for Ramblers UK, Ordnance Survey, and Disability and Access Ambassador for the Countryside, Debbie continues to champion inclusivity and inspire others to explore nature regardless of physical challenges.

NOTE FROM THE AUTHOR

There's something truly magical about stepping outside and feeling the rhythm of the land beneath your feet. Whether it's the crunch of gravel on a canal path or the quiet hush of woodland in early morning light, the outdoors offers something no screen or schedule can provide a sense of: space, stillness and connection.

This book is a celebration of that magic.

But more than that, this is a collection of beautiful stories: portraits of people whose lives have been changed, healed or uplifted by the simple act of walking. With warmth, insight and compassion, I share each journey in a way that feels both intimate and universal. These aren't just walks; they're windows into the resilience of the human spirit. What makes this book truly special is its accessibility. These are walks that welcome, not intimidate. They're designed for real people living real lives – gentle strolls that open doors to discovery, reflection and joy.

This is a book I hope you'll turn to time and time again, for inspiration, for comfort, or simply for the pleasure of reading something crafted with love. Whether you're planning your next walk or seeking a deeper connection with nature and people, these pages serve as both a guide and a companion.

Debbie North, July 2025

INTRODUCTION

Over the past twelve months, I have taken a journey across the UK, meeting people from all walks of life; ordinary folk with extraordinary stories. Each of them has used the outdoors as a way of facing, and often overcoming, the challenges and adversities life has placed before them. Behind every walk lies a story of resilience and determination.

These walks are as varied as the people themselves. They don't always lead to the highest peak or the summit of a famous mountain. But for each individual, their chosen path has been their own Everest – just as demanding, just as meaningful and just as transformative. Each route holds a special place in the hearts of those who shared their stories with me, and in turn, they have left their mark on me.

I am reminded of the words of actor, adventurer, and mountaineer Brian Blessed, whose booming voice and fearless spirit have long inspired explorers of all kinds: 'You can't call it an adventure unless it's tinged with danger. The greatest danger in life, though, is not taking the adventure at all. To have the objective of a life of ease is death. I think we've all got to go after our own Everest.'

This book is a celebration of those Everests – personal journeys that show us that adventure is not always about distance, height or record-breaking feats. It is about courage, connection and the determination to keep moving forward, one step at a time.

GOLDEN KELPIES AT THE HELIX, FALKIRK – A TRIBUTE TO SCOTLAND'S STRENGTH AND SPIRIT

MILES WITHOUT STILES GRADES

I have used the category 'Miles Without Stiles', as it was introduced by Natural England as a grading system and has since been adopted by many national parks, although it is not yet a statutory guideline. This is something I have actively campaigned for in my role as Disability and Access Ambassador, as I firmly believe that if all walks were graded under the 'Miles Without Stiles' system, information about wheelchair-accessible routes would become far more cohesive and accessible to everyone who wishes to wander the countryside.

Miles without Stiles routes are categorised into three grades: 'For All', 'For Many' and 'For Some'. The grades are determined by gradients and surface conditions. It is important to note that these grades are only a guide, so it is advisable to carefully consider your route choice.

FOR ALL
These routes are suitable for everyone, including those with pushchairs and individuals operating their own wheelchairs. The gradient of the paths does not exceed 1:10, and the surface is either tarmac or smooth, compacted stone with a diameter of 10mm (0.4in) or less. Additionally, the path width is a minimum of 1m (3.3ft) with passing places.

FOR MANY
These routes are suitable for assisted wheelchair users and families with more robust, all-terrain type buggies. The existing gradients on these paths do not exceed 1:10, although newly built gradients can be up to 1:8. The surface of these paths is rougher stone with a diameter of 1.6in (4cm) or less.

FOR SOME
These routes are suitable for strong and confident wheelchair users and their helpers. These paths may also be suitable for off-road mobility scooters. There are no limitations on gradients but slopes greater than 1:8 have improved surfacing or handrails. Additionally, there may be some low steps or breaks in the surface up to 10cm (3.9in) in height, and the stone surface material may be up to 10cm (3.9in) in diameter.

THE WATERCUT
MALLERSTANG, CUMBRIA

DEBBIE NORTH

My dad used to say I should have been born in a field.

Maybe he was right; I've never felt more alive than under an open sky, with the scent of fresh earth in my lungs and my feet tracing the rhythm of adventure across the dirt. As a child the outdoors made more sense to me than the confines of walls; indoors, everything felt too close, too still. But outside? There was freedom – unbounded, untamed and endlessly inviting.

I adore the way the world reshapes itself with each season. Spring brings renewal and possibility; summer, warmth and vibrancy. Autumn blazes in fiery reds and oranges before surrendering to winter's quiet stillness. The changing year is like an unfolding story, each chapter full of wonder and discovery.

There is no better place to watch the changing of the year than at the *Watercut*, a striking 2.2m (7.2ft) tall limestone sculpture designed by Mary Bourne. Standing tall and timeless at the head of the Mallerstang Valley, near Kirkby Stephen, Cumbria, this sculpture is at the heart of a walk that is captivating in every season. In spring, the calls of curlews echo through the crisp air, adding a touch of wild beauty to the landscape. Whether bathed in summer sunlight or softened by winter frost, the trail offers an ever-changing canvas.

This was the destination for my walk and a favourite of Andy's – a place where we created sharing memories.

As I followed the steady climb along a bridleway, from The Thrang, the panoramic views over the Eden Valley opened up in front of me. The sheer vastness of the space, where the river meanders below and the Settle–Carlisle railway line snakes through the landscape, hits you immediately.

As a young girl, I wasn't interested in what others my age were doing. I was out climbing trees, exploring riverbeds or building dens from fallen branches. Dinner often had to wait while I lost myself in the landscape, staying out until the sun began to set and the crickets performed their evening chorus.

In my teenage years, walking became something more. It wasn't just about getting somewhere. It became about the journey itself. Growing up in Sheffield, the Peak District was my backyard. I'd explore its hills on school trips or with family, savouring the hours spent walking deeper into its tranquillity. Walking was meditation in motion. The steady rhythm of footsteps quieted my thoughts and gave me space to simply be. That's when the passion took hold, an enduring love affair with the outdoors.

When I moved to Bradford and met Andy, everything changed again. He didn't just share my love of the outdoors, he expanded it. He introduced me to the rugged beauty of the Yorkshire Dales and the majestic peaks of the Lake District, where I discovered mountain walking. What began as a pastime became a need, a calling.

Andy and I walked for miles together, pushing ourselves to climb higher and to conquer new summits. What started as friendship, and a mutual love of adventure, deepened with every step we took. Walking has a way of changing you; slowly, quietly and often without you realising it.

THE MALLERSTANG VALLEY

THE *WATERCUT* | MALLERSTANG, CUMBRIA

In 1999, we tackled Alfred Wainwright's iconic Coast to Coast Walk. For many, it's a bucket-list achievement. For us, it became something more, a journey that marked the beginning of an extraordinary bond. By the end of that trek, we weren't just colleagues or friends anymore. Something deeper had taken root, a connection as inevitable as the pull of the tide.

When we walked the Coast to Coast again in 2003, it was different. We were closer, and every step together felt right. By the time we reached Robin Hood's Bay and the North Sea, Andy knelt – soaked, shivering and, exhausted – he proposed to me. He later joked that fatigue had forced his hand, but I knew better. That place, with its endless sky, sand, and sea, was exactly where our promise was meant to begin.

We married later that year, and the Coast to Coast Walk became a cornerstone of our story, woven into who we were as a couple.

But life, as unpredictable as the trails we loved, brought its own highs and lows. When my health declined, I needed to use a wheelchair. For a time, I was devastated. The black dog of depression was nipping at my heels. How could I explore the world I loved when my body wouldn't cooperate? But Andy wouldn't let me give up. With his support, I found a way. My all-terrain wheelchair, affectionately named 'Harriet', became my new legs.

DEBBIE AT THE *WATERCUT*
SCULPTURE ABOVE
MALLERSTANG VALLEY

In 2015, we set out on the Coast to Coast once again, Andy walking, me in Harriet. That journey marked a turning point. It showed me that life, despite its challenges, could still be lived fully. That's when my career as a writer and keynote speaker began, when I found a new purpose, helping others access the countryside, no matter their physical abilities.

Lost in my thoughts, I follow the track towards the *Watercut*. The path is straightforward and clear, requiring no navigation – just a steady walk along a well-worn bridleway that guides you effortlessly to the top. Reaching the sculpture feels like you've stumbled upon a hidden treasure – a harmonious blend of nature and art that captivates the senses. The landscape seems to echo with memories, each step unearthing moments from the past. One particularly treasured memory for me is recording an episode of Claire Balding's *Ramblings* here. Though Andy was too ill to join us on the day, Claire's thoughtful WhatsApp video call to him from the hilltop brought him into the moment, filling us both with gratitude and love.

The recording was made just days before my darkest day: 29 June 2021. Only eight weeks before, Andy was diagnosed with cancer. The news came like a storm – aggressive and unyielding. Within weeks, he was gone. My partner, my love, my soulmate and my best friend was taken so suddenly that it felt as though the world had shattered into pieces too jagged to hold. The loss was profound, a grief that engulfed every corner of life, leaving behind a silence that echoed with the life and love we shared.

In the depths of my grief, nature called me back. The outdoors didn't heal the loss, it couldn't. But it gave me space to breathe, to reflect and to keep going. Nature reminded me of the enduring rhythm of life, and so, one step at a time, I continued: Walking, wheeling and rediscovering my way forward.

Sat at the foot of the *Watercut* now, I find myself reflecting on the moments that define my love for walking. It's not just about the places I have been to; it's about how nature resets my soul.

Yet, for all the beauty and solitude that nature offers, the most profound moments from my journey over the past 12 months have been shaped by the people I've met along the way. The strangers who have become friends. Every person I've crossed paths with has left a lasting impression, adding a layer to my own journey that I hadn't expected. It is these shared moments of laughter, tears, struggle and discovery that will stay with me long after the walk ended, making every adventure not just about the places I've been, but about the people who've shaped the experience.

THE WALK

IS IT FOR ME?

START/END POINT: The Thrang, near Nateby, Mallerstang, Cumbria
GRID REFERENCE: NY783006
DISTANCE: 5.5km (3.4 miles) there and back
MILES WITHOUT STILES GRADE: For Some
TERRAIN: Compact stone surface along the bridleway
ACCESSIBILITY: This route requires a sturdy powered all-terrain wheelchair.
PARKING: There's off-road parking at the start of the walk.
FACILITIES: The nearest accessible toilets are in the Kirkby Stephen marketplace (CA17 4QN). The Black Bull at Nateby (CA17 4JP) is wheelchair-friendly and has an accessible toilet.

THE ROUTE

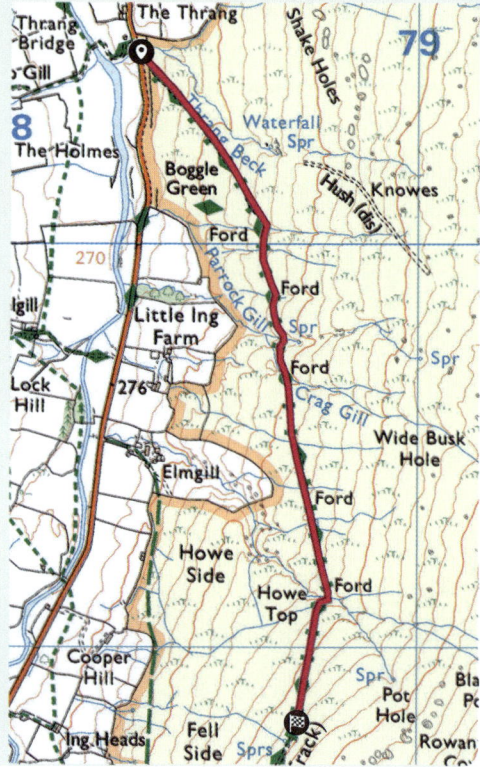

To begin the walk, start at the Thrang, a unique Victorian property and a popular starting point for walks in the Mallerstang valley, Cumbria. It's located about 3 miles south of Nateby village, on the B6259 road. Here is where you'll see signs for the Pennine Bridleway. Pass through the gate and follow the well-marked track upwards. The path is straightforward, so getting lost is unlikely unless you choose to stray from the track, which is not advised. The route stretches just over 1.6km (1 mile) to the *Watercut* sculpture, with a steady climb throughout.

After taking in the views, retrace your steps along the same bridleway to return to The Thrang.

 NEED TO KNOW

A PLACE TO EAT: The Black Bull, Nateby, Kirkby Stephen, CA17 4JP, which has accessible toilet facilities

A PLACE TO DRINK: There are many small cafés in the nearby town of Kirkby Stephen.

A PLACE TO SLEEP: The Canny Grouse, Nateby, CA17 4JR, is a self-catering cottage that has been designed to welcome guests with disabilities.

IF YOU'RE LOOKING FOR SOMETHING ELSE...

A train journey along the **Settle–Carlisle line** is an unforgettable way to experience the rugged beauty of the Yorkshire Dales. Starting in Kirkby Stephen, head south towards the charming market town of Settle, perfect for a scenic break. The train passes through Dent, home to England's highest train station, perched 7.2km (4.5 miles) outside the village.

One of the journey's most iconic highlights is the **Ribblehead Viaduct**, an engineering marvel spanning 396m (440 yards) with 24 towering arches.

This breathtaking route blends history, nature and architecture, making it an essential adventure for lovers of scenic travel.

THE CARLISLE–SETTLE RAILWAY LINE OFFERS ONE OF BRITAIN'S MOST SCENIC TRAIN JOURNEYS

SUTTON BANK

NORTH YORK MOORS NATIONAL PARK

SARA TOWERS

On a bright, crisp autumn day, I had the joy of meeting avid walker Sara Towers at Sutton Bank, North Yorkshire, who was keen to share a trail with me that means so much to her. As the golden light bathed the landscape, Sara welcomed me on a journey filled with personal significance and memories waiting to be rediscovered and enjoyed once more.

We set off from the Sutton Bank car park, making our way towards the Cleveland Way and the iconic 'White Horse'. As the trail merged with the Cleveland Way and wound around Whitestone Cliff, I found myself stopping to admire the stunning view across the Vale of York and the serene waters of Gormire Lake. 'It's absolutely breathtaking,' Sara said. 'You can see for miles – it's like something out of a painting!'

Sara was absolutely right! We sat for a moment, gazing out at the beauty of the vast valley before us. This sweeping panorama, celebrated for its stunning landscapes, has long captivated hearts – including that of renowned veterinarian and author James Herriot, who once described this view as the 'finest in England'.

At first Sara was quiet and deep in thought. Finally, she spoke.

'Being here has made me fall in love with this place all over again. It's filled with so many joyful memories, yet for years I pushed it away. But today, I'm ready to welcome it back into my life.' A bright smile illuminated her face.

I could have lingered there for much longer with the sun warming my skin, but, instead we rose and returned to the walk. As Sara's footsteps fell into rhythm with each turn of my wheels, her voice wove through the quiet, drawing me into a story that began in the heart of the bustling Victorian town of Dalton-in-Furness, near Ulverston, the place where Sara was born and raised.

As one of three children, she fondly remembers the idyllic family days spent on the shores of nearby Coniston Water. Her mum would pack a picnic, and they would revel in the simple joy of being on or in the water all day long. These moments were magical, filled with laughter and a sense of freedom. Yet, despite its proximity to their home, the family never ventured far into the Lake District National Park.

'Little did I know that the landscape I had only glimpsed from afar would soon become my refuge and inspiration,' Sarah said.

When Sara turned 12, her world stretched beyond the familiar. The family spent their summers in their caravan at Torver, a picturesque spot where her mother worked at a local hotel and her father commuted to his day job, leaving Sara and her siblings to their own devices. Together with her sister, Sara embraced this independence, often setting off on adventures in trainers and a T-shirt, to climb the formidable Old Man of Coniston. Sara found solace in these explorations, gradually developing a profound connection with the rugged beauty of the area. As she grew older, this bond deepened and she began to spend more and more time exploring the countryside on her own, savouring the tranquillity and the thrill of discovery.

Life for Sara took an abrupt and dramatic turn when she was just 14. One seemingly ordinary afternoon, she came home from school to find her mother's car packed, ready to leave to start a new life in Kent. The announcement hit her

THE PURPOSE-MADE TRACK AT SUTTON BANK

VIEW ACROSS THE VALE OF YORK

like a thunderclap, rattling the entire family. Sara's mother had always been a complicated figure – sometimes affectionate and often unpredictable. While her departure brought an unexpected sense of relief, it also created a deep emptiness, leaving Sara with feelings of anxiety and uncertainty. The house, once filled with her mother's chaotic energy, now felt hauntingly silent.

'The emotional toll was immediate and overwhelming,' said Sara. 'Anxiety quickly took hold, spiralling into severe health issues.'

Sara was admitted to a children's hospital for two weeks of evaluations and treatment, leading to a diagnosis of mental health struggles. With the help of a psychologist, she began processing her emotions and began to understand that despite her mother's turmoil, she had been a fragile thread holding the family together in her own imperfect way.

At 15, Sara moved to Kent to have some stability, but it worsened her struggles. Her education was disrupted and she left school without qualifications. As her mother's health declined and her aggression towards Sara grew, Sara became homeless. At 16 – too old for social services and too young for council help – she felt forgotten by her father. She eventually found a job picking potatoes to save enough money to return to the Lake District. As Sara spoke, I struggled to grasp the hardships she'd had to endure at such a young age. There was a moment of quiet while I stopped to absorb her story.

We continued to wander along the path, and Sara pointed at a mound of woodland that rose in a peak from the valley floor.

'That's Kilburn Woods,' she said.

I was taken aback by the contrasting colours and the vast skyscape that stretched endlessly above, the clouds casting shadows over the hills. The beauty of it all was overwhelming, with the land unfolding in layers of differing shades of green.

Back in the Lake District, Sara restarted her education by enrolling on a course run by The Prince's Trust (now renamed The King's Trust), which included a YMCA residential programme, work placements and team-building exercises. There, surrounded by a group of misfits who became her family, Sara rekindled her love for the outdoors, learning skills like mountain climbing and watersports. By summer's end, she was offered an apprenticeship at the YMCA, and earned qualifications in canoeing and climbing. By the time she turned 18, Sara had amassed a wealth of experience in outdoor education, a journey she considered the pivotal moment of her life.

After leaving the YMCA, she became a key worker for people with autism, a job she found deeply rewarding.

As we paused by an information board along the trail, curiosity drew me in to read it.

'We're standing on top of the White Horse,' Sara explained, gesturing towards a small patch of white stone just beyond the barrier. 'But the best view of the Kilburn Horse is from over there,' she admitted with a chuckle, pointing into the far distance. Then, with a mischievous laugh, she said, 'I share a special bond with horses.'

I was intrigued. We sat for a while in this picturesque setting and Sara began to reveal yet another remarkable chapter of her extraordinary life.

One day, as she was walking down the street, she spotted an advert for a position at a race school in Newmarket and, despite never having ridden a horse, decided to apply. To her astonishment, she got the job. She moved to

SARA TOWERS AT THE VIEWPOINT AT SUTTON BANK

Newmarket and threw herself into the challenging new environment, learning to ride and building her physical strength. The days were long and the work was gruelling, but Sara made lifelong friends and gained invaluable skills. Her commitment and dedication were rewarded as she was sent on her first placement to the prestigious JonJo O'Neill's Cotswolds Yard. However, this placement ended after a frightening incident with a horse. Nevertheless, her talents had been recognised, and she was given second chance at Donald McCain's stable, where she fully immersed herself in racing.

Sara had found strength in the fast-paced world of horse racing, and was loving life.

'I met Russell while I was working at the stables,' Sara said, 'and we started married life together by moving to Thirsk.'

She began building a future, still working with horses at a local riding stable. But when she became pregnant, a new and unexpected challenge emerged. Postnatal depression crept in, casting a shadow over what she had imagined would be a joyful chapter. The days blurred together, each one heavier than the last. Once confident and determined, she now battled feelings of isolation and self-doubt, struggling to recognise the woman she had once been. The joy she expected was drowned out by exhaustion and an overwhelming sadness. Yet, even in her darkest moments, the resilience that had carried her through the toughest days in racing still flickered inside her, scrambling to find a way back to the surface. Despite the challenges she faced, Sara was unwavering in her determination to rebuild her life. With resilience in her heart and a second baby on the way, she pushed forward, enrolling in college to earn qualifications in English, maths and science. Undeterred, she pushed herself even further, excelling in three A-levels with top marks and accomplishing what once felt out of reach – securing a place in the Medical Microbiology degree programme at Leeds University. But despite having two beautiful children and achieving remarkable success in advancing her qualifications, the relentless shadow of depression still loomed over her.

The COVID-19 pandemic pushed her studies online, adding immense pressure as she struggled to balance motherhood, long hours of study and a lack of human interaction. The resulting stress and burnout took a heavy toll, ultimately contributing to the breakdown of her marriage. One night, overwhelmed by despair, Sara stood on the edge of a decision she could never take back. But fate intervened, and with the help of a crisis team she was given another chance. Her journey to recovery was anything but easy as she grappled with the heartbreak of her marriage ending, the devastating loss of her mother and the aching absence of her beloved dog. Yet, through it all, she discovered an unexpected source of strength: the simple act of hiking. Venturing into the

ENDLESS VIEWS ACROSS THE VALE OF YORK

vast, untamed beauty of the North York Moors with her sons became more than just exercise; it was a lifeline, a way to heal, reconnect and find moments of peace in nature's embrace.

As we wandered deeper along the trail, we paused to watch the gliders from the nearby club, their sleek forms carving silent arcs through the endless blue sky. Sara gazed up, captivated.

'It must be so peaceful up there,' she murmured, her voice laced with longing. 'When my mind feels too full, I think I'd like to be gliding.'

The thought of soaring weightlessly, far above the noise of the world – and the turmoil within – offered a kind of escape that deeply resonated with her. Though she was receiving professional mental health support, she knew recovery was a slow and winding path. But out here, in the open expanse of the Moors, away from the suffocating demands of daily life, she found her own kind of therapy. Each step through the rolling green dales and each breath of crisp, wild air, carried her closer to a feeling of freedom – one that, even if just for a moment, made her believe she could soar.

Making our way back to the visitor centre, we walked through a landscape that seemed to reflect the completion of both our physical journey and the deeply personal one Sara had so generously shared.

The moors of North Yorkshire had witnessed her struggles and triumphs, offering her solace in moments of uncertainty. Though her path forward remains uncertain, one thing is clear: Sara is not defined by her anxiety, but by her courage to keep moving forward. I felt privileged to have walked alongside her, inspired by her resilience and determination. This wasn't just a walk; it was confirmation of the healing power of nature, community and inner strength.

THE WALK

IS IT FOR ME?

START/END POINT: Sutton Bank Visitor Centre, Thirsk, YO7 2EH

GRID REFERENCE: SE514831

DISTANCE: 5.3km (3.3 miles) circular

MILES WITHOUT STILES GRADE: For Many

TERRAIN: Mainly solid track

ACCESSIBILITY: The trail is wide, firm and mostly gentle in gradient, with good signage throughout. It crosses the busy A170, so caution is advised. A mobility scooter is available to borrow from the visitor centre: www.northyorkmoors.org.uk/things-to-do/attractions/sutton-bank-national-park-centre/accessibility

PARKING: There is a large car park, with Blue Badge bays. (Fees apply)

FACILITIES: Accessible toilets are available at the visitor centre.

THE ROUTE

The path to the White Horse is straightforward, featuring gentle slopes and clear signage, making it easily accessible even for those with minimal navigational skills. Follow the route around Roulston Scar and continue on the left track towards Low Town Bank Road. Walk for approximately 1.6km (1 mile), crossing the road with caution. Once across, follow the track on the opposite side. When the path splits, take the left trail through Hambleton Plantation, guiding you back to the visitor centre.

NEED TO KNOW

A PLACE TO EAT: Sutton Bank National Park Centre

A PLACE TO DRINK: The Feathers Hotel, Market Pl, Helmsley, York, YO62 5BH

A PLACE TO SLEEP: The Black Swan, Market Pl, Helmsley, York YO62 5BJ

IF YOU'RE LOOKING FOR SOMETHING ELSE...

Helmsley, the only market town within the North York Moors National Park, with a rich history, culture and beauty, is a must-see gem. The town is nestled on the River Rye along the A170, located 22.5km (14 miles) east of Thirsk.

The town trail takes you to **Helmsley Castle**, which offers wheelchair access and a manual chair for hire.

The trail also includes the stunning **Walled Garden**, where vibrant flowers and charming paths await. Meander through the picturesque back streets that will bring you back to the market square.

THE VILLAGE OF HELMSLEY

THRELKELD TO KESWICK

LAKE DISTRICT NATIONAL PARK

ARRON HART

Longing for adventure and driven by a mission to uncover stile-free, accessible trails, I found myself in the charming village of Threlkeld, in the north of the Lake District. Nestled under the majestic Blencathra Fell, just 6.4km (4 miles) from Keswick, this little gem offers more than breathtaking views; it promises stories waiting to be told. This is also where I met Arron Hart, the inspiring chairperson of the Fillyaboots Rambling Group. Together, we set out on a 5km (3.1 mile) journey along the multi-user track from Threlkeld to Keswick, where I discovered Arron's extraordinary story of resilience, discovery and transformation.

Setting off at a good pace from the pretty village boundary towards the busy A66 and the start of the trail, it's easy to forget that walking hadn't always been a passion for Arron. Growing up as the youngest of six children in a working-class family, outings to the countryside were a luxury his parents simply couldn't afford. Though his parents worked tirelessly, a day in nature seemed out of reach. Arron's first glimpse of the great outdoors, then, came at age seven, when he joined a church group. He vividly recalls the picnic that opened his eyes to a world beyond the city. That day planted a seed of wonder – a yearning to explore more.

But life wasn't kind to Arron during his school years. He faced relentless bullying, endured loneliness and even contemplated ending his life. University offered little respite, as he continued to feel isolated and adrift. Yet despite the hardships, Arron's story is one of resilience – a testament to the human spirit's capacity to overcome.

His turning point came due to an unlikely source: a book. Cheryl Strayed's memoir *Wild* spoke to Arron like nothing else. It tells the story of a woman's 1,770km (1,100 mile) journey of self-discovery on the Pacific Crest Trail. Cheryl's determination to reclaim her life through the transformative power of the outdoors struck a chord with Arron. Inspired by her story, he resolved to step outside, confront his fears and explore the countryside for himself.

At first, Arron thought the world of walking was dominated by privileged individuals with expensive gear; he wasn't sure how a working-class, inexperienced walker like himself would fit in. So, nervous but determined, he reached out to Fillyaboots, a Liverpool-based walking group. To his relief, the group welcomed him warmly, and there he found a diverse, inclusive community eager to support him, regardless of his background. Originally formed to bring together young walkers in their 20s and 30s, the group now embraces members of all ages and backgrounds. Arron quickly learned to navigate routes and read maps with their guidance, and soon, he was leading walks of his own.

EXPLORING THE LAKES THE SUSTAINABLE WAY – ARRON HART ON THE BUS

A game-changing moment came when Arron learned about the accessible bus services in the Lake District.

'That same day, I booked a room at the YHA in Keswick,' he shared with a beaming smile. 'And the rest, as they say, is history!'

His love affair with the Lake District began with explorations around Ambleside and Keswick.

'Walking this railway line towards Keswick feels like I'm walking home,' he told me, his voice tinged with emotion.

One unforgettable evening, Arron decided to hike up Catbells. Halfway up, he paused to take in the stunning autumnal view. Derwent Water was shimmering below, Keswick town nestled in the distance, and the

Skiddaw range standing tall. It was a moment of pure magic and deep spiritual connection.

'That's when I knew this place would always be a part of me,' he said.

And it is easy to see why. Strolling along this trail feels like stepping into a postcard from Switzerland. Towering pine trees stand sentinel, their earthy scent mingling with the crisp mountain air, while clear, babbling brooks meander alongside us, creating a natural symphony. The fast-flowing River Greta races through the valley, a playground for herons and dippers darting between the rocks. In the woods, a flash of rust hinted that a red squirrel was darting playfully through the branches. Every now and then, glimpses of Blencathra and Skiddaw peek through the canopy, teasing those with a thirst for adventure to explore further. The scene is a perfect blend of tranquillity and wild beauty.

The entrance to the Bobbin Mill railway tunnel is one of the most intriguing highlights along the path. Buried for 40 years before being excavated and restored, the tunnel now stands as a preserved relic of the past. Stepping into its shadowy, time-worn walls feels like entering a bygone era. The tunnel's rough stone, shaped by the sweat and skill of workers who blasted through the rock, still carries a rugged charm.

Walking through the tunnel, we chatted about the engineering marvel of its construction, captivated by the immense effort it took to carve such a passage. We discussed the male workforce that brought this magnificent tunnel to life. Arron also reflected on societal assumptions surrounding outdoor activities, highlighting the notion of a 'male bias' – the outdated and often unconscious belief that activities like mountain climbing or hiking are inherently masculine. Historically, societal norms and gender roles have cast outdoor adventure, especially in rugged and challenging terrains, as the domain of men. Outdoor sports, especially mountaineering, are often associated with strength, endurance and toughness – traits traditionally (and unfairly) linked more strongly with men.

'I was at the YHA in Fort William,' Arron began, with the air of a man about to drop some wisdom, or at least a funny story. 'There was this group of guys, all hyped up, swapping tales about how they'd conquered Ben Nevis. You know the type: high-fives, chest bumps, probably planning to start a podcast about it. And there I was, nursing a cup of tea and thinking, *why not give it a go?* And guess what? I did it, and I'm not even the macho type!'

Reaching the end of the track, we passed by the historic Keswick railway station, a relic of the 1860s, when it was constructed for the Cockermouth, Keswick and Penrith Railway Company. Its weathered stone walls and vintage architecture tell stories of a bygone era, when steam trains chugged through the landscape, connecting rural towns and bustling markets. Though trains no longer run here, the station stands as a poignant reminder of the region's industrial heritage and its once-thriving rail network. Strolling past it, you can almost hear the echoes of whistles and the clatter of wheels on tracks, evoking a sense of nostalgia for those early days of travel.

As we walked through the busy market town of Keswick, Arron points out the YHA, his favourite place to stay when he visits the Lake District. Arron relates that, as the chairperson of the Fillyaboots walking group, he is excited to invite anyone to join them. The group always make sure that the cost of their trips is as low as possible, so that anyone can participate, regardless of their financial situation. Whenever they can, they prefer to use public transportation, and they are big fans of the YHA.

'As a young, LGBTQ+, working-class individual, I believe my role shows that the rambler's community and the countryside are open to all,' he says proudly.

Our final section of the walk moves along the shores of Derwent Water, where the calm lake mirrors the surrounding peaks in its glassy surface. The short stroll leads us to the iconic viewpoint of Friar's Crag, one of the most celebrated spots in the Lake District. From there, we absorb the breathtaking vista of the rugged Jaws of Borrowdale, the towering cliffs framing the valley like a natural gateway. The view is both dramatic and peaceful, offering a perfect moment to reflect on the beauty and history of the landscape before us.

For Arron, the outdoors has been a life-saving sanctuary. It gave him the courage to embrace his identity as a gay man, and he was met with unwavering support from his walking group. Arron is now passionately committed to breaking stereotypes and making walking groups more inclusive, especially for the LGBTQ+ community. He is a successful counsellor and behavioural therapist and recently trained to lead outdoor therapy sessions. Reflecting on his journey, he credits the unconditional love and support of the Fillyaboots community for helping him thrive. The outdoors continues to be his sanctuary, offering him peace, perspective and the strength to carry on.

Meeting Arron has been an absolute joy. With his magnetic personality, extensive knowledge and caring nature – not to mention his talent for putting together a fantastic packed lunch – he will leave a lasting impression. Every time I find myself in these mountains now, I'll think of Arron with great fondness. I wish him every success.

And how did we get back to Threlkeld? Arron's favourite mode of transport: by bus, of course!

To learn more about Fillyaboots and their incredible community, visit fillyaboots.org.uk.

THE WALK

IS IT FOR ME?

START/END POINT: At the west end of Threlkeld, just after the village road meets the A6, take the signposted right turn to reach the start of the walk. The walk finishes at Keswick Leisure Centre. The X5 departs Keswick Bus Station hourly from Monday to Saturday. On Sundays the service is slightly less frequent, but still operates.

GRID REFERENCE: NY316250

DISTANCE: 6km (3.7 miles)

TERRAIN: Tarmac path

MILES WITHOUT STILES: For Many

ACCESSIBILITY: This walk is ideal for people with pushchairs and wheelchairs.

PARKING: There is some.

FACILITIES: Threlkeld Coffee Shop, in Threlkeld, Keswick, CA12 4RX, has accessible toilets.

THE ROUTE

The Threlkeld to Keswick Railway Walk traces the path of an old train route that once connected Cockermouth to Penrith. Originally opened in 1865, this railway line played a significant role in promoting tourism in Keswick and providing access to the region for locals residing in the more industrialised surrounding areas. The route offered breathtaking views of the North Lakes, including the edges of Bassenthwaite Lake. However, the railway line was permanently closed in 1973 and subsequently transformed into a footpath connecting Keswick and Threlkeld.

Unfortunately, the path suffered extensive damage during Storm Desmond in 2015, rendering much of it unusable for several years. Following a £7.9 million renovation, it finally reopened in December 2020, and today the newly resurfaced and repaired path is a popular destination for both walkers and cyclists, offering stunning views of the surrounding landscape.

The trail is enhanced by informative panels that span its length, offering insights into the local nature and wildlife, the railway's history, the bobbin mill and the effects of Storm Desmond on both the trail and the surrounding area.

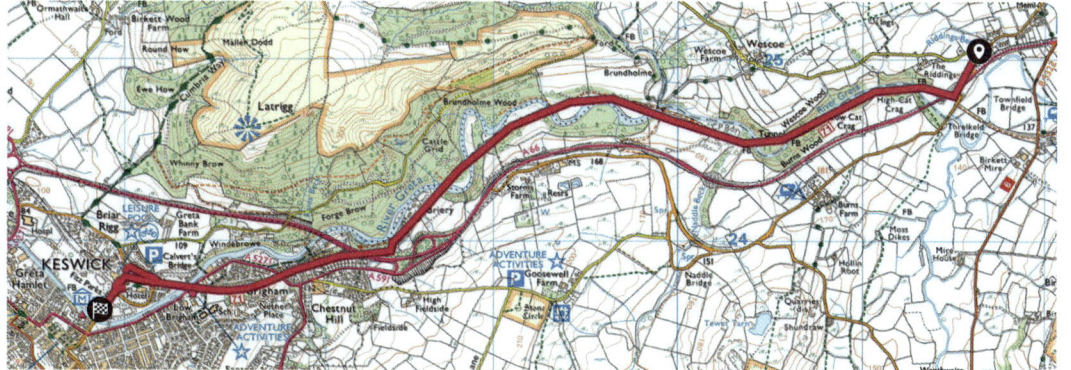

A map and compass aren't necessary, as the walk is straightforward, following a continuous tarmac track. Once you reach town, head down through the streets toward Derwent Lake, where you'll find the paved path leading to the viewpoint at Friar's Crag. For your return journey, the bus station is conveniently located next to Booths supermarket in the town centre.

NEED TO KNOW

A PLACE TO EAT: The community café in Threlkeld

A PLACE TO DRINK: The Wainwright, Lake Rd, Keswick, CA12 5BZ

A PLACE TO SLEEP: Irton House Farm, Isel, Cockermouth, CA13 9ST, has several wheelchair-accessible cottages. The farm is set in 97ha (240 acres) of pasture and woodland and commands possibly one of the finest views found in the northern Lake District.

IF YOU'RE LOOKING FOR SOMETHING ELSE...

Keswick offers several wheelchair-friendly attractions that make it easy to enjoy the area's history, culture and nature. Together, these destinations make Keswick an inclusive and memorable experience for all visitors.

The iconic **Castlerigg Stone Circle**, Castle Lane, Underskiddaw, Keswick, Cumbria, CA12 4RN, perched on a gentle hillside, has a grassy track for viewing these ancient stones and the surrounding panoramic landscape.

The **Pencil Museum**, Southey Works, Keswick, Cumbria, CA12 5NG, is a unique and interactive destination, offering level access to exhibits that tell the surprisingly fascinating story of pencil-making.

For animal lovers, the **Lake District Wildlife Park**, Bassenthwaite Lake, Keswick, CA12 4RD, is a great choice, with accessible paths winding through enclosures.

ORREST HEAD
LAKE DISTRICT NATIONAL PARK

DAWN AND ALAN TOWART

Orrest Head, a stunning hill in the Lake District overlooking Windermere, holds a special place in the hearts of many nature lovers. It was Alfred Wainwright's first conquered fell, celebrated in his 1974 book *The Outlying Fells of Lakeland*, where he described it as 'Our first sight of mountains in tumultuous array across glittering waters, our awakening to beauty.' His deep connection to the region continues to inspire visitors today. In 2021, a £73,000 project introduced the Miles Without Stiles route, making the iconic viewpoint accessible to powered-wheelchair users and families with prams and pushchairs, allowing more people to enjoy the breathtaking vistas that so captivated Wainwright.

Trekking up Orrest Head with Dawn and Alan Towart was both exhilarating and rewarding. Though it was my first time tackling this scenic fell, the Towart clan, seasoned regulars of the trail, made it feel like a familiar and welcoming journey.

Within minutes of crossing the busy A591, the sounds of the main road faded into the distance, replaced by the rustling of leaves and the crunch of boots on the well-trodden path. The climb to the summit was steep, and as we walked, the conversation turned to Alan and Dawn, a couple whose deep connection to the Lake District is immediately evident.

In 2013, Alan, his wife Dawn, and their daughter Sophia moved to Cumbria after the Newcastle company where Alan had worked for 25 years closed its doors. Rather than see it as a setback, Alan embraced the opportunity to transfer to Barrow-in-Furness, drawn by a lifelong love of the Lakes. Having

ALAN AND DEBBIE AT THE VIEWPOINT AT THE SUMMIT OF ORREST HEAD

spent his youth waterskiing on Windermere and sharing holidays here with Dawn, the move felt like coming home. Now, with each step up the familiar trail, their passion for this landscape shone through. It was easy to see why this place holds such meaning for them, a place of adventure, resilience and new beginnings.

As we continued our climb, gaining height quickly, the Langdale Pikes emerged majestically through the canopy of trees. With the breathtaking views unfolding around us, I couldn't imagine a more romantic setting to hear the love story of this couple. They met 23 years ago at a friend's engagement party and hit it off immediately. Alan wasted no time and asked Dawn out on a date the very next day. It was love at first sight for both, and they knew they had found something special. Dawn fondly remembers the moment they locked eyes across the dance floor, and the rest, as they say, is history. Their love has stood the test of time, and it's clear to see that they have something truly special.

And they have passed this love of the outdoors on to their daughter. Sophia was three years old when the family moved to Cumbria, and walking was just the beginning of her own love affair with being out in nature. She was introduced to the exciting world of geocaching, a treasure-hunting activity that involves searching for hidden containers, or 'caches', at specific locations using GPS and other navigational devices. Sophia loved hunting for 'treasure', and as a family they became hooked on their new hobby.

We had climbed the track a little further, following the well-trodden path that wound gently through a tunnel of ancient woodland. Alan announced that, on a previous hunt on Orrest Head, he had found a geocache here at the side of the track.

'And there's one near the summit,' he declared with a cheeky smile, 'but I'm not telling you where!'

For Alan, geocaching has been a source of adventure and connection, leading him to discover new places, form lasting friendships and create cherished memories of hiking with companions. In 2017, Alan was diagnosed with motor neurone disease (MND), a progressive neurological condition that weakens the body and affects movement, speech and even breathing. The diagnosis was devastating, but Alan and his family chose to face it with resilience and positivity.

The day Alan received the diagnosis, he bought a boat for family adventures on Windermere. Dawn initially thought it was impractical, but the boat brought four years of joy, providing a much-needed escape and countless cherished memories. It became a place of peace for Alan and a sanctuary for the family, allowing them to bond and make the most of their time together. Eventually, as Alan's condition worsened, using the boat became too difficult, but it remained a powerful symbol of Alan's commitment to living fully despite his illness.

Alan and Dawn chose to be honest with their daughter about Alan's condition. Though the reality was hard for her to grasp at first, she coined the term 'determinal' to describe their journey – a word the family embraced to focus on determination and resilience instead of despair.

From a young age, Alan embraced judo, a passion Sophia now shares with him. Judo has become more than a sport – it's a vital emotional outlet amid her father's illness. Recognising judo's benefits to their daughter, Dawn and Alan encouraged her involvement, and it has transformed their lives. The family now travels across the UK and Ireland, supporting Sophia as she competes and showcases her remarkable skills. Recently she achieved an incredible milestone, winning gold in the under-40kg, under-16 female championships in Ireland. Like her father, she admires the physical and mental discipline judo demands and finds joy in mastering its techniques.

Despite Alan's wheelchair confinement, he and Dawn continue to embrace their passion for the outdoors, celebrating milestones like their 6,000th geocaching find with loved ones at Orrest Head. Geocaching remains a true inspiration for their adventurous spirits and, now age 13, Sophia still cherishes her collection of discovered treasure.

As we ascended the mountain, gaps in the trees revealed breathtaking views of the lake and the surrounding mountains once again. The route took us past the woodyard and the newly restored Victorian Carriageway, which served hot beverages and delicious cake. We paused for refreshments, and I was deeply moved by the quiet, unwavering love between Dawn and Alan. Unable to hold his own cup, Alan relied on Dawn to steady his drink as he sipped through a straw. Meanwhile, her own coffee sat untouched, growing cold. Yet there was no complaint, no sign of frustration – only a quiet devotion, a love expressed not through words but through the simplest, most selfless of actions.

Living in Newby Bridge, Alan is fortunate to have the newly established West Windermere Way at his doorstep. The accessible trail connects Newby Bridge to Lakeside and extends to Finsthwaite and the Lakeside YMCA. Honoured as a local resident, Alan officially inaugurated the pathway alongside Trudy Harrison, who at the time was Parliamentary Under Secretary of State for Environment, and Richard Leafe, the now-retired CEO of the Lake District National Park. Reflecting on the event, Alan shared, 'I felt like a celebrity for the day!'

Alan has recently embraced newfound freedom with an all-terrain powered wheelchair, which he can operate with his finger. This purchase symbolises his determination to create meaningful experiences for his family and explore the natural beauty around him. The wheelchair has enabled him to enjoy simple yet profound moments, such as picnics on Windermere's shore with Dawn, who reads as Alan watches wildlife. One of his favourite spots is the floating pontoon, where he feels immersed in the lake's tranquility, a nostalgic reminder of his boating days.

Alan's impact extends beyond personal adventures. He starred in an award-winning film by the Motor Neurone Disease Association (MNDA), which was aimed at raising awareness about MND. At the film's premiere, Alan met Her Royal Highness Princess Anne and connected with fellow stars Yvonne, Diana and Mike. The film highlights the resilience of those living with MND and the vital support provided by MNDA, inspiring hope and admiration.

Alan and Dawn's journey, much like Alfred Wainwright's love for Orrest Head, showcases perseverance and the transformative power of nature. Their story inspires others to embrace life's adventures, demonstrating that joy and purpose are possible despite life's challenges.

When we reach the summit, it is clear to see why Alan and Dawn have a deep love for this walk. With the majestic peaks of the Lake District stretching into the distance and the waters of Windermere glistening far below, the view is nothing short of breathtaking. Standing together against this spectacular backdrop, Dawn and Alan's love for the landscape is undeniable, but even more striking is their love for each other. This walk is more than just a climb; it reflects their journey, one of shared adventure, resilience and an unbreakable bond, forever tied to the beauty of the Lakes.

THE WALK

IS IT FOR ME?

START/END POINT: Windermere train station, Station Precinct, Windermere, Cumbria, LA23 1AH

GRID REFERENCE: SD412987

DISTANCE: 3.4km (2.1miles) there and back

MILES WITHOUT STILES GRADE: For Many

TERRAIN: Surfaced paths of tarmac and gravel

ACCESSIBILITY: The path to the summit is steep, and a powered all-terrain wheelchair is recommended for wheelchair users.

PARKING: There's a large layby at the start of the walk, and free parking (3hr) can be found at Booths supermarket (LA23 1QA).

FACILITIES: Accessible toilets are available at Windermere train station.

THE ROUTE

Leave Windermere train station and cross the A591 to take a surfaced road signposted Orrest Head. The walk up to Orrest Head starts from Church Street. There's a large signpost at the start of the climb and from here you are guided by signposts all the way to the summit. Following the path, the route winds through Elleray Woods. As you emerge from the woodland, the summit comes into view.

At an impressive 239m (784ft) above sea level, Orrest Head stands proudly as the highest point on this walk. Take a moment to soak in the panoramic views that stretch all the way to Scafell Pike, the Old Man of Coniston and the Langdale Pikes. After immersing yourself in the beauty of the surroundings, retrace your steps back down into Windermere, cherishing the memories of this unforgettable adventure.

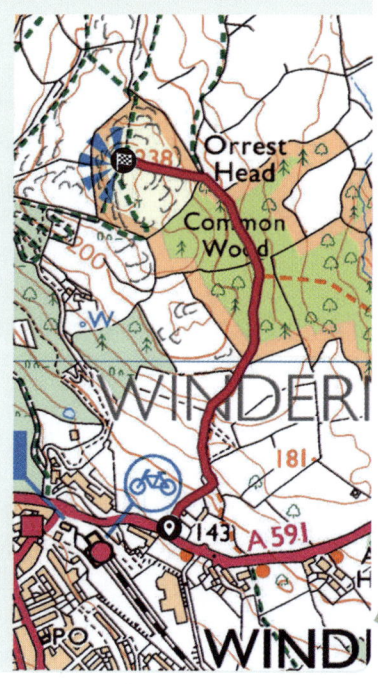

NEED TO KNOW

A PLACE TO EAT: BAHA, 18 Ash Street, Bowness on Windermere, Cumbria, LA23 3EB, serves casual American-style food both day and night and offers accessible facilities for visitors.

A PLACE TO DRINK: Lake View Garden Bar, St Andrew's Lake Road, Windermere, LA23 3DE, features both indoor and outdoor bars, along with wheelchair-accessible facilities.

A PLACE TO SLEEP: Just a short distance from the start of the walk lies Low Wray Campsite, Ambleside, LA22 0JA, featuring accessible pods that are wheelchair-friendly and accommodate up to four people. The YHA Waterhead, Ambleside, LA22 0EU, offers accessible features.

IF YOU'RE LOOKING FOR SOMETHING ELSE...

Anyone Can is an organisation that provides accessible outdoor activities, including canoeing, sailing, paddleboarding and climbing. Whether you're a beginner or experienced, the activities are designed to be accessible to all, allowing everyone to participate and experience the thrill of the outdoors. They usually launch at **Fell Foot (National Trust)**, a stunning lakeside location on Lake Windermere. Here, there is a beautiful stile-free riverside walk, café and lots of picnic space. There's also a Changing Places facility at Fell Foot.

For more detail on accessible water adventures, visit www.anyonecan.co.uk.

PADDLEBOARDING ON WINDERMERE

CONISTON TO TARN HOWS CIRCULAR

LAKE DISTRICT NATIONAL PARK

ALEX STANIFORTH

My journey through the UK to find accessible, stile-free walks led me to the southern Lake District and to Coniston Water. Nestled at the foot of the fells, Coniston is a charming village with slate-roofed cottages, cosy cafés and a rich history tied to both mining and the legendary speed records of Donald Campbell, who was sadly killed during a record attempt at Coniston Water in 1967.

Standing at the water's edge I watched the gentle ripples dance across the surface of the lake, stirred by a soft breeze. On either side, wooded slopes tumbled down to the shoreline, their dense foliage a patchwork of deep greens and golden hues. It was early morning, and the lake's stillness was broken only by the occasional cry of a distant bird or the rhythmic splash of a lone canoeist cutting through the water. In the distance, the rugged peaks of the Old Man of Coniston loomed, their craggy outlines softened by a veil of morning mist.

During my visit, I was joined by Alex Staniforth, a record-breaking adventurer, ultra-runner and the founder of Mind Over Mountains, a charity dedicated to restoring mental health through outdoor experiences. As we began our walk towards Boon Crag Farm, Alex shared how the outdoors has been crucial in helping him overcome depression and anxiety.

At the tender age of 15, Alex had ambitions of becoming a professional long-distance runner. His talent was evident, and he was on a promising path to achieving his goal. However, life had other plans. Illness struck and Alex found himself battling severe depression, compounded by bullying at school. Despite the support available, Alex felt isolated and alone, engulfed by his struggles.

To combat his depression, Alex turned to the outdoors, finding solace and strength in challenging physical feats. One of his early significant achievements was completing the National Three Peaks Challenge at just 16.

'That's a tough challenge, Alex,' I remarked.

'It was,' he replied. Then, with a satisfied nod, 'And I'd do it all over again.'

In 2014, at 18, Alex set out for Everest Base Camp as part of an expedition team. The goal was to summit Mount Everest, but disaster struck before they even reached Base Camp. A massive avalanche claimed the lives of 16 Sherpa climbers, leading to the expedition's cancellation. Despite this harrowing experience, Alex's determination remained unshaken, and began raising funds for a second attempt.

A year later, Alex returned to Everest. This time while on the mountain, a severe earthquake devastated Nepal, resulting in the deaths of three team members. Alex narrowly escaped with his life, but gained a profound perspective on the fragility of existence. This event not only fuelled his efforts to raise money for Nepal but also inspired him to focus on making a difference closer to home.

ALEX AND DEBBIE AT TARN HOWS

HEADING TOWARDS CONISTON

After climbing through the dense forest of Tarn Hows Woods, we find a gap in the trees where we sit for a while, taking in the breathtaking view of the Langdale Pikes. Alex tells me that throughout his life, the outdoors has been his toolkit for managing the ups and downs of his mental health. The challenges he'd faced – depression, eating disorders, epilepsy, stammering and bullying – were daunting, but the natural world provided him with a sanctuary. Being outside, testing himself against the elements, proved to be the most powerful method for confronting his inner demons.

In 2017, Alex embarked on a new project: Climb The UK, a remarkable endeavour that saw him climb to the highest point of all 100 UK counties in 72 days. For Alex, this physical challenge underscored the inadequacies of the mental health support system in the UK.

'It took longer to access NHS mental health services than it did to cycle and run 8,047km (5,000 miles) around the highest county tops of the UK. That's when the lack of support available dawned on me – and I became determined to help others access the outdoors to manage their mental health too.'

Motivated by his experiences, Alex founded Mind Over Mountains. The charity aims to take people into nature, providing a safe space for them to walk and talk with professional support at hand.

Engrossed in conversation, time slipped away effortlessly, and before we knew it, Tarn Hows emerged before us – a shimmering jewel nestled among rolling hills and ancient woodland, the still waters reflecting the ever-changing sky and the surrounding woodland.

'In nature, individuals find it easier to open up about their struggles, away from the intimidating face-to-face settings,' Alex explains. 'The hardest part is often taking that first step, but once they do, the benefits are profound.'

Mind Over Mountains has become a beacon of hope for many struggling with mental health issues. Participants often discover a sense of peace and clarity as they immerse themselves in nature.

Alex's journey is a powerful narrative of overcoming adversity. His achievements as an adventurer and ultra-runner are impressive, but it is his dedication to mental health advocacy that truly sets him apart. By sharing his story and creating opportunities for others to heal, he has transformed his own struggles into a force for good.

But his story is far from over. As a record-breaking adventurer, he continues to set and pursue new challenges, pushing the boundaries of what is possible. His commitment to mental health advocacy remains unwavering. Each step he takes in the great outdoors is an affirmation to his belief in the power of nature to heal and restore.

After stopping at Tarn Hows for coffee, we begin the steep walk up to Hill Fell Plantation. As we climb higher, the landscape unfolds beneath us – a patchwork of emerald fields, winding stone walls and glistening waters stretching towards the distant peaks. The rugged beauty of the fells are even more striking from this vantage point, their craggy summits bathed in soft, golden light.

I am in awe of Alex and his achievements, his determination as unwavering as the ancient hills surrounding us. Through his remarkable journey, he exemplifies how personal trials can lead to profound impact. He has shown that even in the face of immense difficulties, it is possible to find strength, purpose and a way to help others. His legacy is one of courage, resilience and the ability to harness the transformative power of the natural world.

VIEW ACROSS CONISTON FELL

THE WALK

⊙ IS IT FOR ME?

START/END POINT: Monk Coniston car park, Coniston, LA21 8AA

GRID REFERENCE: SD316978

DISTANCE: 7.6km (4.7 miles)

MILES WITHOUT STILES GRADE: For Some

TERRAIN: A mix of forest and tarmac tracks

ACCESSIBILITY: Mobility scooters are available to borrow from the National Trust for rambles around Tarn Hows. See: www.nationaltrust.org.uk/visit/lake-district/tarn-hows-and-coniston/borrow-a-tramper-at-tarn-hows

PARKING: There's a large car park at Monk Coniston (see above); fees apply. An alternative to this walk is to simply park at the National Trust car park for Tarn Hows (LA22 0PP), where there is an alternative car park for disabled visitors who wish to enjoy a relaxing stroll around the lake.

FACILITIES: Accessible toilets are available at the car park in Coniston and at Tarn Hows. There are plenty of cafés and pubs for refreshments in Coniston and there's a small takeaway café at Tarn Hows.

➡ THE ROUTE

Coniston is nestled in the heart of the Lake District, at the base of the Old Man of Coniston and along the western shore of Coniston Water. This charming village serves as an excellent starting point for exploring the area's many mountains, forests and waterways. It also offers a variety of shops, pubs and dining options, as well as guest houses, B&Bs and holiday cottages both in the village and the surrounding area.

Monk Coniston car park is situated on the northern shore of Coniston Water, at the head of the lake. The walk begins from the car park, where you'll take the path leading towards Boom Crag Farm. Here the path turns left toward Tarn Hows Cottage. The trail ascends steeply through the forest, offering a challenging climb for those using an all-terrain mobility wheelchair. This well-trodden route is straightforward and is clearly signposted, making it easy to navigate. Simply stay on the path, and you won't lose your way.

Upon reaching Tarn Hows, you can enjoy a circular walk around the lake. Created in the 19th century, Tarn Hows, manmade beauty spot has become a favourite for walkers of all ages and abilities. It is breathtaking in every season, providing a meditative escape amidst mountain views, particularly in the early morning or evening.

From the top corner of the main car park, take the track through Hill Fell Plantation. Once again, you will have a steady climb, but the views are worth the effort. This track emerges from the woods and connects to a path running parallel to the road, leading you back to the car park.

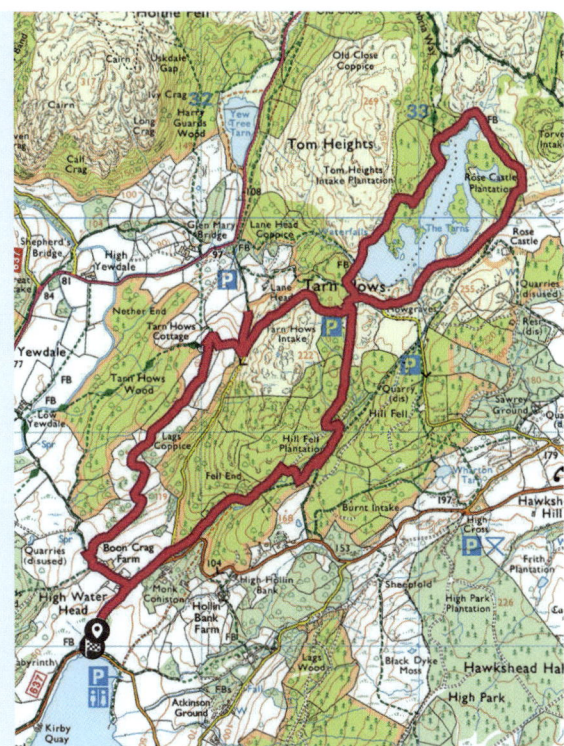

🏠 NEED TO KNOW

A PLACE TO EAT: Chesters By The River, Ambleside, LA22 9NJ, is a lovely little bistro by a waterfall, with accessible facilities.
A PLACE TO DRINK: The Bluebird Cafe next to the pier by Coniston Water (LA21 8AN)
A PLACE TO SLEEP: The Coniston Inn, Coniston, LA21 8AJ, has accessible rooms.

✚ IF YOU'RE LOOKING FOR SOMETHING ELSE…

Gliding across the tranquil waters of Coniston, a boat ride with **Coniston Launch** offers stunning views of the surrounding fells and woodlands. The floating pontoons make boarding easy, ensuring accessibility for those with mobility challenges.

After disembarking at Brantwood Jetty, take a short 15 minute walk to **The Ruskin Museum** (LA21 8DU) to learn more about the 'Story of Coniston' and the many heroes that have lived and worked in the region.

NEWBOROUGH NATIONAL NATURE RESERVE AND FOREST
ANGLESEY

MIKE PALMER

Off the north-west coast of Wales lies the Isle of Anglesey, a place where rugged beauty meets rich history and timeless charm. Famous for its dramatic cliffs, golden beaches and rolling green landscapes, Anglesey has long been a refuge for those seeking peace and inspiration. This was my very first visit to the island, and I was profoundly moved by its serene yet powerful presence, a place that felt both ancient and alive.

It was here that I was to meet Mike Palmer on an accessible walk through Newborough National Nature Reserve (NNR) and Forest, located on Anglesey's southernmost tip. The reserve is a sanctuary of towering pine forests, wild sand dunes and shimmering beaches that open up to the restless Irish Sea beyond. As we followed the trail that wound through stands of pines and alongside vast stretches of dunes, the landscape unfolded like a living painting, each step revealing the extraordinary ability of this island to connect visitors with nature.

 Mike greeted me with a warmth that felt familiar, despite it being our first meeting. His easy manner and genuine enthusiasm for the landscape instantly put me at ease. After a brief introduction to the area, its wildlife and history, we set off into the woodland. The path was wide and firm, a soft carpet of sand mixed with pine needles that crunched beneath my wheels. Above us, a bright blue sky stretched endlessly, dotted with slow-moving clouds drifting lazily across the canopy. The air was fresh, carrying the faint scent of the sea, a gentle reminder that the coastline was never far away.

As we ventured further, the forest revealed its subtle wonders. A sudden flash of rust-coloured fur caught my eye – a red squirrel darting nimbly through the branches. Overhead, the deep, echoing croak of ravens broke the quiet rustling of the trees in the breeze, while on the warm earth below a quick glimpse of a lizard basking in the sunlight reminded me of nature's delicate resilience.

The walk was not just a stroll through nature; it was a steady unfolding of the island's quiet charm, each step drawing us deeper into its gentle rhythms. Mike shared stories from his life, a rich tapestry of quiet strength and dedication. As a retired firefighter stationed at Manchester Airport, Mike had devoted his career to safeguarding the lives of countless individuals in the busy airport community. His calm presence reflected that experience – steady and compassionate. Beyond his career, Mike spoke warmly of his family, revealing himself to be a devoted husband and proud father for whom love was the cornerstone. His stories were laced with deep sincerity, connecting his life's work to the landscape around us.

In the stillness of the woods, as we paused beneath a canopy of towering trees, there was a rare kind of silence; not merely the absence of sound, but a breath held in reverence. It felt as if even the wind and the branches themselves were still, listening.

THE GOLDEN BEACH AT NEWBOROUGH NATURE RESERVE

Mike's voice softened as he spoke of a tragedy that had forever altered his world. His beloved daughter Beth, vibrant and full of promise, had taken her own life at just 17. The weight of grief in his words was palpable, carrying a sorrow no parent should ever bear.

Though pain filled his voice, Mike spoke passionately about Beth, her radiant spirit, boundless talent and infectious zest for life. His words painted a colourful picture of the daughter who was a shining star, radiating talent and joy in every aspect of her life. Her voice soared as she sang, her body moved with grace as she danced, and her quick wit brought laughter to all who were lucky enough to be in her presence. She was a performer through and through, with an unwavering passion for life. Beth was the heartbeat of any gathering, the one who could turn an ordinary moment into something extraordinary. Her zest for life was unmatched, and she lived each day to the fullest, embracing every opportunity that came her way.

A fallen tree at the side of the track, now home to moss and small creatures buried within the decaying wood, made a perfect resting stop along our walk.

DEBBIE AND MIKE ON THE BEACH, ANGLESEY

As we paused here for a while Mike told me how when the COVID-19 pandemic swept across the UK, Beth's world was turned upside down. Lockdowns shuttered her college, stripped away her hobbies and plans, and left her feeling trapped and uncertain. The future she once envisioned faded into a haze of isolation and despair. Despite her family's love and support, Beth's struggles remained hidden, a secret she carried alone.

Mike's voice cracked with emotion as he said, 'If only she had known about PAPYRUS and HOPELINEUK [UK charities working to prevent suicide], perhaps she would still be here, living her vibrant life.'

The realisation that such resources existed that might have saved her had only she found the courage to reach out was heartbreaking.

We pressed on, the forest gradually giving way to vast swathes of sand dunes. Here, the landscape was held together by dense clumps of marram grass, its spiky grey-green blades anchoring the shifting sands against the relentless winds. Mike's presence in this moment felt deeply symbolic. Like the marram grass binding the dunes, he had become a quiet force holding his family together, preventing memories of Beth from being scattered and lost in the winds of grief.

Since that unimaginable loss, Mike has been profoundly transformed. The path forward is marked by remembrance and quiet strength, shaped by love that endures, even in sorrow. For Mike, the forest and beach were more than places of natural beauty; they mirrored his journey through grief, with winding trails that brought waves of emotion, sorrow and, eventually, healing.

While he initially felt angry and confused, Mike began to seek answers and make sense of the tragedy. This led him down a path of exploring near death experiences (NDEs). He discovered that many people who have had such experiences report similar accounts of seeing light, feeling a sense of peace and even having encounters with deceased loved ones. This made Mike hopeful that Beth was in a better place and was at peace. He also read about how NDEs can be transformative, and how they often result in a renewed sense of purpose and gratitude for life.

Then, just three weeks after losing Beth, Mike was introduced to Tim Owen, and a little while later to Andy Airey – two other dads whose daughters had taken their own lives. Despite the dark circumstances, the three dads were determined to try and pull something positive out of the tragedy. Together, they devised a heartfelt plan to raise awareness about youth suicide, hoping to spark important conversations and help others avoid the heartbreak their families had endured. In 2021, they set out on a 483km (300-mile) journey in 2021, driven by their goal to raise money for the charity PAPYRUS. As the 3 Dads Walking, as they became known, walked side by side, a profound sense of unity enveloped them, creating a haven where they could openly discuss suicide and mental health.

Undeterred by their remarkable achievement, other walks followed in 2022 and 2024, totalling 2,253km (1,400 miles). Their impact was immeasurable, as their endeavours resulted in an astounding £1.4 million raised. These three dads continue to march forward, tirelessly dedicating themselves to supporting, empowering, influencing and engaging with communities. And their mission extends far beyond monetary contributions. They work with schools, universities, youth groups and mental health organisations to spread the vital message that suicide is preventable. Through training, awareness campaigns and policy advocacy, they aim to prioritise mental health or push for policies that prioritise mental health, ensuring that support is accessible, and that no young person feels alone in their darkest moments.

Standing on Newborough's beach, where the blue waves lap softly against golden sands, Mike reflected on the enduring presence of Beth. The salty breeze seemed to carry whispers of her laughter, her joy, her love. In this special place, surrounded by the vastness of sea and sky, her memory felt woven into the very heart of the land.

The tide was coming in, and with each wave delicate ripples of water crept further up the beach, slowly reclaiming the sand. Our two dogs darted in and out of the gentle surf, their joyful energy a soft contrast to the quiet stillness that lingered along the shoreline. I watched as the shifting patterns on the sand changed with each retreat and return of the water, every wave smoothing away the last trace, only to inscribe new lines in its place. It struck me how nothing in life remains unchanged. Like the tide, everything moves, reshaping, erasing and quietly beginning again.

Grief, too, is like that ever-changing shoreline. It has no fixed path, no right or wrong course. It rises and falls, shifts and softens, moment by moment. As we walked, Mike spoke gently about the changes he and his wife Helen had faced since losing Beth. Their family home, once alive with laughter, warmth and the familiar comfort of daily life, had become a space too heavy with absence. Its walls, thick with memory, echoed too loudly with what had been, and together they made the heart-wrenching decision to let it go. From its sale, they bought two smaller homes: one in Manchester, close to Helen's work at the primary school Beth once attended, and another on Anglesey, where the rhythm of the sea brought a different kind of peace. For Mike, the coastline offered something elemental, a quiet refuge where the sound of the waves and the expanse of open sky helped soften the weight of grief. Here, on this island shaped by wind and water, he found space to breathe again. One breath. One step. One wave at a time.

MIKE PALMER, MONTY AND TIP

Daily walks with Monty, his faithful dog, became a ritual of healing. Monty's companionship provided unwavering support, turning dark, sleepless nights into moments of quiet peace and motivating Mike to rise each day, even in his darkest moments, to take their daily walks together. The bond between man and dog exemplified the healing power of unconditional love and the restorative embrace of nature. On sleepless nights, Mike found solace in late-night walks with Monty, their bond deepening with each step.

The courage and resilience of Mike, Tim and Andy illuminate a path forward. Their journey proves that even in the shadow of heartbreak, hope can emerge. By turning personal tragedy into a mission of change, they inspire us to confront the youth suicide crisis with compassion and action. Their efforts remind us that every gesture of kindness, every conversation, and every step towards understanding can save a life. Together, we can create a world where no one feels alone in their darkest moments.

THE WALK

● IS IT FOR ME?

START/END POINT: Newborough NNR and Forest, Llanfairpwllgwyngyll, Anglesey, LL61 6SG

GRID REFERENCE: SH404634

DISTANCE: 4.2km (2.6 miles) circular

MILES WITHOUT STILES GRADE: For Many

TERRAIN: A mixture of woodland tracks and sand

ACCESSIBILITY: The forest tracks are mostly solid, but in some areas sand drifts onto the path, making travel in a manual wheelchair more challenging.

PARKING: Beach car park (LL61 6SG); fees apply, but Blue Badge holders can park for free.

FACILITIES: Accessible toilets are located in Beach car park (see above).

➡ THE ROUTE

In 1955, Newborough Forest became the home of Wales's first coastal NNR, encompassing the Newborough Warren and Ynys Llanddwyn. This location is a sanctuary for wildlife, with red squirrels, badgers, foxes, buzzards and owls thriving in this landscape.

Newborough offers a variety of trails to suit every adventurer, including an accessible trail. This well-defined route, free from barriers and set on a solid, level track, ensures that individuals of all abilities can explore the forest with ease. Whether you're walking, cycling or using a wheelchair, this trail offers a seamless way to experience the area's beauty and tranquil atmosphere.

Detailed information regarding accessibility and trail options can be found at the website nationalresources.wales, enabling every visitor to plan their journey into this captivating destination.

NEED TO KNOW

A PLACE TO EAT: Dylan's Restaurant, St George's Rd, Menai Bridge, LL59 5EY, near to the Menai Bridge, serves fresh, local produce.

A PLACE TO DRINK: The Bulkeley Hotel, 19 Castle St, Beaumaris, LL58 8AW

A PLACE TO SLEEP: Penrhos Caravan and Motorhome Club Campsite has facilities for disabled visitors.

IF YOU'RE LOOKING FOR SOMETHING ELSE…

Beaumaris, the name of which derives from the Norman French for 'fair marsh', is home to one of the most remarkable castles in Wales. Built by Edward I as the last of his 'Iron Ring' castles, **Beaumaris Castle** is an architectural masterpiece, though never completed due to a lack of funds. The town itself is also a delight to explore, with pastel-coloured cottages, a scenic seafront and the historic Beaumaris Pier, perfect for crabbing.

Nearby, **Penmon Point** offers stunning views of Puffin Island and Trwyn Du Lighthouse. **Red Wharf Bay's** vast sandy shores and the peaceful Church Island add to the area's rich history and natural beauty.

BEACON FELL

CRAIG-Y-NOS COUNTRY PARK, BANNAU BRYCHEINIOG NATIONAL PARK

KAREN HARRIS

My first visit to the rolling hills of the Bannau Brycheiniog (Brecon Beacons) National Park was an alluring introduction to the natural beauty of South Wales. The vista stretched before me, a stunning blend of rugged, wind-swept mountains, lush green valleys and sparkling lakes. The landscape shifted dramatically with the changing weather and time of day, revealing new layers of its charm at every turn.

I had arranged to meet Karen Harris at Craig-y-nos Country Park, a place steeped in history and alive with the echoes of centuries past. Despite the persistent drizzle, the grandeur of the estate remained undiminished, its imposing silhouette standing in stark contrast to the moody Welsh sky. The knowledge that this was once the home of the legendary diva Adelina Patti, whose voice captivated the world, added an enchanting layer to the atmosphere.

 Even with the weather's best efforts to dampen the mood, my excitement to explore the Country Park and uncover its secrets remained strong. But before setting out on my walk, the promise of a warm cup of tea and a slice of cake, shared with the insightful company of Karen, offered the perfect pause before the adventure truly began.

 From the moment our paths crossed, Karen's magnetic energy pulled me in. Karen, who has worked and volunteered in the social care and disability sectors

KAREN HARRIS AT CRAIG-Y-NOS COUNTRY PARK

for many years, and who has a disability herself, has an optimism and zest for life that are simply irresistible. With every word she speaks, her enthusiasm for Bannau Brycheiniog National Park is contagious, leaving me yearning to experience its wonders first-hand.

As we descended the steep path into the woods, I quickly understood why Wales held such a special place in Karen's heart. The towering Scots pine trees stand like guardians of the park, their branches creaking softly in the breeze. The crisp scent of pine and damp moss fills the air, while the light rain filters through the dense canopy. This isn't just a place she loves – it is a part of her, woven into her memories and soul. With every step, I could see her connection to this wild, timeless land.

Fond memories of delightful family excursions flood her mind, transporting her back to the carefree days of her childhood. She vividly recalls her mother's meticulous preparations for these adventures, as if she were packing for a grand expedition. The car would be filled to the brim with all the essentials – a primus stove, the family teapot, the loose-leaf tea, a trusty washing bowl – it was like having an entire kitchen on wheels. Karen's mother was renowned for her staunch readiness, ensuring that no matter what the day held, they would be well-equipped to face it head-on. No such thing as packing light, Karen follows in her mother's footsteps, with a Kelly Kettle, camping toilet and patchwork quilt ready for comfort breaks in the back of the van she calls 'Daisy'.

After being forced to take ill health retirement, Karen chose to relocate to Wales, where she could finally live in a place of her own choosing without the constraints of work obligations. She has never regretted her decision.

Karen's life has been one marked by health struggles. In her younger years, she was subjected to bullying at school because of her unique qualities. Engaging in physical activities and sports was especially challenging for her, as she was frequently mocked when trying to run, and never picked for the team.

Karen's life took an unexpected twist when she underwent a major life-altering surgery at the tender age of 30. However, she refused to let this setback define her future. Despite grappling with physical obstacles and the responsibilities of being a single mother to two young boys, Karen's resilience shone through. Rather than succumbing to the challenges, she embarked on a remarkable journey of self-improvement by pursuing higher education as a mature student. With enduring determination, Karen embarked on the path to success, ultimately achieving an extraordinary feat – earning a degree in Environmental Science and Geography and master's degree in Environmental Pollution Control.

As we wandered beneath the towering oak trees, their gnarled, twisted stumps adding character to the path, Karen spoke about balancing the demands of full-time studies, part-time work, voluntary work commitments and the tireless care of her two boys. She showed time and time again that she was unstoppable. Her resilience was as rooted in strength as the ancient trees surrounding us, each branch reaching for something greater, a reflection of the determination she carried with her every day. No barrier was too daunting for her to conquer. Karen's story is living proof of the power of perseverance and the indomitable spirit of a woman who refused to let circumstances define her. Her relentless dedication and single-minded spirit serve as an inspiration to all those who face adversity.

While seeking refuge in the woods to escape what was now a relentless downpour, Karen told me about the other obstacles she encountered both in her personal life and professional career. She revealed that she had endured a challenging period where she was incessantly targeted, due to her disabilities, by a clique of toxic individuals. This cruel treatment left her feeling isolated and vulnerable. Additionally, she faced hostility from others due to her reliance on government benefits during that time.

Karen took a sudden turn for the worse when she suffered a terrible fall, resulting in a fractured neck, crushed vertebrae and a head injury that caused her to lose her ability to recall many words. Even when she managed to secure employment, her employer placed immense pressure on her to exceed her own limitations. The only accommodation provided to her, as part of the 'reasonable

WALKING THROUGH THE WOODS OF CRAIG-Y-NOS COUNTRY PARK

BEACON FELL | CRAIG-Y-NOS COUNTRY PARK, BANNAU BRYCHEINIOG NATIONAL PARK

adjustment' policy, was an office chair. This left her solely responsible for managing all other aspects of her work without any additional support. To make matters worse, she was unceremoniously fired from her job while signed off and suffering from a 'breakdown', leading her doctor to recommend she give up her pursuit of a career.

This served as a wake-up call for Karen to prioritise her own well-being and health. So, with her two boys now grown and independent, she made the bold decision to start anew in Wales. Gone were the days of tirelessly trying to fit into a career or overcome her limitations just to find a sense of belonging; she had finally found her true home.

Despite the barriers she faced, she sought solace in nature with the help of her trusty all-terrain mobility scooter, affectionately named 'Kit'.

'To feel the wind in my hair, see and hear the abundant flora and fauna,' Karen says, 'to wander with waterfalls and rivers as companions, and to be embraced by the ever-changing skies – that is my inspiration for my poetry.'

For a few moments, we sat beneath the wooden pagoda, sheltered in its quiet embrace as the lake stretched before us, alive with movement. Cheeky ducks waddled close, eyeing us curiously, while elegant swans glided effortlessly across the water. Raindrops danced on the surface, creating endless ripples that shimmered and faded into the depths. The air was rich with birdsong and the distant rustle of reeds. We let the silence settle, breathing in the calm, the rhythmic patter of rain on water soothing like a quiet lullaby. In that stillness, the world felt softer, as if time had paused to exhale.

When Karen first contacted Bannau Brycheiniog to inquire about wheelchair accessibility, she was hopeful for helpful information. However, what she received was a booklet that seemed to focus solely on the obstacles she would face – mainly stiles, steps and gates. It quickly became apparent that this booklet was only highlighting the places where she couldn't go. Her frustration reached its peak when she arrived at a site and discovered that the only suggestion for her to experience the countryside was to sit in the car and admire the view. This was not the kind of guidance she had hoped for, and it tested her patience to the limit. Karen's motto rang in her ears: 'Don't sit at home and moan about it, get out there and do something about it!'. Determined to make her feelings known, she picked up the phone and voiced her concerns to park staff.

Karen has always enjoyed voluntary work, so when she received an invitation to join the esteemed Local Access Forum for the Bannau Brycheiniog National Park, her heart swelled with pride. With steely determination, she embarked on a noble mission to enhance the park's accessibility for all.

THE AUTUMN COLOURS AT CRAIG-Y-NOS

During our soggy stroll through the intricate network of paths encircling the Craig-y-nos Country Park, Karen graciously divulged her thoughtful and insightful recommendations for enhancing accessibility, which she had previously presented to the authorities. With a discerning eye, she emphasised that not every path necessitated the rigidity of tarmac or concrete, as sturdy tracks would aptly serve the purpose. 'Tarmac everywhere is superfluous,' she confidently asserted. And with the right equipment often available to hire at numerous locations, those with mobility issues can enjoy the countryside au naturel.

Karen related the extensive work that still lay ahead in ensuring the National Park caters to the needs of people with disabilities, but she couldn't contain her elation at the newfound recognition her voice had garnered.

As the rain eased into a gentle drizzle, and a glimmer of sunshine pierced through the clouds, it became clear how the sights, sounds and smells of nature soothe her soul and calm her often-tattered nerves. Despite everything, Karen remains remarkably positive. When asked how she manages to maintain such a sunny outlook, she simply replied that she has both faith and Mother Nature to help her. While she doesn't attend church every Sunday, she believes that nature is her sanctuary and that her prayers are answered there. Karen also shared with me the power of a cwtch, a special type of Welsh hug that goes beyond a simple embrace. Receiving a cwtch from Karen in this haven of tranquillity was truly an honour and a privilege that I will always cherish.

THE WALK

IS IT FOR ME?

START/END POINT: Pen-y-cae, Craig-y-nos, Swansea, SA9 1GL

GRID REFERENCE: SN840155

DISTANCE: 2.1km (1.3 miles) circular

MILES WITHOUT STILES GRADE: For Many

TERRAIN: A mix of forest and tarmac tracks

ACCESSIBILITY: The park offers a fun and safe day out for all the family. Suitable for those who use a manual wheelchair, though there is a steep gradient to climb up to the café.

PARKING: Free parking is available for Blue Badge holders at Craig-y-nos Country Park. The park is also accessible via the X63 bus service, which runs 6–8 times daily between Swansea and Brecon along the A4067.

FACILITIES: Wheelchair-accessible toilets and a café are also on site.

THE ROUTE

Craig-y-nos Country Park is a haven of natural beauty, with towering mature trees lining the numerous winding paths, inviting visitors to create their own scenic trail. The gentle murmur of the river and the shimmering surfaces of two picturesque lakes add to the park's serene charm, drawing a rich variety of wildlife.

For those seeking a moment of rest, the visitor centre and tea room offer a range of hot food, cake and drinks, while picnic spots and benches provide the perfect place

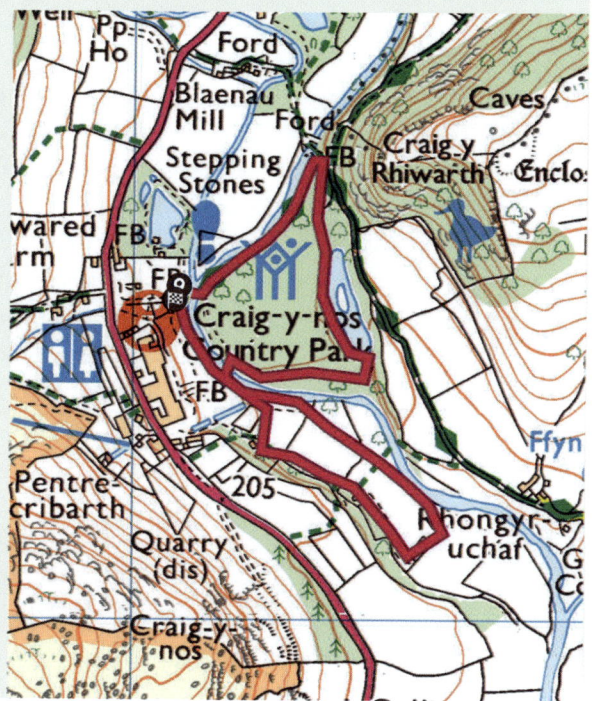

to pause and take in the peaceful surroundings. With its tranquil atmosphere and abundant beauty, the park is an ideal escape for a relaxing afternoon.

NEED TO KNOW

A PLACE TO EAT: The Pen-y-cae Inn, Brecon Rd, Pen-y-cae, Swansea, SA9 1FA, is an award-winning restaurant serving generous portions and high-quality food.

A PLACE TO DRINK: The Gwyn Arms, also in Pen-y-cae, Swansea (SA9 1GP) is a traditional country pub nestled in stunning scenery.

A PLACE TO SLEEP: The Sleeping Giant, Brecon Road, Pen-y-cae, Swansea Valley, Powys, SA9 1FA (has two accessible rooms).

IF YOU'RE LOOKING FOR SOMETHING ELSE...

Big Pit National Coal Museum, located in the Blaenafon Industrial Landscape and a designated UNESCO World Heritage Site, offers a powerful glimpse into Wales' industrial past. Once a working coal mine, it now stands as a tribute to the miners who toiled underground. Visitors can descend 91m (300ft) into the dark tunnels, guided by ex-miners who share first-hand stories of the harsh conditions. Above ground, exhibitions showcase the impact of coal on Welsh communities.

Nearby, **Talybont Reservoir** stretches 4km (2.5 miles) through the Bannau Brycheiniog National Park, surrounded by rugged moorland and dense woodland. Its tranquil waters reflect the rolling hills, offering a stark contrast to the deep, echoing chambers of Big Pit.

THE NEARBY TALYBONT RESERVOIR

THE WYE VALLEY
REDBROOK, GLOUCESTER

BETHANY HANDLEY

From Bannau Brycheiniog National Park, my journey back over the border into England was short. I was heading to Redbrook, a small Gloucestershire village tucked against the River Wye, where the steep, wooded slopes of Wales and England lean gently into one another. It's the kind of place you could pass by without noticing unless, of course, you were looking for it. And I was.

I'd come in search of Bethany Handley – a young poet, disability activist and outdoorsperson whose name had been quietly circulating in the walking and environmental worlds. Her words, both written and spoken, had begun to ripple far beyond her rural roots. Curious, inspired and perhaps a little awed, I arrived eager to meet the voice behind the verses.

 Bethany grew up along the English–Welsh border, surrounded by the beauty of the Wye Valley. From her early childhood, the outdoors wasn't just a backdrop; it was a source of wonder, joy and identity. Whether hiking the green folds of the valley or roaming wooded trails with her family, she learned to feel not just at home in nature, but part of it.

 We left the car park and crossed the Penallt Viaduct – a striking, gently curving skeleton of iron that once carried trains between Monmouth and Chepstow. Now repurposed as a footbridge, it links Redbrook with Penallt in Wales, stretching over the fast-moving waters of the Wye. At the centre of the span, we paused, listening to the rush below. It was there that Bethany spoke quietly about her bond with this landscape and how, over time, it had evolved from something she loved to something she *needed*.

'The Black Mountains in the Brecon Beacons are my sanctuary,' she said. 'I go there to clear my head. There's space to breathe, to think, to just *be*.' That sense of clarity, of belonging, was something she returned to again and again.

Her passion for the outdoors once took many forms: hiking, rock climbing, sailing – all pursuits that filled her with exhilaration. They were more than hobbies. They were a way of seeing and being, connecting her body, mind and spirit to the land.

But when she was 15, everything changed. A sudden chronic illness forced a dramatic reorientation of her life. Over time, she came to rely on a wheelchair, a shift that could have confined her world. But Bethany didn't see it that way. Instead, she embraced the chair as a tool of freedom.

'I hate being pushed,' she told me with a smile that didn't invite pity. And with the help of a power-assist attachment that clips to the front of her chair, she can now take to trails once out of reach. 'The power wheel gives me back my independence. Without it, I'm stuck.'

We followed the old railway line, now a quiet, leafy path curving gently along the valley. The river ran beside us, always close, its voice low and constant. This trail – wide, level, stile-free – is one of the few accessible routes in the area. It's a rare example of what's possible when access is built in, not bolted on.

BATHANY HANDLEY AND DEBBIE AT REDBROOK

THE WYE VALLEY | REDBROOK, GLOUCESTER

Bethany spoke candidly about how people with disabilities are often excluded from the outdoors, not by nature itself, but by human-made barriers: narrow gates, steep tracks, lack of information and a sheer absence of representation. 'Access to nature isn't just about ramps,' she said. 'It's about knowing you *belong* here.'

For her, nature is not just a personal refuge; it's also a political frontier. She's tired of being congratulated for showing up in places she has every right to be.

'I've been called "inspirational" more times than I can count,' she said, laughing, though there was an edge of weariness to it. 'It's as if people don't expect us to exist outdoors at all.'

That exclusion isn't always intentional, but it's everywhere. Even on that day, our walk was cut short by a locked barrier designed to stop vehicles. It stopped us too. We couldn't get through in our wheelchairs. So we turned around and retraced our steps, back along the track where the river hummed beside us and sunlight filtered through leaves like breath. It didn't feel like a defeat, just unfinished. This is a place I know I'll return to. The solitude and quiet of that trail stayed with me, echoing long after we left.

As we walked, Bethany told me about her time at university in Cardiff, a period defined as much by ambition as by disruption. The pandemic hit hard. Like many vulnerable people with disabilities, she spent much of the time in isolation. She caught the virus twice. One night, struggling to breathe, she was refused entry to hospital and treated in a car park.

That moment – inadequate, dehumanising – left deep scars, both physically and emotionally. Yet she kept going. She completed her degree in Media, Poetry and Creative Writing, finding in language a way to make sense of what the world could not explain.

Her poetry is not an escape from that reality, it's a confrontation with it. A form of truth-telling. She writes to illuminate what it means to move through a world that wasn't built with her in mind. Her words carry not just feeling, but clarity. They are acts of resistance, empathy and reclamation.

'Non-disabled people need to speak up too,' she said. 'Otherwise, it's always us doing the emotional labour.'

Her writing asks readers to listen differently, to understand access not as charity, but as justice.

Yet even the tools that enable that access are out of reach for many. Bethany had to crowdfund her power wheel. She paid for her manual chair out of her student loan. These essential devices – lifelines, not luxuries – remain outside the budgets of most people who need them. That's a systemic failure, not a personal one.

'There's this idea that the countryside belongs to a certain kind of person; white, able-bodied, middle class,' she said. 'But that's not true. It never was.' And she's right. Our images of who 'belongs' in nature are built on histories of exclusion, at once colonial, ableist and elitist. To walk freely in the countryside is still, for many, a radical act.

Bethany doesn't consider herself an activist, but her very presence in these spaces challenges the structures that say she shouldn't be there. She dreams of a future where she doesn't have to fight to exist – where the beauty of the world is available to everyone, by design.

That day in Redbrook, walking the old rail path and watching the Wye wind its way toward the sea, I saw what that future might look like. It's not just wider gates and smoother trails, though those matter. It's a culture shift. A change in who we imagine when we picture someone walking through the woods.

Bethany will keep writing, keep walking, keep speaking. Not because she has to but because she believes in a world that welcomes everyone.

And I will return to that path. Not just for the peace it offers, but for what it taught me: that access is not a favour to be granted. It's a right to be honoured. And that, perhaps, is the truest path forward.

CROSSING THE BRIDGE OVER THE RIVER WYE

THE WALK

IS IT FOR ME?

START/END POINT: Penallt Viaduct, also known as Redbrook Bridge, is located on the former Wye Valley Railway, spanning the River Wye between Penallt in Monmouthshire, Wales, and Redbrook in Gloucestershire, England.

GRID REFERENCE: SO536099

DISTANCE: 7.2km (4.5 miles) there and back

MILES WITHOUT STILES GRADE: For All

TERRAIN: Compacted soil and tarmac track

ACCESSIBILITY: The walk is suitable for manual wheelchair users.

PARKING: There's a car park at the start of the walk in Redbrook (NP25 4LZ); fees apply.

FACILITIES: There are no toilet facilities on this walk.

THE ROUTE

The walk Bethany and I shared follows a repurposed section of the Wye Valley Railway, once a vital link between Monmouth and Chepstow, carrying both passengers and freight through the steep-sided valley. Closed in the 1950s, the railway was largely dismantled, but several features remain, most striking among them the Penallt Viaduct.

Built in 1876, the viaduct is an elegant single-track iron structure spanning the River Wye. Its trestled design blends surprisingly well with the wooded surroundings, and today it's used by walkers and cyclists as part of the Wye Valley Walk. From the middle, you can see the river winding away in both directions, fringed with willows and alders. On a still day, the only sounds are birdsong and the noise of the river.

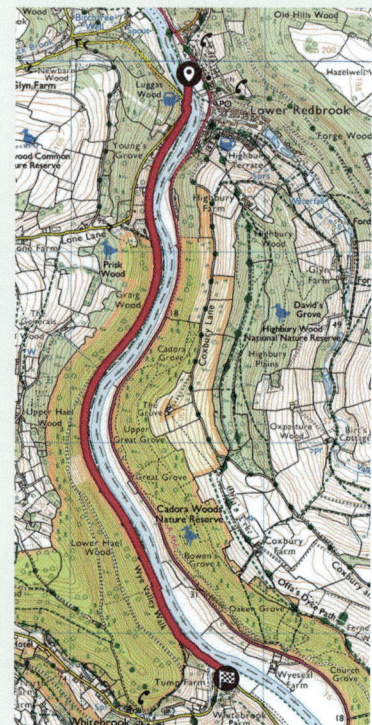

The rest of the trail is flat, accessible and quiet – a rare example of rural infrastructure where people using mobility aids can move freely and independently. It's a reminder of how abandoned industrial routes, if thoughtfully adapted, can become inclusive green corridors linking past to present in more ways than one.

NEED TO KNOW

A PLACE TO EAT: Estero Lounge in nearby Monmouth (NP25 3PS) has step-free access, ample space for wheelchairs and accessible facilities.

A PLACE TO DRINK: The Bell Inn in Redbrook (NP25 4LZ) has wheelchair facilities.

A PLACE TO SLEEP: Homefield Cottage in Itton, Chepstow, Monmouthshire (NP16 6BX) is worth noting. This welcoming cottage offers disabled-friendly facilities and is dog-friendly, making it a rare and inclusive option for those traveling with mobility needs and pets. Its location, nestled in the peaceful borderlands near the village of Grosmont, provides a perfect base for accessing the surrounding countryside.

IF YOU'RE LOOKING FOR SOMETHING ELSE...

If you're looking to explore more of the area's rich heritage, **Clearwell Caves**, just a short drive from Redbrook, offer a unique window into the region's industrial past. These ancient iron mines, now preserved as a visitor attraction, reveal 4,500 years of mining history beneath the Forest of Dean. While not all areas are wheelchair accessible due to the nature of the terrain, the site provides detailed access information and is well worth visiting for those who can manage the uneven paths. It's an atmospheric experience, with underground chambers and storytelling that bring the earth's hidden history vividly to life: see clearwellcaves.com for more information.

NEARBY CLEARWELL CAVES

HERGEST RIDGE
HEREFORDSHIRE

MARIKA KOVACS

As we sat down to enjoy our lunch beneath the towering monkey puzzle trees, I was completely taken aback by the sheer beauty of this serene and peaceful place. The atmosphere was tranquil, so still – as if time itself had slowed down to allow us to fully absorb the moment. The sky, an endless canvas of blue, stretched out in all directions, offering a stunning 360-degree view that enveloped us in its vastness. Above, wisps of clouds drifted lazily, while below, the landscape was awash in a thousand shades of green, each more vibrant than the last. The rolling hills of Hergest Ridge, part of the historic Offa's Dyke Path, undulated gently in the distance, adding a sense of timelessness to the scene. The ridge seemed to merge seamlessly with the sky, creating a harmonious blend of earth and heaven that filled me with a deep sense of peace. Here, in this untouched corner of nature, it is easy to feel a connection to something much larger than us; a reminder of the simple yet profound beauty the natural world offers.

What made this particular walk even more special was my remarkable walking companion for the day, Marika Kovacs. A blind hiker from Hereford, Marika's presence brought an entirely new dimension to the experience. Her steely determination and deep passion for this area were immediately evident. With her walking guide, Angela, by her side, Marika strode out confidently, placing complete trust in Angela to help her navigate the trail. Despite the challenges she has faced, Marika's spirit is unwavering.

Born with infantile glaucoma, a condition resulting from her mother contracting German measles during pregnancy, Marika's vision was

ANGELA GUIDES MARIKA ALONG THE HERGEST RIDGE

compromised from birth. The illness caused damage to the optic nerve and eventual loss of vision. Yet, despite the obstacles presented by her condition, Marika's love for the outdoors and her determination to explore the world around her shine through. Watching her navigate the trail with such confidence and trust is truly inspiring, making this walk one I will never forget.

We began our ascent along the grassy track that winds its way along the Hergest Ridge. Marika suddenly stopped, turned to Angela and asked: 'What's missing from this walk?' Her voice carried a hint of curiosity, as if she was sensing something subtle that the rest of us might have overlooked.

Angela, caught off guard by the question, replied thoughtfully, 'I'm not sure, Marika. What do you mean?'

Marika, with her heightened awareness of the world around her, told us to listen. The only sound that met our ears was the gentle rustling of the wind. The silence was profound, enveloping us in a serene, almost meditative state.

Then, after a few moments, Marika broke the silence with a quiet observation that struck us all. 'The skylarks have gone,' she said softly, her words hanging in the air like the memory of a lost melody.

Marika is fascinated by birdsong and has learned to recognise the calls of most British birds. For her, it is a delight to venture outdoors and listen to the melodies that fill the air. Woodland walks are a particular favourite of hers, as the harmonious birdsong echoing through the forest create a sense of being enveloped by nature. She has come up with a playful rhyme for each bird's call to help her recognise the different species. When she hears the yellowhammer, she enthusiastically recites, 'A little bit of milk and no cheeeeese,' mimicking the distinct rhythm of the bird's song.

Marika's sensitivity to this detail brought a deeper awareness to our walk, transforming what might have been just another peaceful day on the trail into a moment of quiet reflection on the ever-changing rhythms of the natural world.

Marika, who is perfectly capable of navigating her own walks, requires only minimal assistance – just a light guiding hand and occasional alerts about potential hazards or changes in the path's surface. She is such a skilled and confident walker that it's easy to forget she might need a reminder now and then. In fact, there was a moment when I nearly forgot to warn her about a closed gate, and we almost walked straight into it – entirely my oversight!

Marika began walking with Herefordshire Ramblers in the summer of 2012 but quickly realised she wanted to take on a more prominent role. As chair of the group, she played a pivotal role in the Hereford Walking Festival and contributed significantly to the relaunch of the Herefordshire Trail in 2022, a 248km (154 mile) circular walking trail. During the relaunch, more than 100 walkers took part in the event, with Marika walking the first section of the trail.

Marika expressed her desire to lead a walk herself, and from there a unique solution began to unfold. 'I thought we could write the directions of a walk down, and it all started from that. We recorded it on a Dictaphone, then had it transcribed into braille.'

With the support of friends, Marika devised a method that allows her to confidently lead walks. A close friend found an 8km (5 mile) route near Breinton where she could practice. Together they walked the path, her friend describing each detail, which Marika later turned into detailed notes, which in turn became her prompt as she led the walk.

Each walk she now leads involves at least three practice runs using her Dictaphone and braille notes to familiarise herself with the route. Her dedication has paid off, and she has led walks for groups of various sizes, including one for 35 people.

'It takes a long time to get 35 people over stiles!' she joked.

Despite being a capable and experienced walker, Marika has faced challenges which are often met with doubt. She recalls, 'I've had quite a few instances where people have said things like, "You can't do that, we're not covered by our insurance." These are meant to be barriers to stop me from doing what I love! Thankfully, though, the Ramblers have always been supportive of my ambitions.'

During the week, Marika works at the Royal National College for the Blind but she takes every opportunity to get outdoors and absorb the nature around her.

Sight is just one of the senses through which we experience the world, but it often dominates our attention. Marika serves as an inspiring reminder of the importance of pausing to engage and awaken all our senses. By taking the time to listen to the subtle rustle of leaves in the wind, feel the texture of the earth beneath our feet, breathe in the invigorating scents of nature and savour the quiet stillness around us, we can deepen our connection to nature and find moments of peace and clarity.

We walked on, and the disused Victorian racecourse came into view – a popular summer racing venue between 1825 and 1846, its markings still faintly etched along the ridge. Reaching the trig point at the summit of Hergest Ridge, a vast panorama unfolded, stretching from the Black Mountains to the Malvern Hills, with uninterrupted English and Welsh landscapes in between. While we paused for a breathe, I said to Marika, 'I'm closing my eyes to experience what you must see in your mind.'

She responded, 'Don't. My eyes have never seen the view. Instead, listen to it, touch it, smell it, taste it ... that's nature's true power. This is mindfulness, immersed and untethered in the world's pure essence.'

Marika's approach encourages us to move beyond simply observing and to fully immerse ourselves in our surroundings, fostering a more mindful, balanced and enriched way of living. Her example shows that when we tune into the symphony of sensations around us, we open ourselves to a deeper appreciation of life and a more profound connection to nature and each other. In a fast-paced world, her message is clear: slow down, engage your senses and truly feel the world around you.

THE NEARBY HERGEST CROFT GARDENS

THE WALK

IS IT FOR ME?

START/END POINT: Hergest Croft Gardens, Ridgebourne Rd, Kington, HR5 3EG

GRID REFERENCE: SO285567

DISTANCE: 5.1km (3.2 miles)

MILES WITHOUT STILES GRADE: For Some

TERRAIN: Grassy paths and tarmac tracks

ACCESSIBILITY: This walk involves a gentle climb to the summit and requires a robust all-terrain wheelchair to navigate the uneven terrain and inclines.

PARKING: There is a free car park at Hergest Croft Gardens, 450m (1,476ft) up Ridgebourne Road on the right-hand side.

FACILITIES: Accessible toilets are located in Hergest Croft Gardens (see above). The café in the garden centre is wheelchair accessible.

THE ROUTE

This moderately challenging route along Offa's Dyke Path is popular among walkers and runners and offers panoramic views of both Mid-Wales and Herefordshire. It's an ideal walk for those who use an all-terrain wheelchair, as there are no stiles on the route. The trail begins from the car park near Hergest Croft Gardens and follows the Offa's Dyke Path up to the moorland of Hergest Ridge.

The well-marked path ensures easy navigation, guiding visitors through a landscape that inspired musician Mike Oldfield's 1974 album *Hergest Ridge,* which he made during his retreat from the chaos of London to Herefordshire's serene countryside. Along the way, watch for wild ponies and free-roaming sheep – dog owners should keep their pets on a lead. A stop at Hergest Croft Gardens, open March–October, provides a lovely opportunity for refreshments amid beautiful surroundings.

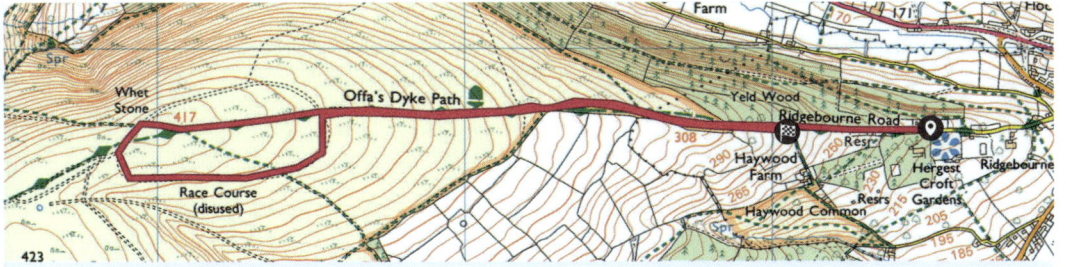

NEED TO KNOW

A PLACE TO EAT: The Mill Race in Walford, Ross-on-Wye (HR9 5QS) has accessible facilities.

A PLACE TO DRINK: Hergest Croft Gardens (see page 68).

A PLACE TO SLEEP: Drovers Rest, Llanerch Y Coed Farm off Watery Lane in Hay-on-Wye (HR3 6AG) has three stone cottages and six luxury glamping tents, providing accessible facilities.

IF YOU'RE LOOKING FOR SOMETHING ELSE…

Nestled beneath the iconic Hergest Ridge with breathtaking views of the Black Mountains, **Hergest Croft Gardens** is a stunning 28ha (70 acre) horticultural paradise. Created over 120 years by five generations of the Banks family, the gardens hold National Collections of maples, birches and zelkovas, along with over 130 Champion Trees, exceptional examples of their species due to their size, age, rarity or historical significance. Divided into six areas, visitors can explore vibrant azalea displays, an enchanting rockery and the secluded Park Wood with its towering rhododendrons. With rare plants, seasonal bursts of colour, a charming tea room and a gift shop, this award-winning 'Hidden Gem' offers a truly memorable experience for garden lovers and nature enthusiasts alike.

THE HIDDEN GEM OF HERGEST CROFT GARDENS

LEIGH WOODS
ABBOTS LEIGH, SOMERSET

DEE CRUTE

Nestled beneath the iconic sweep of Brunel's suspension bridge lies Leigh Woods National Nature Reserve, a sanctuary of serenity just a stone's throw from the bustling city of Bristol. Its well-marked trails weave through the woodland's ancient trees offering a gentle escape for walkers of all kinds. It was here that I met Dee Crute, author, science journalist and photographer. Together, we embarked on an exploration of this woodland wonderland.

Dee was born and raised in Poland, where her love for the outdoors took root early, blossoming into a lifelong connection with nature. For Dee, the wilderness has always been more than a backdrop; it is her sanctuary, a place of healing and discovery. She proudly calls herself a 'disabled adventurer', a title she wears with both defiance and joy.

As we entered the woodland, the air grew cooler beneath the dense canopy of towering oaks, ash and beech, their leaves dancing in the breeze. The forest floor unfolded like a living tapestry, a rich, vibrant mosaic of green. Every step felt like a journey into nature's secrets which lay hidden just out of sight, waiting to be discovered.

'The definition of adventure is anything that brings an unexpected outcome, and it's exciting, isn't it?' Dee exclaimed, her eyes bright with enthusiasm, as if the forest itself was an invitation to something thrilling and unknown. The woods, with their timeless beauty, seemed to echo her words, offering a promise of endless possibilities and the kind of adventure that stirs the soul.

Pausing to let the thought settle, she posed a question that lingered in the crisp woodland air: 'So what is the difference between life and adventure?'

DEE AND DEBBIE IN LEIGH WOODS

Dee went on to share how she had once merely existed; trapped in cycles of pain, stress and anxiety, compounded by post-traumatic stress disorder (PTSD) and autism. But reframing her perspective changed everything.

'Now,' she said with quiet resolve, 'I try to live every day as an adventure, surrounded by nature.'

We reached a clearing, the peaceful surroundings of the coppicing coupes providing a serene backdrop to Dee's words. I listened with interest as Dee shared her remarkable story. Her early life was marked by immense challenges: she was born with developmental dysplasia of the hip (DDH), in which the ball-and-socket joint of the hip fails to form properly. Then she was later diagnosed with Ehlers-Danlos syndromes (EDS), a rare, life-threatening condition that weakens connective tissues. Doctors had warned her parents that her chances of survival were slim, but her family was determined to give her the best quality of life possible. As a baby, Dee spent months in a Pavlik harness to stabilise her hips, followed by years of gruelling physical therapy. Despite these hardships, her spirit remained unbreakable. Through swimming, running and horse riding, she built both strength and resilience, embracing every opportunity to grow, much like the wildlife nurtured in these woodlands, thriving through care and perseverance.

By her teenage years, Dee had defied expectations, living a life that seemed ordinary on the surface. Yet her journey was far from simple. Around this time, she was also diagnosed with autism.

'I had a warrior survivor soul,' she proclaimed, reflecting on her determination to beat the odds.

That tenacity propelled her forward. Through every trial, Dee's unwavering grit and profound connection to the natural world became her compass, shaping the adventurer she is today.

Academically, she excelled, her boundless curiosity and perseverance leading her to university, where she graduated in Biology with honours. She started an integrated PhD programme combining an MSc in Animal Biotechnology and PhD in Reproductive Physiology and Toxicology, but was unable to finish her studies due to the trauma of domestic abuse she suffered. However, she went on to work in the animal physiology and reproductive toxicology department in academia in Poland.

Dee later moved to England with her new husband, a Brighton native, but her dreams of a happy life quickly turned into a nightmare. She endured four years of almost daily domestic abuse, so harrowing that the memories remain too painful for her to speak of even now. The relentless trauma left her petrified of people. At times she became an elective mute, seeking solace not in human company but in the quiet embrace of the natural world.

Her 'warrior survivor soul' gave her the strength to eventually break free and move forward. However, the career she chose as a police officer brought a new kind of pain, as Dee was sexually abused by a work colleague. The impact was overwhelming, affecting her emotionally, mentally and physically. She felt betrayed, as the perpetrator was someone she worked with in a trusted capacity. It shattered her sense of safety and made her question her ability to trust people. She began to experience vicarious trauma. She grew to hate the world, believing she could no longer live in it. She was on a downward spiral and her health was a cause for concern. She also had to face a diagnosis of multiple sclerosis (MS), a chronic disease that affects the brain and spinal cord.

Aware of Dee's medical condition, I had my concerns that our walk through Leigh Woods would be too demanding for her, with its winding trails and steepish slopes, but I never imagined she would tell me that this brief adventure was nothing compared to the long-distance journey she had already completed.

After resting awhile and taking time to soak up the freshness of the woodland, we walked deeper still into the forest. These ancient trees not only shaded our path but also sustained a thriving ecosystem – more than 300 species of fungi grow here, including edible varieties like beefsteak and oyster mushrooms. Dee pointed out a couple of unusual ones nestled among the moss – vivid scarlet elf cups clinging to fallen branches, and the delicate coral-like structure of the yellow stagshorn.

The setting in this part of the woodland had grown quiet, dark and damp, filled with earthy, almost musty smells. What struck me most was how dramatically the mood of the forest shifted from one area to the next. Within only a few minutes of continuing along the trail, the dense woods gradually opened into a sunlit clearing. The light broke through the canopy in golden shafts, warming the ground. It was as if the forest itself was breathing, changing, adapting – each pocket of space holding its own distinct character. We came across a secluded picnic bench in a peaceful spot and settled in with our drinks. As Dee spoke, I listened intently, captivated by her words. The quiet atmosphere seemed to embrace her story, as if the moment itself had been designed for something remarkable to unfold.

At her lowest point, Dee made a life-changing decision: to embark on the 1,014km (630 mile) South West Coast Path, an epic journey along the rugged coastline of England's south-west peninsula. It was a daunting challenge, especially for someone diagnosed with EDS and MS, whose loose and unstable joints made every step a potential source of pain. But Dee was determined.

'I walked it solo, unsupported, with a tent on my back. And yes, I was mostly wild camping,' she explained. The physical strain was immense, and there were moments when she felt like giving up. 'But I wanted to avoid humanity as much as possible and focus on the healing power of nature.'

But nature wasn't her only teacher on this journey. Something surprising began to happen; people started to help her heal.

'If you asked me to describe my adventure in one word, it would be serendipity.' Her face lit up with an infectious smile. Time and again, strangers appeared when she needed them most, offering kindness that rekindled her faith in people. A woman who noticed Dee struggling to walk one day booked her into a hotel for the night. Another stranger gave her a place to stay for three nights so she could rest and recover her strength.

These small acts of compassion, woven into the vast and challenging backdrop of her journey, transformed Dee's perspective. The coastline's wild beauty healed her body, but the kindness of strangers began to heal her heart. For Dee, the South West Coast Path wasn't just a physical challenge, it was a journey back to believing in people and the goodness that exists in the world.

So, what's next for Dee?

With her characteristic blend of determination and patience, she is planning to write a book about her transformative journey along the South West Coast Path and the profound connection she's forged with nature. However, she's in no rush. For Dee, life isn't about racing toward a goal but about savouring the moments along the way. Her mission is clear: to spread the word about the healing power of the natural world, a message she hopes will inspire others to find solace and strength in its embrace. Dee continues to face personal challenges, navigating the lasting impacts of her past and the physical constraints of her condition. But these obstacles make her story even more remarkable.

'If I don't connect with it on a regular basis, I just miss it. It feels like a part of me,' she admits. For her, the wilds aren't just a place to visit, they're a vital part of her identity, a source of balance and peace. As she looks to the future, she's taking it one step at a time, much like her journey along the coast path: steadily, with purpose, and always open to where the trail might lead.

Our circular walk brought us back to the car park. Though it had only been a short journey, the forest had shown us many moods, like the seasons, all rolled into one. I watched as Dee reached out to touch the bark of an old copper beech tree, her fingers tracing its rough surface as if greeting an old friend.

'I'd walk these trails for hours,' she said, her voice soft, 'just listening to the wind and the birds. It reminded me that the world keeps moving, no matter what.'

She turned to me, her expression gentler now. 'I guess I just wanted you to know that even when things seem impossible, there's always something – somewhere – that can bring you back to yourself.'

A lump formed in my throat, but I swallowed it down and offered her a hug – a hug that said *I understand*, and one filled with quiet awe for a woman who, despite everything life had thrown her way, remained positive and grounded.

Who knew that a simple walk in Leigh Woods would uncover such a powerful, heart-warming story – one that doesn't just inspire, but stays with me long after the path ended.

THE WALK

IS IT FOR ME?

START/END POINT: Leigh Woods NNR, Abbots Leigh, Bristol, BS8 3QB

GRID REFERENCE: ST552741

DISTANCE: 3.1km (1.9 miles)

MILES WITHOUT STILES GRADE: For Many

TERRAIN: A mixture of compounded aggregate and woodland tracks. It can get muddy in wet weather.

ACCESSIBILITY: The track is mostly solid, but some sections can be muddy, and exposed tree roots create uneven ground. A manual wheelchair user may find these areas challenging to navigate.

PARKING: Parking is available at Abbots Leigh in Bristol (BS8 3QB); fees apply.

FACILITIES: There are no facilities on the walk.

THE ROUTE

First established in the 19th century with newly discovered conifers from the Americas, Leigh Woods boasts a rich history and an impressive tree collection. You can also explore the arboretum, designed by Humphry Repton in the 18th century.

Visitors can choose from a variety of trails, including the stile-free purple route, or venture further into the network of tracks that weave through the nature reserve. Along the way, you'll encounter rare plants, such as Wilmott's Whitebeam and the Bristol Rock-Cress, and magnificent trees, all of which contribute to the unique charm of Leigh Woods.

The history of this woodland is equally fascinating. In 1909, philanthropist George Wills gifted 32.4ha (80 acres) of Leigh Woods to the National Trust, safeguarding it from housing development and ensuring public enjoyment. Later, in 1949, the Forestry Commission acquired an additional 121ha (300 acres), described at the time as 'devastated woodland' due to extensive felling during the Second World War.

Today, Leigh Woods thrives under the collaborative care of the National Trust, Forestry Commission and Natural England. Their joint efforts have transformed it into a haven of tranquillity and natural beauty, offering visitors a chance to connect with

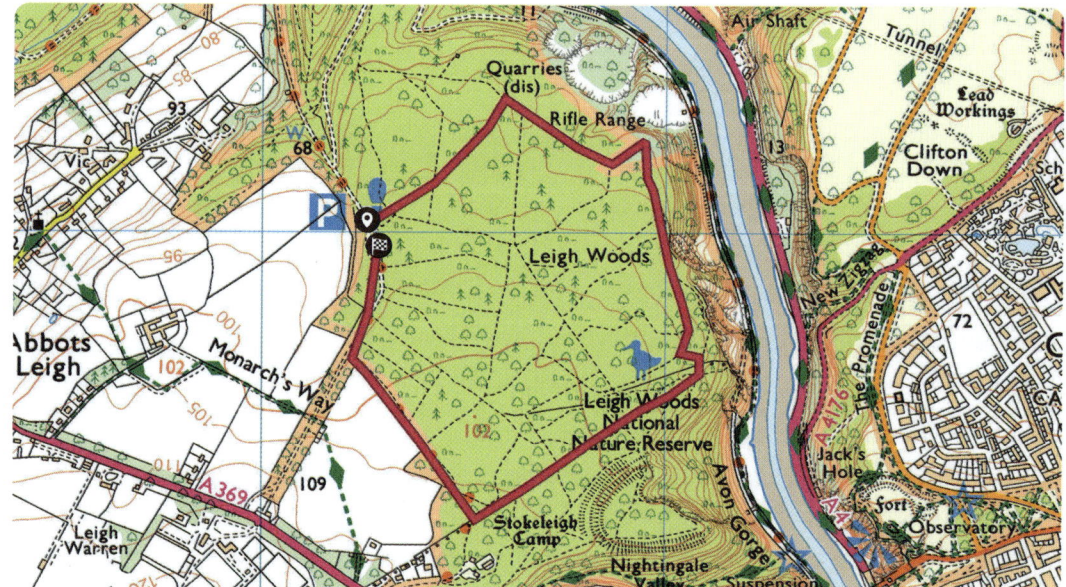

nature and appreciate breathtaking views of the Avon Gorge. Whether you're drawn by history, scenery or the promise of adventure, this is a true gem waiting to be explored.

NEED TO KNOW

A PLACE TO EAT: Ciao Amici is an Italian restaurant in 10–11 Denmark Street, Bristol, BS1 5DQ.

A PLACE TO DRINK: The Garden of Easton, 89 Saint Marks Road, Bristol

A PLACE TO SLEEP: The Camp at The Wave, at Washingpool Farm in Easter Compton (BS35 5RE), offers a glamping experience in stunning countryside, just metres from Bristol's scenic waterfront. They provide two DDA-compliant tents featuring a spacious living area and a roll-under kitchenette for added accessibility.

IF YOU'RE LOOKING FOR SOMETHING ELSE...

All-Aboard Watersports at Baltic Wharf in Bristol is an accessible centre designed to welcome everyone wishing to take part in watersports such as sailing, canoeing, kayaking and swimming. The site features accessible ramps and lifts, a hoist for boarding boats and canoes, and a gentle ramp leading to the water's edge. Inside there are accessible toilets, a wet room with a shower chair, a changing table and an overhead hoist.

KINGS WOOD
ST AUSTELL, CORNWALL

PAT SMITH

When I was first told about the meeting point location for my walk with Pat Smith, I couldn't help but wonder what to expect. The address led me to a business park, and I braced myself for an industrial landscape, far from the peaceful countryside stroll I had envisioned. But as soon as I arrived at Kings Wood near St Austell, my doubts vanished. The air was crisp with the gentle rustling of leaves filling the silence. And then, I met Pat.

Known affectionately as 'Action Nan', Pat is a force of nature in her own right. Her energy is boundless, her passion for the outdoors undeniable. She doesn't just explore nature – she protects it, champions it and inspires others to do the same. From the moment we exchanged greetings, her enthusiasm was contagious. She spoke with such warmth and purpose that I felt instantly drawn in, as if I were about to embark on something truly special. With Pat, even the simplest walk became an adventure, a chance to uncover hidden wonders that most would overlook. This was no ordinary stroll, and Pat was no ordinary guide. I was about to see the world through her eyes where every path holds a story, and every step is an opportunity to make a difference.

    As we strolled along the well-trodden trail, a favourite among dog walkers and a perfect route for families with buggies, Pat mused, 'Life is what happens while we are planning other things,' a quote often attributed to John Lennon. The words lingered for a while; a reminder of how fleeting moments can be.

    It was heartening to see families together, embracing the outdoors, where conversations replaced notifications and laughter filled the space usually occupied by screens. In a world where parents often snatch only a few minutes each day to check in with their children, who, in turn, are absorbed by playing games or watching YouTube videos on their digital devices, this shared experience felt like a small rebellion against modern distraction'. 'I believe the outdoors belongs to everyone,' Pat added, and as a gentle breeze carried the scent of the sea, it was hard to disagree.

Born in Worcestershire, Pat grew up with a deep and enduring love of the outdoors, along with an unquenchable curiosity to explore and discover all it had to offer. Family holidays in Cornwall were a cherished tradition, and even as a child, she felt an unshakable connection to the rugged beauty and charm of the region. Cornwall always seemed to be calling her, a place where she felt at home. She spent her childhood wandering through the woods, constructing treehouses and dens, and transforming each day into a new escapade.

When Pat married her husband, David, her dreams of a life tied to the outdoors began to take shape. Together, they shared a profound appreciation for Cornwall, a passion so strong that they even spent their honeymoon searching for a farm to call their own in the county. Theirs was an ambitious dream: to set up a dairy farm from scratch while raising two young children. The challenges were immense – back-breaking work, long days, and the daunting task of building a new life in unfamiliar territory. But the couple were undeterred. With determination and teamwork, they made the move and poured their hearts into creating a thriving farm.

ACTION NAN PAT ON HER MISSION TO CLEAN UP THE BEACHES

As we walked further along the popular trail in Kings Wood, I was relieved to find that the path was an easy, flat walk – perfectly accessible for me to navigate in my manual wheelchair. Running parallel to a gently babbling brook, the route followed the course of the St Austell River, its clear waters weaving through the landscape like a silver ribbon. As we moved along, the air was filled with the earthy scent of damp leaves and fresh water, a reminder of the delicate balance that makes this habitat so special.

And while we walked and talked, Pat shared that many years later, after she and her family made the move to Cornwall, she is still truly living the dream she set out to create; her life a reflection of the power of determination and embracing change.

'I'm a great believer that it's never too late to try something new,' she says, her voice steady and filled with the quiet confidence of someone who not only believes in these words but has shaped her life around them. Pat's nickname, 'Action Nan', couldn't be more fitting. With boundless energy and an insatiable love for adventure, she is always seeking her next challenge.

Although Pat's significant hearing loss often makes social situations challenging – she feels lost in a crowd, missing parts of conversations and sometimes feeling excluded – she finds solace in nature. There, the pressure to keep up disappears, and her other senses take over. As we walked along the trail, she embraced the stillness, noticing the world in a way others might overlook. She pointed out intricate patterns on a leaf and the textured markings on tree bark. And when she breathed in the crisp sea air she was tasting its salty freshness. In the countryside, she is not defined by what she cannot hear but by the deep connection she feels with the world around her.

At the age of 50, Pat embarked on a completely new adventure when a friend introduced her to sailing. What began as a casual outing quickly became a passion, and over the next six years she dedicated herself to mastering the craft, earning her qualifications as a Day Skipper and Yacht Master and undertaking thrilling voyages, including a crossing of the Atlantic Ocean and two journeys across the Gulf of Mexico.

But Pat's drive to push boundaries didn't stop there. At 57, she set her sights on an even more daunting challenge: cycling the entire length of Britain, from John O'Groats to Land's End, along with a friend. The odds were stacked against her: she was recovering from a hip replacement and navigating the demands of her age. Yet determination carried her through. 'I just believed I could do it,' she recalls. 'And I did. Every mile was gruelling, but it was exhilarating. I loved every minute.' The ride was more than a personal accomplishment; it raised much-needed funds for a head scanner at Treliske Hospital, blending her passion for adventure with her desire to give back.

Pat's reputation as a formidable adventurer was further cemented in April 2016, when she embarked on a 483km (300 mile) continuous walk along Cornwall's section of the South West Coast Path. Through this remarkable feat she raised over £8,000 for the RNLI, reflecting her deep connection to Cornwall's coastal heritage.

Her inspiring journey has not only earned her widespread recognition but also established her as one of Cornwall's most beloved and motivational figures. Through every challenge she has faced, Pat has shown that courage, curiosity and an unwavering belief in oneself can lead to truly extraordinary accomplishments.

Kings Wood, a fragment of ancient woodland over 400 years old, stands as a living relic of the past, once belonging to the realm, the Earl of Lancaster, and the Forestry Commission. Today, it is lovingly managed by The Woodland Trust. As we walked beneath the towering trees, Pat paused, her eyes scanning the forest floor. With a sigh, she bent down to retrieve a discarded plastic bottle, an empty drink can, crumpled food wrappers and a plastic bag filled with dog waste. 'I can't abide rubbish,' she remarked, her voice firm yet resigned, as she carefully picked up each piece, determined to leave the woods cleaner than she found them.

Pat's journey as an environmental activist began in 2017, when she watched Jo Ruxton's eye-opening documentary, *A Plastic Ocean*. Seeing the staggering amount of rubbish polluting the world's oceans, much of it accumulating within her own lifetime, was a turning point. The film brought into sharp focus the contamination of marine ecosystems and the devastating impact on sea life, compelling Pat to act. Determined to make a difference, she founded the environmental campaign group Final Straw Cornwall that same year, launching a grassroots movement to tackle the growing issue of plastic waste. The campaign focused on persuading hospitality businesses and their customers to eliminate plastic straws, highlighting the damage caused by single-use plastics. Under her leadership, Final Straw Cornwall expanded, inspiring sister groups across the country. The campaign's efforts contributed to a landmark victory in October 2020, when the UK government banned the sale of plastic straws, drink stirrers and cotton buds.

By 2018, Pat had completed her New Year's resolution of 52 beach cleans in a single year, a commitment that symbolised her tireless dedication to protecting Cornwall's coastline. 'I won't stop,' she said at the time, 'our beaches need me.'

Her work quickly captured the public's imagination, earning her national media attention. As a Litter Heroes Ambassador in 2019, Pat's efforts were recognised far and wide. She appeared on the BBC's *The One Show*, was interviewed by Jeremy Vine on Radio 2, and was featured in The Times, which produced a short film about her for their *Amazing Humans* series. 'It was one of those surreal moments that takes you completely by surprise,' Pat recalls, reflecting on the overwhelming support and recognition her efforts received.

But Pat's influence extended far beyond media coverage. Speaking at Westminster on the critical issue of litter and plastic waste, she became a powerful advocate for environmental change.

Despite these major large-scale achievements, Pat remains just as committed to small, everyday actions. For her, change starts with simple habits – saying no to a plastic straw with your drink, bringing a reusable bag to the supermarket, or encouraging others to make small, eco-friendly choices.

Her passion for preserving Cornwall's beauty and protecting the planet for future generations has also led her to organise local litter-picking groups. She founded the St Austell Tidy Up Team, Mevagissey Clean Team and Charlestown Chums, all of which work tirelessly to keep their communities free of rubbish.

'I am passionate about the legacy we're leaving for our children and grandchildren,' Pat says. 'We cannot carelessly contaminate our world and expect the next generation to clean up after us.'

Emerging from the woodland into the seaside village of Pentewan (Cornish: *Bentewyn*, meaning 'foot of the radiant stream'), the salty breeze carried the scent of the ocean, mingling with the echoes of history. Once a thriving medieval fishing hub with stone-quarrying, tin-streaming and agriculture, Pentewan's charm endures, its harbour whispering tales of the past.

Today, at 76, Pat's commitment to environmental activism remains unwavering. Whether driving change on a national scale or simply picking up litter along her local beaches, she proves that small acts can ripple into something extraordinary. As the sun dipped lower, casting golden light over the waves, Pat's radiant smile reflected the warmth of the day; a reminder that passion and purpose never fade.

PENTEWAN BEACH IN CORNWALL

THE WALK

IS IT FOR ME?

START/END POINT: Kings Wood. Starting in the car park just off Pentewan Road (B3272) just after London Apprentice. Ends at Pentewan village.

GRID REFERENCE: SX008496

DISTANCE: 2.9km (1.8 miles) one way

MILES WITHOUT STILES GRADE: For All

TERRAIN: Compacted soil path, can get muddy in places after rain

ACCESSIBILITY: A flat, level track with a wide and well-defined path, making for easy walking even after rain. The compacted surface provides a firm footing, though occasional exposed tree roots and small stones may be present along the way.

PARKING: There is a small car park just off Pentewan Road (B3272) just after London Apprentice and the Kings Wood restaurant.

FACILITIES: Accessible toilets van be found in Trevithick and Trays Farm Shop and Café (PL26 7AR), the café at Kingswood Business Park, and in nearby Pentewan village.

THE ROUTE

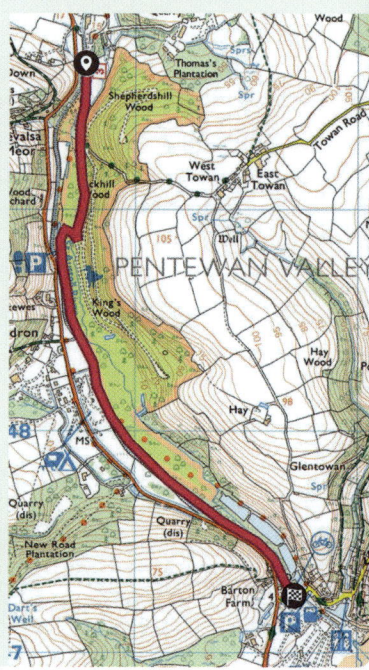

The walk from Kings Wood to Pentewan village offers a rich tapestry of natural beauty and historical intrigue. As you begin your journey at Kings Wood, the ancient semi-natural woodland provides a haven for a variety of bird and insect species, including the delicate holly blue butterfly, which flits among the undergrowth.

The wood's designation as both Ancient Semi-Natural Woodland (ASNW) and Planted Ancient Woodland Site (PAWS) ensures that this lush landscape is not only a picturesque retreat but also a vital conservation area. Following the path along the old track bed of the horse-drawn tramway, you step back in time to when the Pentewan Railway was a vital artery for the bustling China clay industry. This tramway, which once transported goods to the busy port, takes you past reservoirs and sluices that were used to flush sand out of the harbour, a testament to the area's industrial past.

As you approach Pentewan, with its historical roots reaching back to the Domesday Book, the village unfolds with its quaint charm. This was once a self-sufficient community, home to tradesmen and sailors. With pub names like The Ship Inn, The Jolly Sailor and The Hawkins Arms echoing the region's maritime history, Pentewan's legacy as a bustling port town is still alive in its stories and its wide, sandy bay. The village's name, derived from the Cornish words for 'headland' and 'sand-hill', hints at the landscape's natural allure, as you'll finish your walk at The Round, the circular hill that stands over the bay.

 NEED TO KNOW

A PLACE TO EAT: Enjoy fish and chips at Pentewan Plaice, Pentewan, Saint Austell, PL26 6BT.

A PLACE TO DRINK: The Cove Café, 3 The Square, Pentewan, Saint Austell, PL26 6DA, serves hot and cold food and drinks. The Cornish pasties are very good!

A PLACE TO SLEEP: Bosinver Farm Cottages in Trelowth, PL26 7DT, offers four accessible cottages.

 IF YOU'RE LOOKING FOR SOMETHING ELSE…

The Eden Project, located in Bodelva (PL24 2SG), is a world-famous eco-park with large glass domes called biomes. The biomes emulate different natural climates, such as tropical rainforests, the Mediterranean and Western Australia, and is home to a vast collection of plants and nature.

Visitors can explore the stunning biomes and beautiful outdoor gardens, enjoy fun exhibits and learn about global environmental issues and sustainability. With 12ha (30 acres) to explore, plan on spending at least four hours here.

THE NEARBY EDEN PROJECT IS WELL WORTH A VISIT

RIVER OTTER ESTUARY
BUDLEIGH SALTERTON, DEVON

ISAAC KENYON

Emerging from the fog on an early January morning was the faint outline of a solitary walker, his steady stride cutting through the mist. This was Isaac Kenyon, my guide for a walk around the River Otter estuary in the town of Budleigh Salterton, Devon. Covering 33ha (82 acres), this protected landscape is more than a serene expanse of saltmarsh and tidal waters; it is a designated Site of Special Scientific Interest (SSSI), renowned for its rich biodiversity and the striking Triassic sandstone cliffs at Otterton Point, a paleontological treasure trove.

As the fog wove ghostly patterns across the water, we caught sight of a heron standing motionless like a sculpture on the sandbank, while a kingfisher, distinctive by its splash of iridescent blue, perched delicately on the edge of the bridge. 'This is home,' said Isaac, his voice filled with warmth and a sense of belonging. The scene was a prelude to a walk that promised to deepen my love for wildlife and offer the chance to learn more about Isaac – a philanthropic, world-record-breaking British eco-adventurer.

'This landscape is so different from the one I grew up in,' Isaac remarked as we began our walk along the estuary. Isaac spent his childhood in one of Luton's most deprived areas, a community shaped by persistent challenges such as limited job opportunities, poverty and high rates of crime. In this environment, vulnerability was seen as weakness, and outdoor spaces, where nature should have offered refuge, were far from safe. Together with his younger brother, and with few places for outdoor play and exploration, Isaac spent hours indoors immersed in computer games.

However, there was something else, other than a game console, that piqued his curiosity: dinosaurs. As a young boy, he was obsessed with the *Jurassic Park* films, which sparked his early fascination with prehistoric life.

Family outings to Lyme Regis, a haven for fossil enthusiasts, were a highlight for Isaac. He combed the beaches for ancient relics and scanned the cliffs for hidden fossils. Ever curious, he was full of questions: Why is there a hill here? What shaped the cliffs this way? Why did dinosaurs go extinct? This fascination with his surroundings eventually fuelled his passion for understanding Earth's geological history.

Isaac's enthusiasm for the subject was still palpable as he spoke, his gaze fixed on the rugged cliffs at Otterton Point. 'The cliffs are a nationally significant site for biodiversity,' he said. 'These cliffs reveal Triassic sandstone rocks that hold fossils of ancient reptiles.'

Heading towards the saltmarshes, Isaac told me about his first real escape from Luton, which came when he left for university to pursue a degree in Geology and later a Masters in Geoscience at Royal Holloway, University of London, in Egham. The leafy, affluent surroundings of Surrey were a stark contrast to anything Isaac had known, and while his studies had given him the chance to see more of the world, they also took a toll on his mental health. Exhaustion and academic burnout crept in, worsened by the relentless pressure of 18-hour days, difficult deadlines and an environment with little understanding of, or support for, mental health challenges. At school, where

ISAAC KENYON AT THE RIVER OTTER ESTUARY

vulnerability was perceived as a sign of weakness, there had been no education about the importance of mental well-being. So with very little in the way of support well into university, Isaac found himself navigating a struggle that had long been overlooked in his life and education.

It was during this lowest point that he discovered the restorative power of nature.

'The best 15 minutes of my day was walking through the woodlands to my department,' Isaac explained. 'It was the one place where no one demanded anything of me; it was a sanctuary for headspace, where I could connect with my senses and find clarity.'

What started as a short 15-minute daily walk soon expanded into longer rambles, with Isaac exploring the paths from his base in Egham towards the River Thames and Windsor. It was during these moments of quiet reflection and connection with nature that Isaac realised he needed the outdoors to truly thrive. The impact was profound. Not only did his mental well-being improve, but his academic achievements soared as well.

After completing his studies, he found employment in the energy sector, focusing on sustainable energy – a career that he enjoyed, and for five more years he lived in London, but the city lifestyle took a toll once again on his mental health. Despite the capital's reputation as being one of the greenest cities in the world, Isaac was not coping in an urban environment and was struggling with the disconnect from nature, which led him to question the impact on the mental well-being of those who have limited access to nearby natural spaces. It made me think of the pelicans that inhabit St James's Park – a surprising sight in the heart of the bustling city.

The contrast between these urban green spaces and the wild, untamed beauty of the Budleigh Salterton Nature Reserve is striking. As we walked along the track, skirting the water's edge at low tide, the reserve revealed its vast mudflats and saltmarshes. Wading birds like curlews, redshanks and oystercatchers move through the shallows here, foraging for food. Nestled along the tranquil River Otter Estuary, this unique habitat offers a peaceful retreat for birdwatchers, walkers and anyone seeking to immerse themselves in Devon's coastal landscape.

It was quite clear that Isaac was determined to make a difference. He became a trustee for Mind in Mid Herts, a charity that works to provide prevention, social support and recovery resources for mental health in the community. He also trained as a Mental Health Peer Supporter, taking action to raise awareness, challenge stigma and create safe spaces for open conversations about mental health.

Seeking a lifestyle more aligned with his values, Isaac secured a part-time remote job and relocated to a small village near Budleigh Salterton in Devon. Here, surrounded by nature, he found a renewed sense of peace and purpose, and continued to advocate for mental health and his love of the outdoors.

'I love living near the sea because of the sense of wonder and connection to nature it provides,' he says. 'The sea itself also offers a sense of peace and inspiration.'

For someone so passionate about history and biodiversity, the sea offers Isaac a constant reminder of the Earth's vast and ever-changing story.

By timing the tides perfectly, we managed to cross the bridge, which disappears beneath the water at high tide. From there, our journey continued into a more rugged landscape, with Otterton Mill as our destination. The mist that had enveloped us began to lift, and sunlight started breaking through the swirling grey.

'It's going to be a warm day,' Isaac remarked.

He was right. Once the sun fully emerged, the day turned hot.

In the years since, Isaac has gone on to truly embrace the opportunities that being outdoors brings, pushing the boundaries of physical and mental endurance. He has even broken world records and achieved world-first expeditions, from rowing across the Atlantic Ocean in just 40 days to swimming the English Channel, and cycling across countries. In 2023, Isaac took on his most symbolic challenge so far: a gruelling Ironman triathlon (swimming, cycling and running) while wearing a 15kg weighted vest. The vest represented the invisible burden of mental health struggles that many men endure in silence, a burden Isaac knows all too well.

Isaac is now an ambassador for the mental health benefits of getting outdoors. He works with groups like the Scouts and schools in underprivileged areas to inspire young people to connect with nature. He is also co-founder of the community interest company Climate Explorers, which aims to inspire individuals to reconnect with nature and discover practical ways to address climate challenges through adventurous exploration of the outdoors. Reflecting on his journey, Isaac feels a deep sense of fulfilment.

'I've learned so much about myself through my work with nature,' he said. 'I'm happiest when I'm on an adventure.'

Whether those adventures are big or small, he emphasises their importance to rediscovering balance, resilience and joy. By sharing his story, Isaac hopes to encourage others to embrace the outdoors, reconnect with the natural world and find their own path to well-being and self-discovery. 'Without nature and the outdoors, I don't know how my mental health would cope.'

Upon reaching our destination, we enjoyed coffee and cake at Otterton Mill, recharging before starting our walk back to Budleigh Salterton.

THE WALK

IS IT FOR ME?

START/END POINT: Lime Kiln car park, 1 Granary Ln, Budleigh Salterton, EX9 6JD
GRID REFERENCE: SY072821
DISTANCE: 1.6–3.2km (1–2 miles) circular, depending on the route chosen
MILES WITHOUT STILES GRADE: For Many, though some sections are For All
TERRAIN: The trail consists of a mix of compacted aggregate and surfaced paths. Some areas can become muddy in wet weather and certain sections are rocky, making them challenging to navigate in a manual wheelchair.
ACCESSIBILITY: Budleigh Salterton Beach is a wide stretch of pebbled shoreline.
PARKING: Lime Kiln car park is located right at the edge of the beach and serves as the starting point for the walk around the Nature Reserve.
FACILITIES: The nearest accessible toilets are located at Otterton Mill, Budleigh Salterton, EX9 7HG also has a café and a craft shop – both highly recommended for a visit.

THE ROUTE

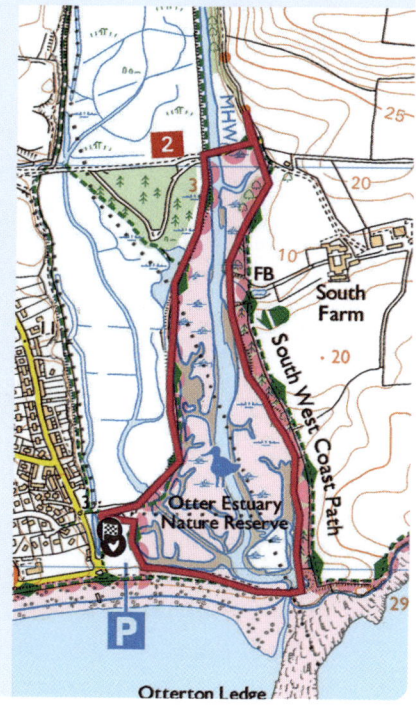

The River Otter and its estuary have been shaped by centuries of human activity. In the early 19th century, an embankment was built to reclaim land for farming, and later the area was modified to accommodate a railway line and a refuse tip. However, the Lower Otter Restoration Project has reversed these interventions, returning the estuary to its natural state as it existed before these alterations. This ground-breaking project reached a significant milestone in 2024 with the completion of the construction phase highlighted by the 70m (231ft) 'Elizabeth Bridge'. Today, the Lower Otter is managed by the Pebblebed Heaths Conservation Trust.

The Otter Estuary is a thriving ecosystem and is home to multiple species of fish, birds and other marine life. Birdwatchers can spot wading birds such as ringed plover, curlew, black-tailed godwit, dunlin, common sandpiper, redshank and Brent goose. Occasionally, rarer birds like avocets and glossy ibises make an appearance. The estuary's diverse bird population changes throughout the year due to migratory patterns, offering visitors a unique experience with every visit.

The estuary is not only a haven for birds but also home to otters, and England's first native wild beaver population in over 400 years. Once hunted to extinction in England for their fur, meat and a scent used in perfumery, beavers have made a remarkable resurgence on the River Otter.

For visitors, the estuary offers an accessible walking route that begins at the back of the car park. A viewing area provides opportunities to spot birds like egrets and curlews while offering information about the local wildlife, including the beavers.

A purpose-built track on the left-hand side of the estuary provides access for manual wheelchair users, leading towards South Farm Road. Depending on the wheelchair's capabilities, visitors can take a circular route that crosses the estuary (which floods at high tide) onto a bumpy gravel path that leads back to the car park via the Elizabeth Bridge. For those seeking a greater challenge, the route can be extended from the South Farm Road bridge to Otterton Mill.

Whether you're a birdwatcher, a conservation enthusiast or simply a lover of the outdoors, the River Otter Estuary offers a rich and rewarding experience for all.

NEED TO KNOW

A PLACE TO EAT: When in Devon, you have to sample a cream tea. Try The Salt Cellars Café in Budleigh Salterton, EX9 6SG

A PLACE TO DRINK: The Sir Walter Raleigh in Budleigh Salterton, EX9 7ED, is a traditional English pub that is wheelchair accessible. Dogs are also welcome.

A PLACE TO SLEEP: The Victoria Hotel in nearby Sidmouth, EX10 8RY, has accessible rooms and a swimming pool.

IF YOU'RE LOOKING FOR SOMETHING ELSE...

Nestled near Sidmouth on the Jurassic Coast, the **Donkey Farm** is home to hundreds of rescue donkeys. The farm offers a peaceful, family-friendly environment with lovely views of the valley and sea. The sanctuary is dog-friendly, welcoming pets on leads. Many of the paths are wheelchair accessible, making it a perfect spot for the whole family.

ASHDOWN FOREST
EAST SUSSEX

ANITA KERWIN-NYE

Having grown up with stories of Winnie-the-Pooh and Christopher Robin, I was thrilled to visit the very place that inspired these beloved tales. Exploring the 2,630ha (6,500 acres) of ancient woods and heathland that sparked A.A. Milne's iconic stories of a bear with 'very little brain' and a boy full of wonder feels like a true adventure. A royal hunting ground in Norman times, Ashdown Forest is now one of the largest public access areas in the South East UK, offering boundless opportunities for discovery.

No one was better suited to guide me through the forest than Anita Kerwin-Nye. Her lifelong passion for nature took root in places such as Ashdown Forest, where she first experienced the outdoors as a powerful source of learning, healing and personal growth.

In the words of Winnie-the-Pooh, 'A grand adventure was about to begin.' So, with this in mind, we set off towards a cluster of mainly Scots pine trees known as 'Friends Clump'. Golden light streamed through the branches, drawing us towards the heathland's embrace beyond.

From a young age, Anita loved spending time in nature. Her late father would take her to the beach for overnight fishing trips, and some of her earliest memories are of him pointing out the stars. Her mother, on the other hand, would hold back her fears when Anita climbed another mountain or canoed another river. Anita loved adventure.

Nowadays, though, she no longer embarks on long-distance walks, nor climbs or canoes as she once did. But she still enjoys a slow, gentle stroll.

As we made our way towards the deeper woodland, the landscape shifted

ANITA AT ASHDOWN FOREST

around us. One moment, the open heath stretched wide, bathed in golden hues, and the next we stepped beneath the towering oaks. Their ancient trunks, thick and gnarled, bore the marks of time, their bark rough and deeply grooved. High above, branches intertwined to form a dense canopy, filtering the sunlight onto the mosses and ivy which carpet the forest floor here. The contrast is striking; where the heath is open, warm and windswept, the oak forest is cool, shadowy and rich with the earthy scent of moss mingled with the damp aroma of bark and the faint sweetness of wild mushrooms hidden in the undergrowth.

'This is so beautiful,' I said to Anita.

'Being able to access this countryside sparked a lifelong passion for nature and outdoor learning,' she replied. 'My early experiences shaped my career that focused on harnessing a transformation with outdoors in education.'

This dedication led Anita to create influential initiatives like The Communication Trust and Whole School SEND (Special Educational Needs and Disabilities), both aimed at helping children with disabilities access enriching educational opportunities.

A mother of four and a self-described 'serial social entrepreneur', Anita seamlessly integrates her personal and professional commitment to the outdoors. Her passion for connecting people with nature extends beyond her work, shaping her family's lifestyle and activities. Whether it's gardening together, tending to their allotment or exploring natural spaces near water and dark sky sites, Anita ensures that nature is a constant presence in her life.

In 2018, Anita joined the Youth Hostels Association (YHA) as Director of Strategy and Engagement, where she led initiatives to reconnect children with outdoor learning, particularly in response to the challenges of the COVID-19 pandemic. Then, in 2024, she began her role as Director of the South Downs National Park, focusing on balancing landscape protection with increasing public access. She is also the lead of 'Every Child Should', a campaign advocating for every child's entitlement to a broad set of experiences and enrichment by the age of 18.

Later, she spearheaded the creation of the DEFRA-funded Generation Green programme, an initiative that has made transformative strides in connecting young people to the natural world. The programme successfully engaged over 115,000 participants across England, providing many participants with their first meaningful connection to nature. Generation Green not only introduced young people to the beauty of National Parks and green spaces but it also created job opportunities and cultivated a workforce focused on advancing a green recovery. Among its standout achievements, the programme facilitated day trips, residential stays and self-led experiences for nearly 39,500 young participants. These efforts played a crucial role in addressing inequalities in access to nature and ensuring diverse communities could experience the benefits of the outdoors.

As we meandered through the forest, a sense of calm washed over me. Overhead, branches swayed gently, their rustling blending with the distant, rhythmic call of a bird, deepening the tranquillity of the moment. Anita paused, trailing her fingers along the rough bark of an ancient oak.

'There's something so peaceful about this place,' she murmured.

I inhaled deeply, letting the crisp, wooded scent settle within me. In the stillness, time seemed to slow, and for a while the outside world faded. A quiet sense of belonging filled me – an unspoken connection to something older, wilder and infinitely vast.

Anita encouraged us to stop just for a while and embrace the quiet magic of the forest.

'My children love these woods,' she said, her voice warm with appreciation, 'and I can visibly see any tension and anxiety leave their bodies when they are here. This is their safe space.'

Here, among the trees, they were free, free to explore, to breathe, and to simply be.

Anita's latest challenge, one she has fully embraced, comes in the form of her role as Director of Fundraising, Marketing and Communications at the Wildfowl & Wetlands Trust (WWT), through which she leads initiatives to highlight the importance of wetlands and drive vital conservation efforts.

I was giddy when Nutley Windmill appeared at the end of the woodland path. Standing proudly against the sky, this historic gem is the last open-trestle post mill in Sussex, one of only five left in the country and the only one still working. Its weathered timbers and sturdy sails offered a glimpse into a bygone era when wind powered corn grinding. Seeing it nestled in the landscape felt like stepping back into the golden age of traditional milling. Though not mentioned in Winnie-the-Pooh stories, the windmill evokes the enchanting world of woodland tales, filling me with sheer joy as if I had stepped into a beloved storybook. After passing the windmill, our woodland path opened to a panoramic view across the moors – a patchwork of rolling heath and distant hills fading into the horizon. We paused to soak in the vastness and tranquillity before returning to Friends Car Park, completing our circular walk. Anita and her husband, Matt Overd, co-founded Walking Pace, a project dedicated to making walking accessible and enjoyable for all. Celebrating walkers of every ability and distance, Walking Pace shares insights, promotes innovation and highlights stories from the walking community.

A standout initiative is the One Mile Walks programme, a national effort curating walks approximately one mile long. These routes provide detailed information on accessibility, facilities and other considerations to ensure inclusivity. By collaborating with outdoor advocates, charities, protected landscapes, and community groups, Walking Pace is building a network of routes that anyone can enjoy.

'One mile is approachable,' said Matt. 'You can see so much in just one mile, and the key is finding routes people of all abilities can enjoy.' He explained that while many resources exist for longer or more challenging hikes, few cater to shorter, accessible walks. By focusing on these, Anita and Matt help remove barriers to the outdoors, encouraging movement and fostering connection with nature. Their work promotes physical health while building inclusivity within the walking community, proving every step matters.

Meeting Anita was awe-inspiring. Brimming with energy, feisty, funny, and remarkable, she achieves more than expectation. Her dedication and spirit are a powerful reminder of the strength and drive within us all. Whether through her resilience, humour or unwavering commitment, Anita exemplifies living life fully and with purpose.

THE WALK

IS IT FOR ME?

START/END POINT: Friends car park, Crowborough Rd, Nutley, East Sussex, TN22 3JA

GRID REFERENCE: TQ456289

DISTANCE: 2.6km (1.6 miles) circular

MILES WITHOUT STILES GRADE: For Many

TERRAIN: Grassy paths and sandy tracks. It can get muddy in wet weather.

ACCESSIBILITY: Please note that the paths may be challenging for manual wheelchair users due to some raised tree roots.

PARKING: Friends car park (see above); fees apply, though Blue Badge holders park for free.

FACILITIES: There are no facilities on this walk. However, the Ashdown Forest Centre (Colemans Hatch Rd, Wych Cross, Forest Row, RH18 5JP) has accessible toilets and a Changing Places facility.

THE ROUTE

You're spoilt for choice at Ashdown Forest, with so many paths to explore! The term 'forest' may be misleading, as much of this landscape is open heathland, although there are stands of trees and deeper forest areas throughout (which get extremely muddy during wet periods).

The forest is also classified as a Special Protection Area for wild birds. Among its most notable visitors is the nightjar, which migrates from Africa to breed here. You may also spot lizards, deer, rabbits, foxes, badgers and a dazzling array of butterflies. Note, the area is also open to free-roaming livestock during the summer months, with cows, sheep and even wild Exmoor ponies grazing the heathland.

The walk that we completed was straightforward and easy to navigate, making it unlikely for anyone to get lost. For more details about the area, its unique features and particular trails, visit the Ashdown Forest website at ashdownforest.org.

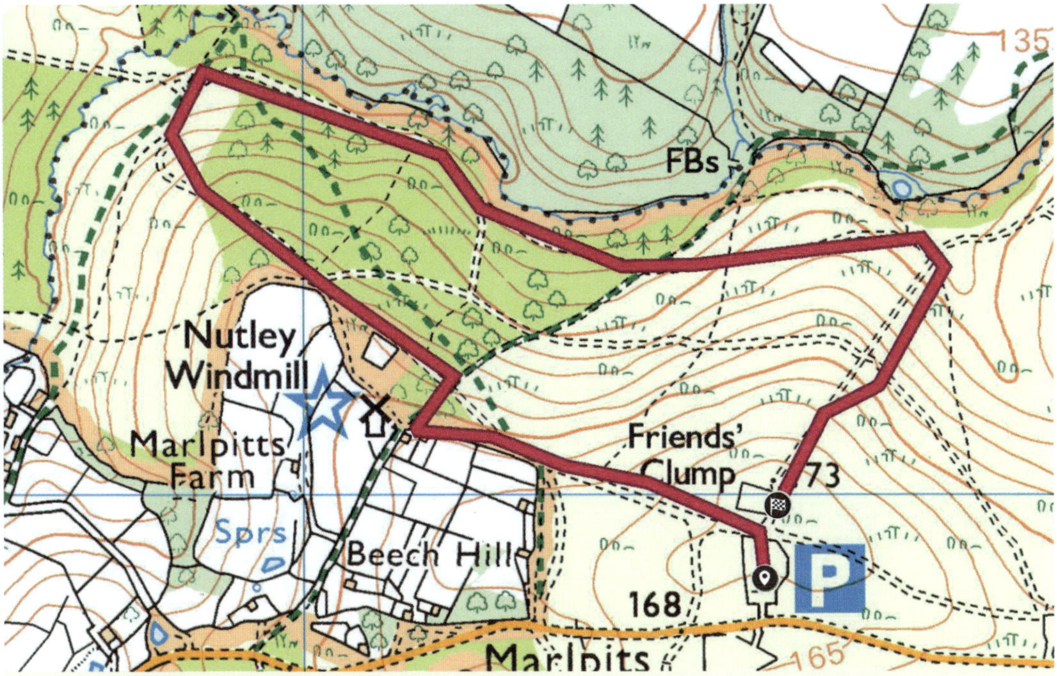

NEED TO KNOW

A PLACE TO EAT: The Coffee House (TN22 3NF) in the pretty village of Nutley serves tea and coffee, along with paninis and homemade cakes and pastries. Open Tue–Fri 7am–4pm and Sat–Sun 9am–3pm.

A PLACE TO DRINK: You'll find a range of excellent local beers (along with delicious pub food) at The Coach & Horses in nearby Danehill (RH17 7JF).

A PLACE TO SLEEP: Nutley Edge Cottages (TN22 3EE) offer two wheelchair-accessible cottages.

IF YOU'RE LOOKING FOR SOMETHING ELSE…

A 30-minute drive from the Ashdown Forest, the **British Wildlife Centre** in Lingfield boasts one of the finest collections of native species in the country, with more than 40 different animals on display, ranging from tiny harvest mice to majestic red deer. All animals are housed in spacious enclosures designed to mimic their natural habitats. Every half hour, you can enjoy Keeper Talks, offering an up-close look at the animals and insights into the challenges they face in the wild. The centre is a fantastic spot for wildlife photography and is just 10 minutes north of the town of East Grinstead. It also offers free parking, a coffee shop, picnic areas and wheelchair access.

HEARTWOOD FOREST

NR ST ALBANS, HERTFORDSHIRE

EMMA HARRISON

Heartwood Forest, just outside the town of St Albans, is a serene and expansive woodland that, remarkably, except for a few areas of ancient woodland, is entirely new. It began its journey in 2008 with the goal of reclaiming and preserving the land for future generations. Spanning 347ha (858 acres), it now offers a diverse landscape of newly planted areas and sections of older woodlands, making it a beloved spot for locals and visitors alike.

It was in this forest, which gets its name from the heart-shaped leaves of the lime trees that grow within it, that I was to meet Emma Harrison. I was so looking forward to meeting this remarkable lady after I'd heard her story of surviving a rare disease that left her disabled. Emma has been tirelessly rebuilding her physical strength by finding solace and empowerment in the outdoors.

As we set off on our walk, the air was crisp, and the soft crunch of wheels on the gravel paths filled the air, creating a steady cadence as we made our way forward. Emma walked beside me, each step a powerful reflection of her remarkable strength and determination.

Our route took us along the Magical Meander, a winding trail that leads to the enchanting Magical Wood. Along the way, we were greeted by a collection of beautifully carved wooden animals, each one representing the local wildlife that thrives in the area. These intricate sculptures, crafted by chainsaw artist

Will Lee, were sponsored by the Disney Store and add a whimsical touch to the landscape; the hare with long, elegantly pointed ears, poised in mid-leap as though caught in the breeze; nearby, a playful badger seems to emerge from the wood, its paws raised in a charming gesture of curiosity, exuding a sense of mischief. Further along, a toad is carved with great precision, its bumpy skin and wide eyes capturing the creature's quiet, watchful nature. Each sculpture is a stunning tribute to the creatures of the land, their personalities and essence brought to life through the skilful hands of the artist.

The trail itself is part of a much larger project, which has brought together thousands of locals in creating something truly special. As we walked, Emma's resilience seemed to mirror the project that surrounded us, making this walk not only a physical journey but an inspiring one. For Emma, this place is more than just a park; it's a sanctuary. She has a deep personal connection to the forest, finding peace for quiet reflection and healing in its tranquil environment.

After graduating from Chelsea Art College with a degree in Interior and Special Design, Emma was poised to make her mark in the world of design.

EMMA HARRISON IN LANGLEY WOODS

It was in Southeast Asia's vibrant heartland of Myanmar that Emma encountered not just a new culture, but a profound awakening. Myanmar's beauty and its people enchanted her, but it was the stark contrast of their daily struggles that deeply moved her. Amid the lush landscapes and ancient temples, she witnessed the harrowing reality faced by many – poverty that gnawed at the edges of hope and a healthcare crisis marked by one of Asia's highest adult HIV prevalence rates.

Emma was particularly struck by the isolation and discrimination faced by individuals living with HIV. They were not just battling a health crisis but were also entangled in a web of social stigma that depicted their condition as a personal punishment or moral failing. It was in this crucible of hardship that Emma's resolve hardened, and her compassion took shape. Driven by a sense of justice and a desire to make a tangible difference, she envisioned a project that would not only address immediate needs but also empower those marginalised by society. In Myanmar, where teak wood is both abundant and revered, she saw an opportunity for transformation. Her idea was to leverage her design skills to create a social enterprise that would uplift men living with HIV by teaching them the craft of woodworking. By equipping these individuals with carpentry skills, Emma helped them craft beautiful furniture and integrated them into a meaningful, productive workforce.

Over the next three years, Emma dedicated herself to this mission, immersing herself in the local community and working tirelessly to dismantle the stigma surrounding HIV. The furniture crafted by her trainees was more than just a product; it was a symbol of their reclaimed dignity and newfound purpose. Emma found profound fulfilment in witnessing the ripple effects of her work: lives transformed, self-esteem rebuilt and a community gradually shedding its chains of shame.

It felt almost ironic that Emma, who had built a career in designing wooden furniture, was now enjoying the healing benefits of this vibrant new forest. In Myanmar, she had worked among towering, mature teak trees, making the contrast with the young trees at Heartwood even more striking. But while these trees are still young, their potential is undeniable. Emma appreciates the beauty of these saplings with a deeper understanding, knowing that, like her own journey, they have the power to grow, evolve and flourish with time.

In 2015, Emma's life took an unforeseen and harrowing turn when she found herself facing a health crisis that would challenge her resilience in ways she never expected. Yet, much like the landscape around her, she found strength in the transformation.

It began with a persistent fever that stubbornly refused to relent, accompanied by severe headaches, debilitating nausea and a rash that crept across her skin. The full extent of Emma's situation became clear when, encouraged by her friends, she sought medical help at the SOS International Hospital. Despite her mounting concerns, she hadn't fully understood the severity of her condition. Within the hour, the doctor had diagnosed that she had contracted dengue fever, which triggered a rare autoimmune response known as transverse myelitis.

But, against all odds and coming dangerously close to death, she survived one of the world's most deadly diseases. However, the massive autoimmune response her body mounted against the fever led to a severe spinal cord injury at the C6 level, leaving Emma with left-side weakness, balance issues and limited movement in her hands. While the dengue fever itself was a self-limiting illness from which Emma fully recovered, the spinal cord injury caused by the transverse myelitis resulted in permanent disability. The consultant's grave concern and the urgency of a blood transfusion underscored the seriousness of her illness.

DEBBIE AND EMMA EXPLORE THE MILES OF TRACK AROUND HEARTWOOD FOREST

The days that followed were a blur of emergency responses and frantic medical interventions. Emma was swiftly transferred to Thailand, where she began receiving crucial initial treatment. Her battle with transverse myelitis took on an international dimension when the British Embassy contacted her family to arrange her medical evacuation back to the UK.

'It took 16 hours to get back, but I don't remember much of it. By the time I had to get off the plane I couldn't move.'

The sense of urgency and the weight of her condition were palpable as she was admitted to the Tropical Diseases Hospital in London, a place specialising in the very ailments she was now fighting.

When Emma was finally discharged from the hospital, her life had been irrevocably altered. This once-vibrant woman who had dedicated herself to empowering others in the far-flung reaches of Myanmar now found herself facing disability.

'The illness had done more than just sap my strength,' she explained. 'It had attacked my nervous system so severely that doctors initially believed that I had suffered a stroke.'

Emma was left to confront an unrelenting new reality, one that threatened to define her by its limitations. Yet, in the midst of her struggles, a flicker of resilience sparked within her. Refusing to accept a life of dependency, Emma harnessed the same inner strength that had always driven her to inspire others, and she set her sights on the ultimate goal: reclaiming her health. She knew that her recovery would be neither quick nor easy, but she was determined to find a way.

Emma was convinced that the key to her recovery lay in reconnecting with the outdoors, in rediscovering the natural world that had once brought her so much peace and clarity. Her journey began with a relentless search for a physiotherapist who could offer more than just conventional rehabilitation.

We took refuge from the midday sun in the ancient forest of Pudler's Wood, where the dense canopy offered welcome shade. It was a truly beautiful autumn day.

'Coming here in spring is magical,' Emma said. 'The ground becomes a carpet of bluebells.'

I had no doubt it must be breathtaking, yet I felt that visiting this place in any season would be a wonderful experience. Having rested for a while, Emma and I began to walk and as we did, she told me about the excruciating early days of her rehabilitation.

'The simple act of standing was a monumental effort,' she recalled, 'each step a painful reminder of the physical toll the illness had taken.'

As Emma strode confidently through the trees, it was evident that she was a woman of determination. During her recovery she pressed on, pushing past the discomfort, refusing to let the lingering fear of her body failing hold her back. With unwavering support from her therapist, who recognised her deep need to heal in nature, she slowly began to regain strength. Her body was fragile, but her mind was relentless – a force of sheer willpower that propelled her forward, even on the darkest days.

'Every step I take out here reminds me that I'm stronger than I think.'

Week by week, Emma's perseverance began to pay off. The tentative, shaky steps that had once seemed impossible grew stronger and more confident. The outdoors became her sanctuary, a place where she could push her limits and measure her progress. With each new walk, she gained not just strength, but hope. Slowly but surely, she began reclaiming her independence one painful step at a time.

Though Emma had fought her way back to walking, the battle was far from over. The lingering effects of her illness left her body still frail, her muscles prone to weakness and her energy easily drained. Yet, Emma's spirit was anything but diminished. Instead of resigning herself to a life of limitations, she set her sights on an audacious goal – qualifying as a Mountain Leader.

The decision was not just about reclaiming her physical abilities; it was about proving to herself that she could still conquer challenges, no matter how insurmountable they seemed. Emma knew the path ahead would be gruelling; the mountains she needed to climb for her qualifications were formidable, not just because of their height but because of the toll they would take on her recovering body. Every step would be a test of endurance, every ascent a measure of her willpower.

The journey was as slow and painful as she had anticipated. With each climb, Emma pushed her body to its limits, scaling rugged terrains that demanded both physical strength and mental resilience. Her progress was not swift, but it was steady, and that was what mattered. The assessors who watched her tackle these mountains were left stunned. They had seen many candidates attempt the rigorous tests required to become a mountain leader, but none had faced the challenges with the kind of tenacity Emma displayed. They were in awe of her determination to complete each challenge, one gruelling step at a time.

The resilience of the wildlife at Heartwood Forest mirrors the strength Emma found within herself to complete her Mountain Leader training. Just as the diverse range of animals – including owls, yellowhammers, linnets and Eurasian skylarks – thrive in the ever-changing landscape, Emma's journey was a powerful demonstration of the human spirit's capacity for growth and renewal. Heartwood Forest, a sanctuary of woodlands and meadows, is a place where life constantly evolves, much like Emma's own path. In the same way the warblers and fieldfares find their home in this forest, Emma found her new sense of purpose and strength through her training. By earning her qualifications, she proved not only to herself but to others that with determination, the human spirit can overcome even the greatest of challenges. Now, as a qualified Mountain Leader, Emma dedicates herself to helping others who, like her, have discovered the healing power of the outdoors. Just as the forest continues to grow, Emma's journey is one of ongoing transformation, inspiring others to find their own strength in the face of adversity.

Through her guidance, Emma offers more than just physical training; she provides a lifeline to those who need to rebuild their confidence and rediscover their potential. Emma's journey from the depths of illness to the peaks of mountains is a story of perseverance, hope and the unwavering belief that even the most daunting challenges can be overcome.

THE WALK

⊙ IS IT FOR ME?

START/END POINT: Heartwood Forest, QMMR+PW, St Albans, AL4 9DG

GRID REFERENCE: TL167108

DISTANCE: 4.2km (2.6 miles) circular

MILES WITHOUT STILES GRADE: For All

TERRAIN: Surfaced paths of tarmac and gravel

ACCESSIBILITY: While there are some hard-surfaced paths, most of the terrain is grass or natural earth, which can become muddy and slippery after rain.

PARKING: Free parking at the forest for Blue Badge holders; there are five designated spaces.

FACILITIES: There are no facilities at this site.

➡ THE ROUTE

When you arrive at Heartwood Forest, you'll find a large car park with numerous information boards that offer a variety of suggested walks, catering to different interests and fitness levels, and ensuring a perfect trail for everyone.

For those who prefer to plan ahead, the Woodland Trust provides a wealth of useful information at heartwood.woodlandtrust.org.uk. Here you can explore detailed maps, discover the history of the forest, and find tips on what to look out for during your walk. The website also features updates on events and activities, making it a valuable resource for visitors looking to fully immerse themselves in the natural beauty of Heartwood Forest.

As you set out on your walk, take a moment to appreciate the carefully preserved environment, home to a diverse range of wildlife and plant species. The trails are well-marked and designed to blend seamlessly with the natural landscape, providing a peaceful and rejuvenating experience. Whether you're exploring the Magical Wood with family, searching for woodland characters or simply enjoying the serenity of the forest, Heartwood offers a perfect escape into nature.

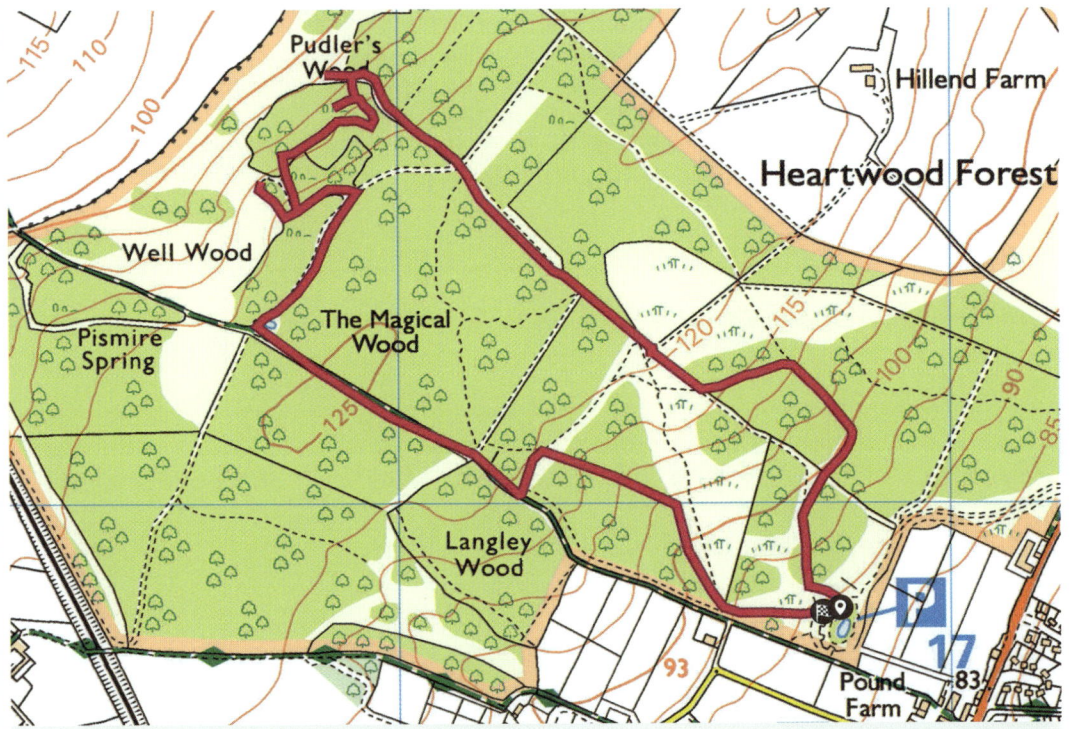

NEED TO KNOW

A PLACE TO EAT: Denbies Wine Estate in Dorking (RH5 6AA) is wheelchair accessible.

A PLACE TO DRINK: The Watermill is a cosy gastropub in Dorking (RH4 1NN) and is wheelchair accessible.

A PLACE TO SLEEP: The White Horse on Dorking High Street (RH4 1BE) is a 13th-century inn that has two accessible rooms.

IF YOU'RE LOOKING FOR SOMETHING ELSE…

Dorking Museum & Heritage Centre is a hidden gem, offering an engaging, multisensory experience for visitors of all ages. Run entirely by passionate volunteers, the museum brings local history to life with interactive exhibits, from fossils and medieval artifacts to the town's role in the 2012 Olympic Road Race. Children will love the dressing-up costumes and hands-on displays, while history buffs can explore archives, guided walks and South Street Cave tours. The museum beautifully showcases Dorking's rich heritage, from famous residents to its iconic chickens! A must-visit for anyone curious about the area's fascinating past.

SUTTON PARK

SUTTON COLDFIELD, WEST MIDLANDS

DARREN HARRIS

I recently had the pleasure of meeting Darren Harris in the scenic surroundings of Sutton Park, located in the West Midlands not too far from Birmingham. Spanning over 970ha (2,400 acres), Sutton Park is renowned as the largest urban park in Britain. This expansive green space offers a diverse range of attractions for visitors, including a small visitor centre, a donkey sanctuary and vast open fields where cows and ponies roam freely, adding to the park's idyllic charm. Dotted with several wildlife ponds, the park provides a perfect spot for picnics, walks and wildlife observation, making it a favourite destination for families and nature enthusiasts alike. Conveniently situated less than 3.2km (2 miles) from Darren's home, and only 9.7km (6 miles) from Birmingham's city centre, Sutton Park proved to be the perfect backdrop for our engaging conversation.

Starting at Palace Hill, we entered Sutton Park through Town Gate and followed the tarmac track towards Wyndley Pool. From there, the path led us onwards to another of the park's seven lakes: Powell's Pool. Originally built in the 18th century to power a watermill, the pool now holds its history quietly beneath calm, reflective waters.

Darren often comes running here, drawn by the peace and natural beauty that surround the trail. Originally from Wolverhampton, he's now made his home in nearby Sutton Coldfield. The move was a natural fit, offering both excellent transport links and immediate access to green space, something he deeply values. He usually travels by train and visits Sutton Park regularly.

For Darren, running here isn't just exercise, it's a way of reconnecting with the stillness, of finding rhythm in nature.

Darren's life journey began at a young age when he was diagnosed with bilateral retinoblastoma at just 15 months old. The condition, which severely affected both his eyes, led to the removal of his left eye and treatment with radiotherapy for his right eye. As he grew older, the damage to his tear ducts resulted in corneal scarring, further diminishing his vision. By age ten, magnifying glasses were no longer effective, prompting Darren to learn braille to navigate his world.

Growing up, Darren faced significant challenges. He found inspiration in his grandmother; a wheelchair user whose resilience and faith became a beacon of strength to him. Though he loved playing sports, his vision issues made activities like catching a ball difficult, leading to feelings of exclusion and isolation, especially towards the end of primary school. Despite these obstacles, his love for sports remained steadfast.

As we walked on, the urban feel of the park at the start of the walk had faded, giving way to coarse heathland and gorse. It was here that Darren reminisced about his school days, lost in thought amid the peaceful surroundings.

SUTTON PARK IS RENOWNED AS THE LARGEST URBAN PARK IN BRITAIN

DEBBIE AND DARREN EXPLORING THE MILES OF TRACK AROUND SUTTON PARK

Darren's secondary education at Worcester College for the Blind, a prestigious institution with a rich history of supporting visually impaired students, was a turning point in his life. At Worcester, Darren encountered peers who were redefining the boundaries of what was possible. One particularly influential moment came when he saw a fellow student using echolocation to ride a bike unaccompanied, a technique that sparked a newfound admiration for the capabilities of blind individuals.

As we continued on, Longmoor Pool shimmered into view, like a piece of sky laid gently on the earth, cradled in the arms of ancient woodland and open heath. The surface was glassy and still, so calm it mirrored the slow-drifting clouds above. Reeds edged the water, rustling softly in the breeze like whispers in a forgotten language. The hush of the landscape held us in its grasp until Darren's laughter broke through, bright and effortless, lifting the quiet like sunlight breaking through mist.

He was telling one of his many tales from school, his eyes glinting with mischief. 'There was this time,' he began, 'when a bunch of us were playing a game of blind football during break.' It had been thrown together spontaneously – no uniforms, no referees, just friends running and laughing, the ball ringing with every kick thanks to the small bell hidden inside. 'But then,' Darren said, laughing, 'the ball went over the fence onto the field – and the bell stopped ringing. We couldn't find it.' With the absurdity of childhood logic, the boys had come up with a solution. 'We all lay down, head to toe, and rolled across the grass until someone hit the ball. It was a comical sight to see!'

He chuckled at the memory, the sound rising like a birdcall above the hush of the pool.

Then, more thoughtfully, he added, 'Of course, in real blind football, things are way more serious. The players are incredible. They don't just rely on the bell – they've trained their hearing, their awareness. They know the pitch inside out.'

I listened as he described how players move with confidence, guided not just by sound but by instinct and hours of practice. Coaches shout cues, goalkeepers call positions, and every pass is deliberate, every dribble controlled.

'It's all about trust,' he said. 'Trust in your teammates, in your senses and in your own body.'

We took a break from our ramble and sat beside Longmoor Pool, the quiet returning, thick and still. A dragonfly skimmed across the water's surface, wings catching the light. And I thought about the boys rolling in the grass, the silence of a still bell, and extraordinary coordination required to chase a dream in the dark. It made me smile.

Darren's time at Worcester College for the Blind was transformative in so many ways. There he could fully embrace his passion for sports, trying out a wide variety of activities alongside peers who, like him, were pushing the limits of what they thought possible.

However, despite the enriching environment, Darren faced a painful and unexpected challenge: he was bullied due to his skin colour. This type of bullying was a constant struggle for Darren, and it led to confrontations that sometimes got him into trouble.

Despite these difficulties, Darren's resilience shone through. He refused to let the negativity define his experience. Through sheer determination, he excelled academically, leaving Worcester with both GCSE and A-levels and, most importantly, a strong foundation for his future.

Darren's educational journey continued at the University of Sheffield, where he pursued a degree in Mathematics. He had a significant advantage over most first-year students at the university, as he was already accustomed to living away from home. University life was a mix of academic challenges and social adventures. The lack of braille resources meant that Darren had to rely on borrowing notes and getting them transcribed or read aloud, making his studies a long and arduous process. Despite this, he thrived academically and enjoyed the vibrant social scene.

People who got to know Darren often asked why he chose such a challenging subject like mathematics to study at university. He would laugh and joke about the Greek symbols used in mathematical equations, saying, 'Joe Bloggs doesn't understand Sigma or the squiggles of other symbols,' and adding, 'I don't even know what Pi looks like.' The complexity of the subject made it difficult to find a support worker who could help.

Upon completing his studies, Darren ventured into the IT sector but remained deeply committed to sports.

Darren spoke about the next chapter of his life, reflecting on the path that had brought him here. With each step we took, the rich tapestry of Sutton Park revealed itself, ancient woodlands, wide open heath and still, glassy pools, each holding traces of the past. Framed by the park's calm beauty, his words carried a quiet sense of fulfilment and gratitude. The rhythm of our walk seemed to echo his journey – measured, thoughtful, shaped by challenges faced and experiences that left their mark.

The path to Blackroot Pool was dry underfoot, the late afternoon sun picking out flecks of quartz in the gravel. Trees stood tall and steady, their green canopies reflected cleanly on the surface of the water, untroubled by wind or weather. Built to power a watermill, the pool now lay still – its industrious past softened into peace. But it wasn't hard to imagine energy here. Drive. Purpose. Blackroot seemed like just the place to reflect on the life of someone who had built something extraordinary from quiet beginnings.

Upon completing his studies, Darren ventured into the IT sector, and also began playing blind football for England. The team was entirely amateur, with no funding or support. Players had to raise their own money for kits and transport costs, but their passion for the sport kept them going. Training took place in Hereford, and Darren made his debut in 1996. That same year, he went on holiday to Atlanta, USA, where he had the chance to experience the Paralympic Games as a spectator. Watching the athletes compete, Darren felt inspired – it was at that moment he knew he wanted to become a Paralympian.

Darren shifted focus to judo, a sport in which he could compete in the Paralympics. In 2004, he made a bold decision, quitting his job to train full-time in preparation for the 2008 Beijing Paralympics. After the Beijing Games, Darren returned to football in time for the London 2012 Paralympics, determined to make his mark in both sports.

Sport remains a central part of Darren's life. His athletic accomplishments extend beyond football and judo – he has run marathons, competed in triathlons and cycled from Land's End to John O'Groats. His journey as an athlete continues to inspire others, as he shows no signs of slowing down.

We stopped at the water's edge at Blackroot Pool to watch a lone swan carve a 'V' through the stillness. Darren asked me to describe the scene, my words becoming his sight. The swan glided across the surface of the pool, its white feathers catching the sunlight like polished ivory. It moved with effortless elegance, barely disturbing the water beneath it. Each motion was deliberate and slow, as if time bent gently around its passage. The ripples that followed fanned out in widening arcs – soft, silver-edged trails that shimmered briefly before dissolving into the stillness. Its long neck curved like a question mark, poised and watchful, while its black eyes remained fixed ahead, calm and certain. In the quiet, the only sound was the subtle whisper of water folding

DARREN HARRIS IN SUTTON PARK

around its body, smooth as silk. It didn't need to rush. It was simply present, proud and perfectly at ease in its element. No roar of crowds, no flashing lights – just quiet persistence, mirrored in the ripples. Like Darren, Blackroot Pool has known both momentum and stillness. And in both, there is strength.

As we approached the car park where our journey began, the park had now come to life, with families making the most of the open space. Laughter echoed through the air as children ran freely across the grass. Prams rolled smoothly along the stile-free paths and picnic blankets were spread beneath towering trees. The late afternoon sun cast a golden glow, wrapping the scene in warmth and contentment.

Today, Darren is a proud father of two children and embraces the responsibilities that come with being a parent. He loves family life and the joy that his children bring him. Even from a young age, his children were a great support to him. On the walk to school, they would instinctively point out obstacles like wheelie bins and uneven paths, helping him navigate the world more easily. Darren finds great pride and humour in how naturally his children adapted to supporting him, and their bond has only strengthened through the shared experiences of daily life.

Sutton Park will always hold a special place in Darren's heart. It's a sanctuary where he finds solace and rejuvenation, a place where he can run freely, unwind from the stresses of daily life, and take a moment to refuel both physically and mentally. But his characteristic sense of humour is never far away, as he jokes about the possibility of encountering cows during his daily runs...

THE WALK

IS IT FOR ME?

START/END POINT: Sutton Park, Park Rd, Sutton Coldfield, B73 6BT

GRID REFERENCE: SP112961

DISTANCE: 6.6km (4.1 miles) circular

MILES WITHOUT STILES GRADE: For All, if staying on the tarmac track

TERRAIN: Surfaced paths and solid ground

ACCESSIBILITY: There are three main entrances to the park: at Palace Hill, access via Town Gate; at Flying Field, access via Boldmere; and at Jamboree, access via Streetly Gate. Parking fees apply. There are some steeper sections on the walk which can get muddy. These paths are better suited for sturdy powered all-terrain wheelchairs. Purpose-built tracks for manual wheelchair users have been created around the park – ask at the visitor centre for more information.

PARKING: There is a charge for the car parks from Easter until September, and on Sundays and Bank Holidays. At other times parking is free. Check signs in the car park for full details.

FACILITIES: Accessible toilets are available near the car park at Palace Hill, via Town Gate.

THE ROUTE

Steeped in history, Sutton Park was first established as a royal forest by the Anglo-Saxon kings of Mercia in the 9th century, before evolving into a Norman medieval deer park by the 12th century. In 1528, King Henry VIII granted the land to the people of Sutton Coldfield at the request of Bishop John Vesey, securing its place as a cherished public space.

The park's name itself holds traces of its past, with 'Coldfield' possibly linked to the charcoal burning that once thrived here. But today, Sutton Park offers a breathtaking mix of open heathland, ancient woodlands, seven tranquil lakes and rich wetlands. It's home to a diverse array of wildlife, including grazing cattle and wild ponies.

Parking is available around the perimeter, but those arriving by train can easily enter through Town Gate. A great way to start your visit is by collecting a map from the

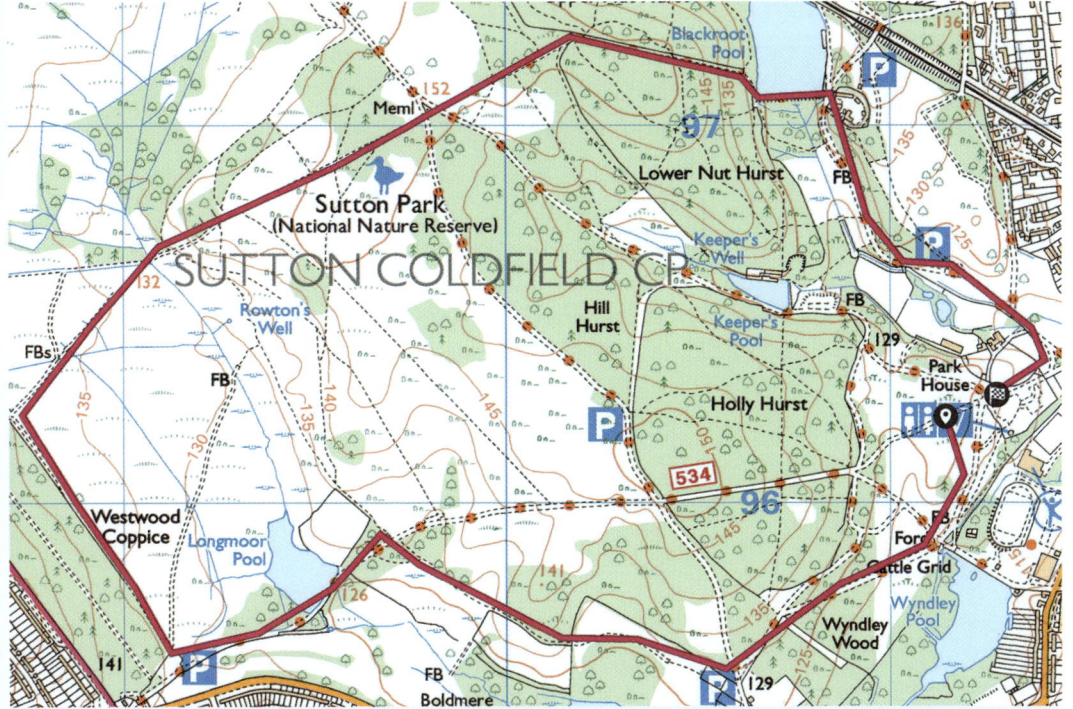

visitor centre before setting off on one of the many scenic trails. Wander towards Holly Hurst Woods or seek out the historic Jamboree Memorial Stone. Follow Lord Donegal's Drive to Banner Gate, where a charming café offers a welcome break.

From there, a path leads toward Longmoor Pool; at the woodland's entrance, turning right will take you to Powell's Pool before leading on to Wyndley Pool and back to the visitor centre.

NEED TO KNOW

A PLACE TO EAT: Miller and Carter, Sutton Park, Boldmere Gate, B73 6LH

A PLACE TO DRINK: The Four Oaks, Belwell Lane, Sutton Coldfield, B74 4TR

A PLACE TO SLEEP: New Hall Hotel & Spa, Walmley Road, Sutton Coalfield, B76 1QX

IF YOU'RE LOOKING FOR SOMETHING ELSE…

Sutton Sailing Club, founded in 1952, sits on the tranquil waters of Sutton Park. It welcomes sailors of all levels to enjoy sailing, racing and social events in a beautiful setting. Learn more at www.suttonsc.org.uk.

STANSTED PARK
STOUGHTON, WEST SUSSEX

STEPHANIE JANE QUINTRELL

Nestled between Chichester and Portsmouth, within the picturesque South Downs National Park, lies Stansted Park, a sprawling 728ha (1,800 acre) estate of stunning landscaped parkland and ancient forest. Steeped in history, the estate's earliest records reveal its use as a royal hunting ground in medieval times, frequented by monarchs such as, Richard the Lionheart and King John. Today, my walk through this storied landscape promised a unique twist, as my companion, Stephanie Jane Quintrell, joined me not on foot but on horseback.

Walking together through the tranquil countryside Stephanie shared her extraordinary journey; one that embodies remarkable resilience, unwavering courage and an indomitable spirit of adventure.

From her beginnings as a successful career woman and devoted army wife, Stephanie faced the profound challenge of adapting to life as a wheelchair user. Undeterred, she went on to make history as the first wheelchair-dependent person to ride horseback across the Pyrenees mountain range. Her story is a powerful example of overcoming immense personal obstacles and redefining the boundaries of possibility.

As we made our way up the wide driveway towards Stansted House, the grand estate slowly revealed itself through the bare branches of winter trees. The Georgian-style mansion stands with timeless elegance; its symmetrical façade adorned with large sash windows that gleam in the cold afternoon light. The crisp air carried whispers of history, and for a moment, it felt as though we had stepped into another era, where the past and present intertwine.

Stephanie, known to many as Steph, grew up amid the rural landscapes of Hampshire, where the lush forests and rolling hills became her playground. The quiet country lanes and winding bridleways nurtured her deep love for nature and the outdoors, a passion that has stayed with her ever since.

As a child, horses were everything to Steph. It all began on her tenth birthday when her parents arranged riding lessons as a special treat. Little did they know that this would ignite a lifelong passion. From the moment she sat in that saddle, Steph was hooked. She spent every spare moment thinking about horses, reading about them and dreaming of the day she could have one of her own. At 12, that dream became a reality when she got her first horse.

Horses quickly became the focal point of Steph's life. They brought her joy, peace and a sense of purpose. As she grew older, her love for these magnificent animals never waned. Riding was more than just a hobby; it was a way of life.

Our walk took us to Rosamond's Hill, a quiet, evocative rise nestled in the eastern reaches of the Stansted Park Estate. Surrounded by a patchwork of open pasture and shaded woodland, its gentle slopes unfold into serene vistas of the South Downs, with glimpses of Stansted House framed by the trees. The hill, rich in historical resonance, offers an elevated calm – a subtle yet striking feature of the estate where nature and heritage meet in perfect harmony.

When Steph married Jon, a serving soldier in the Royal Electrical and Mechanical Engineers (REME) since 2001, horses naturally remained a significant part of their shared life. Both fiercely independent, they each

THE HISTORIC STANSTEAD HOUSE IN ALL ITS CHARM

STEPHANIE AND DEBBIE EXPLORING THE STANSTEAD ESTATE

had their careers, hobbies and circle of friends. Steph had imagined they would continue living 'unaccompanied' until Jon retired from the Army. The arrangement suited them well. Their young son was happy and settled in nursery, and Jon made every effort to be present at home whenever possible. It was a comfortable, balanced life they both deeply valued.

But in July 2019, at the age of 28 and with a young son who was just two years old, Steph's life took an unexpected and devastating turn. What began as a seemingly routine day quickly spiralled into a nightmare. Steph became suddenly and severely unwell. Within 48 hours, she had lost her ability to walk and became wheelchair dependent. Over the next two weeks, her condition worsened: she lost the use of her fingers on her right hand, began experiencing seizures and entered a daily battle with chronic pain and exhaustion.

After numerous medical consultations and tests, Steph was diagnosed with complex functional neurological disorder (FND), a condition that affects how the brain and body send and receive signals. In addition, she was diagnosed with fixed dystonia in her right hand, dystonia in both feet and ankles, and Fowler's syndrome, a condition affecting bladder function.

The impact on Steph's family was profound. Steph had always been an active, independent person, and suddenly she needed help with even the simplest of tasks. Her career, her hobbies and the life she had known were all put on hold as the family adjusted to this new reality. But as difficult as it was, this experience brought clarity to what mattered most. They realised that their family needed to be together, not just in spirit but physically as well. So, just four months after her diagnosis, Steph and their son packed up their lives and moved 290km (180 miles) to join Jon at his posting.

Feeling isolated in her new environment, Steph found connection through the Forces Wives Challenge (FWC), a social enterprise that brings together women with partners in the armed forces (serving or veterans) through adventure and challenge. It was within this community that Steph returned to riding, embarking on an adventure that would profoundly shape her future.

Eighteen months after her diagnosis, and with the support of her husband, Steph returned to the saddle. The experience was transformative.

'The minute I was back in the saddle, I felt like a spark had been ignited within me again,' she recalls. Riding provided her with a sense of freedom and empowerment that had been missing since her illness.

Steph's return to riding wasn't just about personal fulfilment; it was also about setting an example for others facing similar challenges. And the bridleways weaving through the Stansted Park Estate have long been a place of adventure for Steph. These trails, winding beneath towering beech avenues and through ancient oak and chestnut groves, hold memories of carefree rides and quiet reflection. In spring, the woodland floors burst into life with carpets of bluebells, while autumn transforms the trees into a fiery tapestry of red, orange and gold. But beyond their beauty, the paths became something more, a reminder of resilience. When Steph's life took an unexpected turn, the familiar rhythm of hoofbeats on soft earth brought comfort and clarity. The trails she had once ridden for pleasure became a symbol of perseverance, guiding her forward through uncertainty. That day, as we ventured out together, we followed these same bridleways, not just as riders and walkers, but as friends embracing the journey, one step, one stride at a time.

In June 2023, Steph achieved something truly extraordinary. She became the first wheelchair-dependent person to ride horseback across the Pyrenees mountain range, following the historic Second World War freedom trails from France to Spain. This achievement was part of the FWC's 'Ride to Freedom', a gruelling 130km (81 mile) trek through mountainous terrain, reaching altitudes of 7,218km (2,200m). The route, which closely follows the paths taken by Allied servicemen and women and Jewish refugees fleeing Nazi-occupied France during the war, was both physically and emotionally challenging.

For Steph, the journey was not just a personal challenge, but also a powerful statement of resilience and solidarity. The FWC team, composed of eight military wives, each brought their own personal struggles to the expedition. Together, they aimed to demonstrate the transformative power of adventure, and the strength found in unity. Steph's participation in the ride, without the physical and mental support of her husband for the first time, was a monumental step in her journey of recovery and self-discovery.

Jon understands the importance of adventure and challenge in maintaining mental and physical well-being. He often joins Steph on her countryside explorations, walking alongside her as she rides Bubba, her beloved horse. Their shared love for the outdoors and for each other has been a cornerstone of Steph's recovery and resilience.

Steph's role as a military wife has also played a significant part in shaping her outlook on life. Despite the difficulties, she remains a devoted mother to her energetic young son. Her disability has not diminished her ability to be an active and engaged parent. Whether she is bum-shuffling around a soft play area or exploring the countryside with her son, she is determined to provide him with a childhood filled with love and adventure.

Looking to the future, Steph remains focused on pushing the boundaries of what is possible. She continues to advocate for greater accessibility and opportunities for people with disabilities, using her platform to raise awareness and inspire others. Her work with Equine Para-Adventures is just one example of how she is making a difference in the lives of others.

In addition to her advocacy work, Steph is also looking forward to new adventures. As Jon approaches retirement, the two are beginning to plan their next chapter. Whether it's exploring new trails with Bubba or embarking on new challenges, Steph is determined to continue living life to the fullest.

As we followed the bridlepath through the estate, Stephanie gave her horse a canter, the rhythmic drum of hooves echoing through the trees. I could feel the earth vibrate beneath me, the energy of the moment filling the crisp air. Watching her ride with effortless grace, it was impossible not to admire her strength and determination. Her story is one of extraordinary courage. From the sudden onset of a debilitating condition to becoming a trailblazer in equine adventure, she has shown that life's challenges, no matter how daunting, can be overcome with resilience, support and a passion for living. She is a powerful reminder that even in the face of overwhelming adversity, we can still find ways to pursue our dreams, inspire others and live a life of purpose and joy.

Stephanie Jane Quintrell's story is one of extraordinary courage and determination. From the sudden onset of a debilitating condition to becoming a trailblazer in equine adventure, she has shown that life's challenges, no matter how daunting, can be overcome with resilience, support, and a passion for living. Her journey is a powerful reminder that even in the face of overwhelming adversity, we can still find ways to pursue our dreams, inspire others, and live a life of purpose and joy.

THE WALK

⊙ IS IT FOR ME?

START/END POINT: Stansted Park, Stansted House, Rowland's Castle, PO9 6DX

GRID REFERENCE: SU753104

DISTANCE: 6.5km (4.1 miles) circular

MILES WITHOUT STILES GRADE: For All

TERRAIN: On tarmac roads (suitable for wheelchair use), no stiles

ACCESSIBILITY: The paths are well signposted, making them easy to navigate and allowing you the freedom to explore at your own pace.

PARKING: There is parking available at Stansted Park Garden Centre, on the estate (PO9 6DU).

FACILITIES: Toilets are available at the house and garden centre.

➤ THE ROUTE

From the car park, head towards the Orange Grove, where the first glimpse of Stansted House emerges through the trees. As you walk, the path skirts the edge of Lumley Woods, where towering conifers, ancient broadleaf trees and neatly coppiced woodland create a rich tapestry of greenery.

Following the tarmac road, you'll pass through mixed woodland behind Lumley Seat, a haven for wildlife. Fallow and roe deer move quietly among the trees, their presence sometimes only revealed by the rustling of leaves or a fleeting silhouette in the distance. Muntjac deer are becoming an increasingly common sight, adding to the estate's thriving biodiversity. This landscape, steeped in history, is even mentioned in the Domesday Book of 1086.

Taking a sharp right turn past a dense oak copse, the trail leads to a crossroads – turn right here to head towards the cottages. The well-signposted paths make navigation easy, but be prepared for muddy and slippery sections, especially after rainfall (wellies are highly recommended).

The grounds and walled gardens are open year-round. The arboretum, Pavilion Tearoom, Stansted Park Garden Centre, farm shop and even a charming maze provide inviting stops along the way. Past the bustling café area, tranquillity returns, with

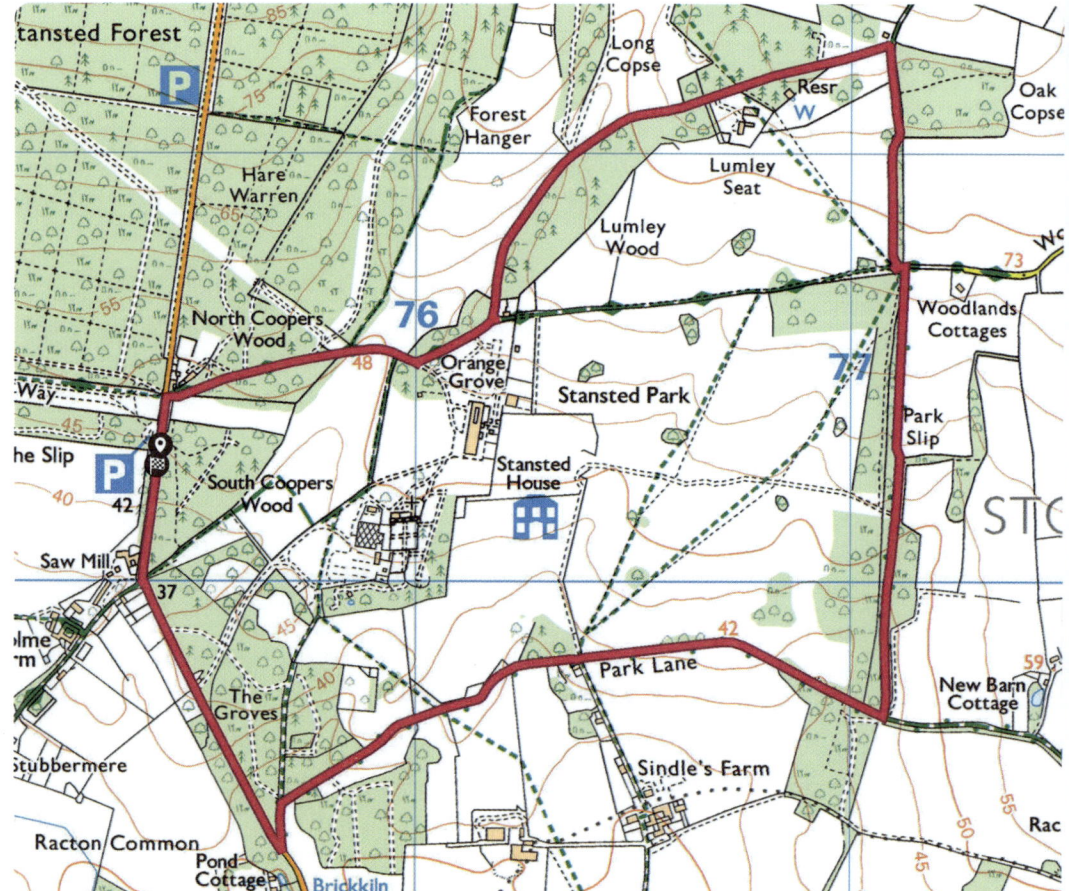

quiet spots perfect for soaking in the beauty of this historic estate.

In spring, the bluebell woods are a breathtaking sight, a sea of violet carpeting the forest floor. The views stretching across the Hampshire–West Sussex border add to the sense of space and grandeur. For those wishing to extend their walk, take a detour and enjoy a ramble in Stanstead Forest or towards Rowlands Castle.

🏠 NEED TO KNOW

A PLACE TO EAT: Stansted Park Garden Centre is wheelchair accessible.

A PLACE TO DRINK: The Barley Mow pub in nearby Walderton (PO18 9ED) has accessible facilities.

A PLACE TO SLEEP: The Lakeside Coastal Resort on Hayling Island (PO11 9NR) has disabled facilities.

IF YOU'RE LOOKING FOR SOMETHING ELSE...

Wetwheels Solent, in Portsmouth, offers an unforgettable, fully accessible powerboating experience for people of all abilities. From the first contact, their team is incredibly helpful, answering questions and easing any concerns. They ensure a smooth and supportive boarding process, securing wheelchairs safely and providing waterproof capes for comfort. Once on the water, the sense of freedom is unmatched, and disabilities fade away as the boat speeds through the waves. Best of all, everyone gets a chance to take the helm, creating smiles that last long after the trip. It's an inclusive, joyful adventure and is perfect for families, leaving you exhilarated and wanting more!

THE WETWHEELS SOUTH WEST BOAT IN PORTSMOUTH

FOLKESTONE WARREN

KENT

GINI MITCHELL

The salty breeze rolled in from the sea as I arrived at Folkestone Warren, a wild and dramatic stretch of coastline where land meets water in an untamed embrace. Here, towering cliffs frame the horizon, their chalk faces worn by centuries of wind and waves. Below, a tangle of woodland and shingle beaches unfold, a haven for wildlife and a sanctuary for those seeking solitude in nature. It was here, amid the rugged beauty of the Kent Heritage Coast, that I was meeting Gini Mitchell, a woman whose passion for the outdoors was as fierce as the elements that shaped this landscape.

Gini arrived in her all-terrain mobility scooter, a bright smile on her face despite the biting wind. Her presence was immediately warm and welcoming, and as she extended a hand in greeting, I could tell she was someone who had spent a lifetime defying limitations. The founder of Wild with Wheels, a Disabled Forest School Leader, and a North Downs Way Ambassador, Gini has dedicated her life to making nature accessible to everyone, regardless of mobility or disability.

'This place is special to me,' she said, gazing out over the vast expanse of shingle beaches and rolling cliffs. 'I spent my childhood exploring these landscapes. Losing access to them was devastating. That's what drives me – ensuring no one else has to feel that way.'

Folkestone Warren, with its crumbling cliffs, seafront trail and hidden paths, had always been one of Gini's favourite places to explore. However, as her neuromuscular condition progressed, she found herself facing barriers that many able-bodied people take for granted: uneven terrain, locked gates and inaccessible paths. But rather than accept defeat, she took action, leading a campaign to make the Warren more accessible. After three years of determined advocacy, a new gate was installed, opening up this incredible landscape to those who had previously been excluded.

That gate might not seem like much to some people,' she said, pointing towards it, 'but for wheelchair users and mobility scooter riders, it's the difference between being shut out and being free.'

As we began our walk, the sound of waves crashing against the shore below filled the air. Overhead, seagulls circled, their cries blending with the rustling leaves of the trees that line the clifftop. The path was wide enough for both our mobility scooters to navigate comfortably, something that hadn't always been the case.

'Growing up, I spent all my time outdoors,' Gini said as we followed the trail. 'On foot or on horseback, I was always out in the countryside, learning about nature, listening to the wind in the trees. It's where I felt most at home.'

Even as she spoke, I could see how deeply connected she was to the landscape. She pointed out native plants, describing their uses and historical significance. She paused to admire a red admiral butterfly resting on a thistle and gestured toward a pair of kestrels hovering over the grasslands. Her knowledge of the flora and fauna of the Kent countryside was astonishing, and it was clear that even though her mobility had changed, her passion for nature had not diminished. But losing access to these spaces had been more than just frustrating – it had been heartbreaking.

THE FERRY TERMINAL AT DOVER, TAKEN FROM THE CLIFFTOP

'It felt like a part of me was being taken away,' she admitted. 'That's why I started fighting, not just for myself but also for others who face the same struggles.'

The path soon opened up to reveal a breathtaking view. The sea stretched endlessly to the horizon, its surface rippling with the motion of the tide. Below us, rockpools sparkled in the sunlight, remnants of the changing coastline that had shaped Folkestone Warren over millennia. It was here that Gini shared the story of Wild with Wheels.

'Wild with Wheels offers guided, interactive walks specifically designed for people with mobility impairments, learning disabilities and mental health conditions. I wanted to create something that allowed people with disabilities to experience nature in a way that is meaningful and fulfilling.'

GINI EXPLORING THE BEACH AT FOLKSTONE WARREN

The walks are more than just an opportunity to enjoy nature; they are immersive experiences.

'We do things like leaf rubbing, storytelling, wildlife spotting,' Gini says, her eyes shining with enthusiasm. 'It's about connection. Connection to nature, to history, to each other.'

These experiences aren't just about accessibility; they're about restoring a sense of adventure.

'When we remove barriers, we remind people that they belong here too,' she says.

As we continued along the trail, the path became rockier, the landscape wilder. The remnants of old landslides created an eerie yet beautiful terrain, where trees leaned at odd angles, their roots gripping onto the soil like twisted fingers. Folkestone Warren is a place constantly in motion, shaped by the forces of nature – much like Gini herself, who refuses to be held back by limitations.

Her advocacy for improved accessibility extends beyond leading walks. She has spent the past two years working with local councils, organisations and landowners to create real change. She has spoken at events, worked as a public speaker and collaborated with accessibility groups to design toolkits that can be used nationwide.

'People assume the countryside is for everyone,' she said, steering her scooter carefully over a bump in the path. 'But for many disabled people, it's still full of obstacles. That's why I keep pushing for change. One gentleman told me that by joining our activities, it got him out of the house,' Gini says, her smile full of pride. 'That's what this is about: bringing people together. Breaking down barriers. Making sure that everyone has the chance to experience the joy of the natural world.'

The sun began to dip lower in the sky, casting golden light over the cliffs. The sea shimmered, reflecting the fading daylight. It was a perfect moment, a reminder of why spaces like this should be accessible to everyone.

Before we parted ways, I asked Gini what freedom meant to her. She looked out over the landscape, taking a deep breath.

'Freedom means everything,' she said. 'It means I'm back in the world I love. My scooter lets me explore, find new routes, push boundaries. When we're out on recce trips, people can't believe where I can go. But that's the point – if we break down barriers, the possibilities are endless.'

As I left Folkestone Warren, I felt profoundly inspired by Gini's passion, determination and unshakable belief that the countryside should be open to all. She isn't just reclaiming the landscape for herself – she's opening it up for countless others, ensuring that nobody has to miss out on experiencing the beauty of the natural world.

THE WALK

 ## IS IT FOR ME?

START/END POINT: East Cliff Pavilion car park, Wear Bay Rd, Folkestone, CT19 6BL

GRID REFERENCE: TR246377

DISTANCE: 2.9km (1.8 miles) one way

MILES WITHOUT STILES GRADE: For Some

TERRAIN: Uneven tarmac surface, concrete walkway and sandy paths

ACCESSIBILITY: There are some steep sections, and due to the potholes and cambers this route is not suitable for manual wheelchairs.

PARKING: East Cliff Pavilion car park.

FACILITIES: There are toilets at the car park.

 ## THE ROUTE

Folkestone Warren is a stunning landscape where land, sea and sky meet in a dramatic display of nature's power. This walk combines coastal cliffs, fossil-rich shores and wildlife habitats, making it a haven for nature lovers, geologists and historians alike.

Once a lively Victorian beauty spot with a railway station, gardens, ponds and tea huts, Folkestone Warren has since been reclaimed by nature, though traces of its past remain. Begin your walk from the small off-road parking area via a RADAR key gate. The initial track is rough and uneven – unsuitable for manual wheelchairs.

North of the railway lies hart's-tongue wood, a humid, fern-covered woodland alive with birdsong – over 150 species are found here. South of the line, chalk grassland supports grazing cattle that help preserve the ecosystem. The Warren itself is a vast landslip, where shifting clay and chalk gradually move the cliffs seaward.

Follow the track towards the beach, where a concrete walkway leads beneath the cliffs – an excellent spot for rockpooling and fossil hunting, especially ammonites. Enjoy sweeping views of the White Cliffs and East Cliff as you explore this ever-changing landscape. Whether for fossils, wildlife or sea air, Folkestone Warren offers an unforgettable coastal adventure.

NEED TO KNOW

A PLACE TO EAT: The Rock Salt Restaurant in Folkestone (CT19 6AA) offers locally produced food.

A PLACE TO DRINK: The Pilot Beach Bar in Folkestone Harbour (CT20 1QH) offers a varied drinks menu and a lovely outdoor setting.

A PLACE TO SLEEP: The 4-star Burlington Hotel (CT20 2HR) offers stunning views across the English Channel and has wheelchair-accessible facilities.

IF YOU'RE LOOKING FOR SOMETHING ELSE...

No visit would be complete without seeing the **White Cliffs of Dover**. An iconic British landmark, the Cliffs stand as a symbol of homecoming, wartime defence and resilience. Rising 107m (350ft) above the English Channel, their striking white chalk faces, accented by black flint, have inspired generations and are designated a Site of Special Scientific Interest (SSSI), a Special Area of Conservation (SAC) and part of the Kent Down National Landscape

A wheelchair-friendly path leads to a viewing point, offering breathtaking vistas, while the National Trust Visitor Centre café provides fresh meals and refreshments, perfect for enjoying alongside the world's busiest passenger port below.

MILLENNIUM QUAY
PORTSMOUTH, HAMPSHIRE

PAULINE NIXON

It was hard to believe I was sitting on the seafront in Portsmouth, waiting for Pauline Nixon, a woman I had only met once but who had left a lasting impression of friendship. Our paths first crossed at the launch of the charity Access the Dales, hundreds of miles north at Ravenseat Farm in the Yorkshire Dales. Pauline had come with her father and son, Theo, to celebrate the special day, alongside her father's birthday. What stood out most, then, was the instant connection I felt with Pauline. That connection deepened when I observed a quiet yet powerful moment during the lively festivities. Pauline had discreetly taken Theo to the car, as he was becoming fractious, and she was attempting to feed him despite his obvious reluctance. Eating had always been a challenge for Theo, and he has gone on to be fitted with a gastrostomy (feeding tube). Watching Pauline handle the situation with such grace and composure, without drawing attention to the situation, I couldn't help but admire her quiet strength. In that moment, I truly understood the isolation she must sometimes feel, yet also the deep love and dedication that defined her journey.

Despite the hundreds of miles that separate us, I had a feeling that Pauline and I would become great friends. I set off on the lengthy voyage from my home in Yorkshire to hers in Hampshire, to meet with her and learn more about her story, and to uncover the wonders Portsmouth had in store for us.

Portsmouth, situated on Portsea Island in the Solent, is a vibrant city on the South Coast of England. Not only is it famous for being the home of Henry VIII's warship the *Mary Rose*, but it also boasts a bustling ferry port that offers regular sailings to France and the Isle of Wight. The city is rich in history, with captivating murals adorning the walls of some buildings, showcasing the bustling harbour life of yesteryear and depicting scenes of majestic tall ships anchored in the harbour, the lively atmosphere of the public houses and the recruitment of reluctant sailors by press gangs.

Pauline was eager to show me the Millennium Promenade, an accessible 4.2km (2.6 mile) trail connecting Portsmouth Historic Dockyard to Southsea Castle. As we set off on our stroll, the morning sun making the sea sparkle and the gentle breeze carrying the salty scent of the sea, I realised how little I knew about her son's medical condition.

Theo (who was at school while we walked) was diagnosed with Wolf-Hirschhorn syndrome (WHS) at a young age, a rare genetic condition caused by a partial chromosome deletion. It affects every aspect of his life, leading to distinct facial features, significant developmental delays, intellectual disability, low muscle tone (hypotonia) and seizures. He requires Pauline's full-time care, a role she embraces with pure dedication.

We rested a while by the iconic harbour walls, which have stood for centuries, a reminder of the city's illustrious maritime history. A variety of

THE SPINNAKER TOWER, PORTSMOUTH

PAULINE, THEO AND DEBBIE FIRST MET AT RAVENSEAT AT THE LAUNCH OF ACCESS THE DALES

vessels were coming and going, from small fishing boats to large cruise ships.

Pauline, a native of Carlisle, embarked on a journey to pursue her dreams in London at the tender age of 18, accompanied by her then boyfriend. The vibrant city life captivated her, and she started working in post-production at the BBC, where she stayed for 14 years (apart from a couple of years working with writer and broadcaster Clive James). She started a relationship with a colleague, and they had a son, James, together. Unfortunately, it wasn't a happy relationship, and they parted ways, leaving her a single mum for five years. It was a difficult time: she was working full-time, living in London and away from family.

Back on our walk, the vibrant energy of Gunwharf Quays, with its blend of modern elegance and historic charm, mirrored the twists and turns of life itself. As we took in the bustling waterfront, Pauline reflected on the journey that had brought her to this part of the world. After years in London, her path led her to new beginnings on the South Coast.

Time had ushered in change, and with it came love and family. After a long friendship, romance blossomed again at the BBC when she met John. They soon married, and shortly after, the family made a move from London to Hayling Island, a beautiful spot off the Hampshire coast. Pauline continued to commute to London until the happy arrival of Clara, a lovely sister for James.

Pauline and John were overjoyed when they later discovered they were expecting their third child. Throughout her pregnancy, Pauline cherished every moment and relished in the anticipation of welcoming a new life into their family. However, as her pregnancy neared its end, she began to feel uneasy. It had been a couple of days since she'd last felt the baby kick and her concern grew. She decided to visit the hospital for a check-up, and doctors decided it was time for Theo to make an appearance. He was delivered by emergency C-section at 35 weeks. Despite his small size, there were no health concerns.

However, while Pauline was nursing Theo she noticed that, despite his intake of milk, he wasn't gaining weight. He suffered badly with reflux and his body couldn't take any extra food. Theo was referred to the paediatrician for 'failure to thrive' (FTT), a term used to describe children who haven't been able to develop and grow as expected. It deeply saddened Pauline when she was advised to stop breastfeeding and switch to formula milk.

Then Theo was admitted to hospital and stayed there with Pauline alongside him. After a month of careful observation and testing, the doctors finally diagnosed him with WHS. The news understandably came as a shock to the family, as there was no apparent cause for his condition. Adjusting to this new reality, the family knew that their lives would be forever changed.

As we continued our walk, we arrived at Vernon Creek, a historical site running inland from the harbour, where ships were beached for repairs from the 12th century before the development of the dockyard. Today, the area has several attractive water features, including three torpedoes used as seating, which were discovered in a building on the site, and an old crane left by the MOD when it sold the site, which is beautifully floodlit at night. Alongside the creek stands a painted wooden ship's figurehead, originating from the fourth HMS Vernon, a 50-gun frigate first launched on 1 May 1832.

As we admired the creek, our conversation turned back to Pauline's story.

Pauline fully immersed herself in the responsibility of caring for Theo while delving into research about the rare illness that affected only 1 in 50,000 children in the UK. With two other children to think of, she was determined to maintain a sense of normality in her family's life.

'There was a time of immense difficulty when my daughter had to be admitted to the hospital. I found myself torn between being there for her and ensuring that Theo, who was at home, received the care he needed.' Reflecting on this particularly challenging period, Pauline shared how she'd experienced emotional turmoil, grappling with the decision of which child's health to prioritise.

Theo attended a mainstream nursery until the age of five before transitioning to a special school. During this time, Pauline often felt drained and recognised the need for moments to clear her mind and manage the emotional stress of her daily routine. She found solace in nature and the outdoors, and she and Theo would enjoy walks together. Pauline would carefully place Theo into his wheelchair before embarking on a stroll through the countryside. Although Theo cannot speak, he often expresses his emotions through sounds, and Pauline believes that he enjoys their outings. They've even completed several long-distance walks, tackling a different section each time.

'Right now, we're taking on the South Downs Way. I'm lucky to have a wonderful group of friends who are joining me on this adventure, but it's not without its challenges. One of them is lifting Theo and his buggy over stiles. However, being out in nature makes it all worth it.'

Our walk then took us to The Camber Docks. The Bridge Tavern stands with its rustic brick façade, its windows glowing warmly from within. A large, vibrant painting adorns its outer wall, capturing the rich, storied life of the Point through scenes of fishermen hauling in their catch, bustling market vendors and lively dockworkers.

As we took in the sights, Pauline shared her love of walking, no matter the weather. She finds solace in the open space, feeling the elements, admiring the views and embracing the peace it brings.

Despite her busy life as Theo's carer, she still manages to work part-time as a music teacher for children with disabilities and those living in deprived areas. She finds her job deeply fulfilling, believing that the magical moment when a child beats on a drum after months of practice is priceless. She is also a member of a local choir, where singing keeps her spirits high.

PAULINE, THEO AND HER DAD AT GORDALE SCAR IN THE YORKSHIRE DALES

Pauline shares the exciting adventures with Theo on social media, always maintaining a positive and upbeat tone in her posts. However, beneath the cheerful façade, she sometimes feels overwhelmed by the pressure of being a full-time carer. People often label her as inspirational, but comments like 'Special parents are given special children' and 'You only get what you can cope with' can be difficult for her to digest. There was one instance when Pauline had had a tough morning with Theo and she decided to express her true feelings on social media. Reading her heartfelt words was heart-wrenching, but it struck a chord with many of her followers.

As we approached the gun battery in Portsmouth, the imposing stone walls rose before us, weathered by centuries of salty sea air and countless storms. Peering through the battlements, we could see the vast expanse of the Solent stretching towards the horizon, where ships of all sizes glided across the water. The sunlight cast long shadows across the cobbled pathways and for a moment it felt as if we had stepped back in time. I imagined the soldiers who once stood guard, watching for approaching enemies.

The sight of the gun battery, the imposing stone walls rose before us, weathered by centuries of salty sea air and countless storms, transported us to a time when Portsmouth stood as a formidable coastal defence. Gazing out over the Solent, we reflected on the city's rich maritime history. The rhythmic crash of waves against the shore seemed to echo the passage of time, a reminder of both resilience and change.

Lost in the moment, Pauline shared how thoughts of Theo's future often weighed heavily on her as he grew older. Yet, she had found hope in walking and immersing herself in nature. Despite the constant movement of Portsmouth's busy port, we discovered a sense of peace along the seafront. Sitting quietly, we listened to the soothing symphony of the ocean—the rhythmic lull of the waves, the distant cries of seagulls, and the clanging of yacht masts swaying in the breeze. It was a powerful reminder that one does not need to climb mountains to experience the healing embrace of the natural world.

Pauline's contagious optimism and her unyielding passion for nature are so powerful that if they were bottled up and sold as a cure, countless individuals would reap the benefits.

THE WALK

IS IT FOR ME?

START/END POINT: The Spinnaker Tower, Gunwharf, PO1 3TT

GRID REFERENCE: SU629000

DISTANCE: 3.5km (2.2 miles) one way

MILES WITHOUT STILES GRADE: For All

TERRAIN: Tarmac tracks

ACCESSIBILITY: Fantastic accessibility for everyone to enjoy, with level paths that make it easy to navigate while you take in the stunning sea views.

PARKING: There is disabled parking at Gunwharf Quays car park, PO1 3TZ.

FACILITIES: Accessible toilets are located at Point Battery, Portsmouth, PO1 2FS.

THE ROUTE

The Millennium Promenade is a scenic 4.2km (2.6 mile) route that weaves through Portsmouth's rich maritime history, connecting Portsmouth Historic Dockyard to Southsea Castle. Whether starting at the dockyard or Southsea, this walk offers a captivating journey through time, blending historic landmarks with modern attractions and stunning waterfront views.

Marked by a distinctive stone chain motif, the promenade symbolises the deep-rooted connection between Portsmouth and Gosport, as well as the

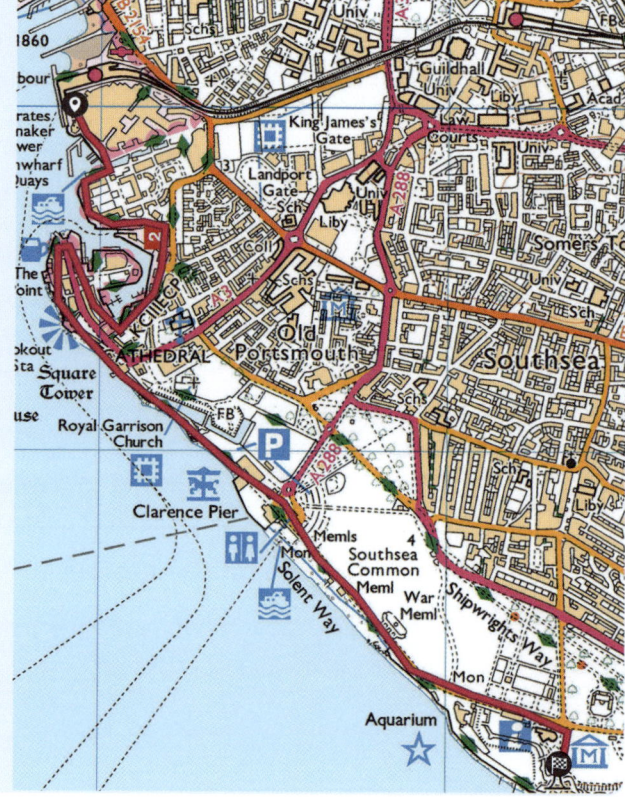

city's past and present. Along the route, visitors will pass Gunwharf Quays, home to the Spinnaker Tower and a bustling shopping and leisure complex, before continuing into Old Portsmouth, where historic pubs, cobbled streets and the original fishing docks provide a glimpse into the city's seafaring heritage.

From Clarence Pier to Southsea Castle, the path transitions into an open promenade lined with plaques and totems that highlight points of interest along the way. Column-mounted lanterns illuminate the walk, inspired by the traditional blue lights strung around the harbour. The route itself is paved with high-quality natural stone, reclaiming waterfront land that was once inaccessible to the public.

 NEED TO KNOW

A PLACE TO EAT: Spinnaker Towe, PO1 3TT, is wheelchair accessible. The iconic structure houses The Clouds Cafe, 105m (344ft) above the harbour. Recommended for afternoon tea.

A PLACE TO DRINK: Clarence Pier pub and restaurant in Southsea, PO5 3XX, serves traditional pub grub.

A PLACE TO SLEEP: The Royal Maritime Hotel, Queen St, Portsea, Portsmouth, PO1 3HS, is a stone's throw away from Portsmouth's historic dockyard, and has plenty of options for food and excellent accessible facilities.

IF YOU'RE LOOKING FOR SOMETHING ELSE...

The **Mary Rose Museum** offers an extraordinary exhibition showcasing the remains of Henry VIII's iconic warship, which sank in 1545 and was eventually raised in 1982. Visitors can explore thousands of genuine Tudor artefacts, from weapons and tools to personal items like wooden bowls and nit combs, offering a unique glimpse into life aboard a Tudor warship. The ship itself is displayed in a stunning atmospheric setting across three levels, immersing visitors in the sights and sounds of the 16th century.

The museum also hosts Relaxed Opening Mornings once a month, lowering sound effects and increasing lighting for those with sensory sensitivities. A highlight is the 4D immersive theatre experience, 'Dive the Mary Rose', which brings to life the ship's sinking, rediscovery and excavation using CGI, archive footage and multi-sensory effects like sounds, smells, bubbles, wind and movement. The museum features further interactive displays, video projections on the ship and guided tours, making it a must-visit for history enthusiasts and families alike.

FOLKESTONE COASTAL PATH
KENT

TINA, CAS AND FREDDIE BUSH

With no person in the UK living more than 113km (70 miles) from the sea, British identity is deeply tied to the coast. The King Charles III England Coast Path is a long-distance trail that, when complete, will celebrate our island nation by following 4,303km (2,674 miles) of the English coastline, making it the longest coastal path in the world.

Walking an already-complete section of the path in Folkestone, Kent, I was treated to spectacular views of the English Channel, a scenic boardwalk across a pebble beach and a climb to the historic Martello Towers, small coastal defence forts built in the early 19th century to protect against French coastal attacks during the Napoleonic Wars. Yet, what truly made this experience unforgettable was that I enjoyed this walk in the company of the Penfold Gang, an extraordinary family whose warmth and camaraderie made every step more special. Penfold Adventures is an inspiring project by young Freddie, aka 'Penfold', who is on a mission to walk the entire coastline of England, Wales and Scotland to raise awareness for mental health and post-traumatic stress disorder (PTSD) in young people. Hailing from south-east England, Freddie's journey is not just about the miles covered but also the connections made along the way. Meeting Freddie is like stepping into pure sunshine; his vibrant personality and boundless energy are infectious, leaving everyone around him smiling. His passion for the cause is evident in every mile he walks, making this adventure not just a physical challenge but a journey of hope and inspiration.

Freddie was joined by his two mums, Tina and Cas, who had lovingly adopted him at the age of three. This journey back to Folkestone was emotional for the family. Not only was it Freddie's birthplace, but it was also the special place where Tina and Cas first met him.

As we reached the promenade, we came across the weathered remains of Sandgate Castle. Built between 1538 and 1540 by Henry VIII as part of England's coastal defences, much of its front has since been claimed by the relentless force of the sea. The crumbling stone and timeworn walls stand as a reminder of the past, blending history with the ever-changing coastline.

Seeing the castle sparked Freddie's curiosity. Keen to learn, he eagerly asked about the castle's history, his questions thoughtful and insightful beyond his years. It was remarkable to hold such an engaging conversation with a boy who is only nine years old, his enthusiasm and intelligence shining through. This moment reflected how far he has come in his short life.

DEBBIE AND FREDDIE ON THE PROMENADE IN FOLKSTONE

Having passed the brightly coloured beach huts that capture the charm of a traditional English holiday, the smooth tarmac path gradually gave way to a wooden boardwalk stretching across the pebble beach. This shift in terrain mirrored Freddie's own journey. Like the boardwalk providing a way forward over difficult ground, Freddie continues to move ahead, navigating life's obstacles with resilience and determination.

At the age of three, he was diagnosed with PTSD and anxiety, conditions that revealed themselves in deeply challenging ways. His behaviour swung dramatically; hyperactivity filled his days, while his nights were haunted by relentless nightmares. Violent outbursts would erupt, leaving Tina and Cas heartbroken and helpless as they watched their son struggle.

To make matters worse, it felt like the external agencies and the primary school he attended offered little meaningful support. The school was ill-equipped to meet Freddie's unique needs, leaving Tina and Cas feeling isolated and overwhelmed. They were desperate for guidance on how to navigate and support Freddie through the complexities of childhood PTSD.

As such, Tina and Cas have often faced the struggles of Freddie's challenging and distressing behaviour in solitude. They've endured criticism from all sides, including accusations that Freddie's behaviour stemmed from their poor parenting, and judgemental stares from strangers when Freddie's outbursts became uncontrollable. Each moment of judgement and misplaced blame has been a painful reminder of the lack of understanding and support they've longed for.

The challenges put a strain on Tina and Cas's relationship, and some of their friends turned their backs on them during the tough times. After facing negative reactions from neighbours, they decided to relocate.

'Initially, we were angry,' Tina said, 'but looking back, it was a blessing. We now live in a welcoming village in Hampshire, where our family and Freddie's needs are understood.'

Having crossed the boardwalk, we reached the harbour and the former Folkestone railway station – a haunting yet beautiful relic of the past that has now been transformed into a trendy restaurant and market area. Dominating the scene, though, was the impressive steel swing bridge, a feat of engineering designed by George Ellson, Chief Engineer for Southern Railway. Built in 1930, its sturdy frame, weathered by time and salt air, sits upon stone piers that were built to accommodate the heavier trains that came into the station. As we admired the bridge's intricate workings, Tina and Cas yet again seized the opportunity to nurture Freddie's ever-growing curiosity. They shared the history of the harbour, explaining the mechanics behind the bridge and how it once played a vital role in the area's transport network. Freddie listened intently, his young mind absorbing every detail, eager to understand the world around him. Every walk with Tina and Cas became more than just a journey; it was a chance for Freddie to learn, explore and connect with the history woven into the landscape.

When Freddie was placed with Tina and Cas, his health was poor; he was weak and breathless after even short walks and lacked muscle strength. Determined to improve his well-being, they began walking together, starting with short steps. Freddie quickly grew to enjoy his time in the outdoors and excelled there. When his stress became overwhelming, Tina would keep him out of school. Instead of him struggling with the confines of a classroom, she would take him hiking in the countryside, which helped them both to clear their minds and reduced Freddie's anxiety. Though there were the daily struggles to get ready for school, Freddie always embraced the chance to put on his hiking boots and outdoor gear. He would swiftly take the lead, picking up the pace and even grumbling that Cas was holding him back. Tina and Cas were impressed by his progress and observed that, as they continued walking, Freddie was beginning to control his extreme behaviour.

Such was Freddie's progress that, when he turned seven, the family decided to take on the 154km (96 mile) West Highland Way, from Milngavie to Fort

THE IMPRESSIVE MARTELLO TOWERS STANDS PROUD ON THE CLIFF TOP

THE PROMENADE AT FOLKESTONE OFFERS SCENIC VIEWS

William in Scotland, camping along the way. To their surprise, Freddie's confidence vastly improved. He began engaging easily with fellow hikers and even started conversations. This breakthrough in social skills was a huge milestone, and hearing Freddie express happiness was unforgettable.

In 2022, the family tackled their biggest challenge so far – the 278km (173 mile) Camino Portuguese. Starting in Lisbon, the journey took them along Portugal's Atlantic coast and into the heart of Spain. Another success for Freddie.

During our walk along Folkstone sea front, there were moments when Freddie's excitement threatened to escalate, but Tina and Cas handled it with remarkable skill, avoiding major disruptions. Cas instinctively stayed behind with Freddie while Tina and I continued ahead. What stood out was the seamless teamwork between Tina and Cas. Cas provided the attention and empathy Freddie needed, while Tina maintained structure and reassurance for the group. Seeing this partnership in action was truly inspiring.

Parenting is a challenge, but raising a child with PTSD is even harder, especially when there is limited resources and guidance. Determined to ease the struggles they've faced, Tina and Cas now advocate for better access to information and support, aiming to make early intervention available to all families.

Freddie is now much more stable, and he attends a tutoring group and socialises with other children. It is hoped that he will soon join a school that specialises in educating children with PTSD.

Finally, we reached our destination: one of the Martello Towers. The stone tower stood tall on the clifftop, its unmistakable round shape outlined against the skyline. Having weathered the centuries, it still commanded the landscape with its formidable presence. Built as part of a series of coastal defences, the tower seemed to hold centuries of history within its thick walls. From its elevated position, we could see the rolling waves of the English Channel stretching far into the horizon. The grey clouds that had followed us since our starting point gradually gave way, offering a glimpse of blue sky, which cast a soft, melancholic light over the scene.

But even as we reached this historical landmark, Freddie's journey was far from over. His determination to keep moving was evident – his goal is to walk the entire length of the Coastal Path. With each step, Freddie moves closer to his goal, with Tina and Cas by his side, supporting and encouraging him every step of the way.

Freddie shares his adventure on a website that Tina has created: the affectionately named 'Penfold's Adventures'.

'So, why are you called Penfold?' I asked Freddie. There was a hint of mischief in his eyes, as if he's been waiting for this question.

'It's because I'm the go-to person for health and safety,' he answered. He glanced at Tina and Cas with a knowing smile before turning back to me with a proud grin. 'It's my job to evaluate all potential dangers and risks. But I must admit, I have a fondness for Danger Mouse.'

And true to his word, he gently steered me away from the edge of the clifftop.

Freddie thrives on the chance to explore the wild. Each hike feels like a quest, full of new and exciting adventures. He loves challenging himself, and no matter the weather or terrain, the Penfold Gang never give up. They'll keep exploring trails and appreciating nature's beauty together, with Freddie always eager to hike with his mums.

THE WALK

⊙ IS IT FOR ME?

START/END POINT: On the promenade near Hythe Swimming Pool, CT21 6AR

TERRAIN: Tarmac paths and boardwalk

ACCESSIBILITY: There is a level path along the seafront, with a section on a boardwalk. Lift access to the cliff top is also available.

PARKING: CThere is parking at the car park on Mount St, Hythe CT21 5AL

FACILITIES: You'll find lots of pubs and cafés with accessible toilets in the harbour area.

➡ THE ROUTE

The Folkestone coastal path begins with a flat, level promenade that offers a relaxing stroll along the shoreline. Along the route, various public artworks, originally created for the Folkestone Triennial – an arts festival held here every three years – add cultural flair to the natural beauty. This boardwalk extends the pedestrian route, starting at The Stade and passing by the iconic viaduct and the restored railway station. It connects visitors to the vibrant bars and cafés on the Harbour Arm, eventually leading to the Lower Leas Coastal Park and the historic Leas Lift.

Taking the lift to the clifftop, the walk continues toward the Martello Towers. This was my turnaround spot. While the Penfold Gang pressed on with their journey, I retraced my steps along the same path, reflecting on the history we'd just passed and the resilience of the people who have walked this coast over millennia. The views and the sense of history make this walk unforgettable – especially with Freddie's unrelenting drive to keep going, no matter the distance.

🏠 NEED TO KNOW

A PLACE TO EAT: The Lazy Shack, The Fishermans Landing Beach, Range Rd, Hythe, CT21 6HG, offers delicious seafood with stunning views of the harbour.

A PLACE TO DRINK: Visit Folkestone's Harbour Arm (CT20 1Q) to get an unbeatable view of the coastline with a drink and a quick bite to eat.

A PLACE TO SLEEP: The Rocksalt (CT19 6AA) is situated in the harbour and has accessible rooms.

✚ IF YOU'RE LOOKING FOR SOMETHING ELSE…

A 20-minute drive north from Folkestone is **Dover Castle**, which offers a mix of accessibility features and challenges. The site provides wheelchair access to some areas, including the visitor centre. But many historical parts, such as the castle keep and tunnels, involve uneven terrain and steep steps, making them difficult for visitors with mobility impairments. Some areas are accessible via lifts, but pathways can be narrow. Accessible toilets and parking spaces are, however, available. The free train service from the visitor centre to the entrance is a helpful feature for those with mobility challenges, though some areas remain difficult to navigate. Despite its barriers, Dover Castle is worth a visit, even if it is just for the views over the Solent.

DOVER CASTLE REWARDS EVERY VISITOR WITH BREATHTAKING VIEWS ACROSS THE SOLENT

HOLMWOOD COMMON
DORKING, SURREY

GENNY BROWN

Holmwood Common is a serene expanse of ancient woodland southeast of Dorking in Surrey, where the rustling leaves and birdsong create a haven for reflection and ambition. For those who frequent the woods, the sight of Genny Brown power-hiking through the forest, often with a digger tyre trailing behind her, has become an inspiration. Since moving to the area in 2021, her dedication has caught the attention of locals, sparking curiosity and admiration.

Genny's story begins far from Surrey, on the sun-drenched Caribbean island of Aruba. Growing up on the tiny island – just 32km (20 miles) long – Genny often dreamed of a life beyond its golden beaches. Her adventurous spirit led her to Canada, where she pursued her degree in a country where she knew no one. This bold move would foreshadow her greatest challenge yet: becoming the first woman from Aruba to ski to the South Pole.

From a young age, Genny exhibited a knack for turning challenges into opportunities. Her entrepreneurial journey began with a heartfelt mission to uplift others. Recognising the struggles of vulnerable young people, particularly single teenage mothers struggling with childcare, poverty and education, Genny launched a 12-week mentoring programme inspired by Centrepoint, a charity supporting homeless young people. For two years, her initiative provided practical skills, emotional support and empowerment to young women navigating daunting circumstances. Witnessing their transformations reinforced her belief in the power of resilience and determination.

Her success with the programme caught the attention of head hunters at an Italian oil firm, who offered her a prestigious grant scheme and a new platform to expand her impact. True to her adventurous nature, Genny embraced this unexpected opportunity, continuing to evolve and inspire. But life had its own tests in store.

Holmwood Common is a peaceful retreat, filled with native trees and plants, with dense woodlands dominated by towering oak trees. Many of these oaks have grown from acorns, unintentionally planted by jays storing food for the winter. As we wandered through the common, we noticed the abundance of insect life – especially the dragonflies and midges hovering over the sunlit Black Brook. The cycle of nature was strikingly evident. This peaceful scene was a fitting backdrop to hear about Genny, who, while on holiday in Turkey, received an insect bite that triggered a mysterious and devastating health crisis. Months later, Genny's hair began falling out, and she was overcome by debilitating fatigue, excruciating body pain and severe memory loss.

GENNY, DEBBIE AND TIP EXPLORING HOLMWOOD COMMON

Doctors initially suspected early-onset Alzheimer's, a crushing diagnosis for someone so vibrant and independent. Genny found herself bedridden, relying on her mother, who flew in from Aruba to care for her. Tasks as simple as bathing and dressing became insurmountable. Yet, even in her darkest moments, Genny's spirit refused to fade.

Her journey to a diagnosis was fraught with frustration. Dismissed and misdiagnosed repeatedly, she encountered a particularly shocking moment when a junior doctor told her, 'Black people don't get this ill.' Hurt but undeterred, Genny began questioning the biases and systemic gaps in healthcare. Her persistence led her to an infectious disease specialist in London, who acknowledged that she was battling a viral disease, though the exact cause remained elusive. The possibility of lifelong antibiotics and antivirals loomed over her, but Genny was determined to find a clearer path.

After collapsing on the street, Genny decided to take matters into her own hands. She sought private medical consultations, eventually landing an appointment with a naturopath specialising in infectious diseases. It was there, three years after her symptoms first appeared, that she finally received a diagnosis: Lyme disease. Relief and frustration intertwined as she learned that Lyme disease, especially in Black patients, was often overlooked. Until 2021, there had been no medical references documenting how its characteristic rashes appeared on darker skin tones – a critical oversight that delayed her diagnosis.

The road to recovery was anything but straightforward. Genny underwent multiple courses of antibiotics, revamped her diet to manage a newfound gluten sensitivity and fought to reclaim her health. Lyme had left her battling relentless fatigue, weakened immunity and aphasia, a condition that disrupted her ability to speak and process language. It took a gruelling year of treatment and lifestyle changes before she began to feel even a shadow of her former self.

As we wandered through the woodland, our eyes were drawn to a particularly striking mushroom nestled at the base of a moss-covered tree stump. Its cap, a deep, rich shade of crimson, was glossy and smooth, contrasting beautifully with the earthy tones of the surrounding leaves and fallen twigs. The edges of the cap curled slightly inward, giving it a delicate, almost fragile appearance. Below the cap, the pale, creamy stalk was firm and sturdy, standing tall amid the surrounding undergrowth. The air around the mushroom carried a distinct, earthy scent – fresh and damp, reminiscent of wet soil after a rainfall. As I leaned in closer, I caught a faint, almost sweet aroma, mixed with the sharpness of decaying wood and the musty scent of the forest floor. It was a smell that was both inviting and mysterious, as if the mushroom itself was a hidden secret of the woodland.

Much like this mushroom, Genny found herself in the midst of something unpredictable and transformative. Just as she had started to regain strength, menopause triggered a devastating relapse, forcing her to confront her limits once again. But rather than succumbing to the setback, she found clarity in the challenge. Amid these obstacles, a spark of determination ignited within her. 'What's the craziest thing I can do to raise awareness of Lyme disease?' she asked herself one day, and in that moment, a new purpose took root, much like the mushrooms that emerge from the depths of the forest.

The answer came unexpectedly when a colleague introduced her to a guide who organised Arctic expeditions. Inspired, Genny set her sights on an extraordinary goal: to mark a decade of living with Lyme disease by becoming the first Black woman to ski solo and unsupported to the South Pole. The journey to Antarctica is as monumental as the dream itself. Starting from scratch, Genny began rigorous training, aware that her health required careful management. She earned navigation qualifications, demonstrating her discipline and determination. Along the way, she found a mentor in Helen Turton, a winter mountain leader and Nordic ski instructor, who not only provided technical guidance but also supported her through the unique challenges of living with a chronic illness.

Genny's unconventional training regimen includes pulling a digger tyre – a practice that builds the strength and endurance needed for polar skiing. During the COVID-19 lockdowns, her tyre-pulling workouts on Tooting Common became a community spectacle, sparking conversations and helping her to form unexpected friendships.

Genny will push her limits even further when she spends six weeks in Norway to hone her skiing skills and tackle a seven-day mountain crossing challenge across the Hardangervidda range. Camping and skiing in sub-zero temperatures will no doubt test her resolve, but Genny approaches the challenge with unyielding determination. Her story is often likened to a real-life Cool Runnings – a Caribbean woman chasing an icy dream of her own.

Emerging from the forest, we came to the Old Football Pitch, the site of the village's former football field. The open sky above stretched wide, filling us with a sense of freedom, while the distant sound of children laughing and playing added to the light-hearted atmosphere. The warmth of the sun on our faces and the gentle breeze made it feel like a perfect moment of respite. Such a peaceful scene is a stark contrast to what lies ahead for Genny in 2026 – a gruelling 21-day consecutive ski expedition and the demanding glacier safety course that will push her limits in ways we can hardly imagine. These milestones are essential to gaining the approval of her logistics team for the Antarctic expedition.

Once everything is in place, she will embark on the journey of a lifetime, flying from Chile to base camp and waiting for the perfect weather window to begin her trek to the South Pole.

Genny's journey is not just a physical challenge – it's a testament to the resilience of the human spirit. Despite the setbacks and the lingering effects of Lyme disease, she continues to forge ahead, driven by a desire to raise awareness and inspire others to dream beyond their circumstances.

Following the track that would eventually lead us back to the car park, we passed the viewpoint, 110m (361ft) above sea level. From this vantage point, the spire of St Barnabas Church on Ranmore Common is visible in the distance, along with the iconic viewpoint at Box Hill.

For the people of Holmwood Common and beyond, Genny is more than just a determined hiker pulling a tyre through the woods. She is a beacon of hope, a living example of perseverance, and a reminder that the most inspiring journeys often begin in the face of adversity. As Genny prepares to conquer the icy wilderness of the South Pole, her story continues to uplift and motivate everyone she meets. And as she carves her trail through the snow, she will carry with her the resilience, courage and unyielding spirit that have defined her remarkable journey, inspiring others to face their own challenges with the same strength and determination.

THE WALK

◉ IS IT FOR ME?

START/END POINT: National Trust car park, Inholms Ln, North Holmwood, Dorking, RH5 4JH

GRID REFERENCE: TQ169470

DISTANCE: 5.6km (3.5 miles) circular

MILES WITHOUT STILES GRADE: For Many

TERRAIN: Woodland trails, compounded soil and slight incline in some sections but mostly level.

ACCESSIBILITY: Several paths are accessible for manual wheelchair users, though some areas may be muddy. Certain woodland paths can be uneven, with tree roots making the ground uneven in places.

PARKING: Free parking is available at the Inholms car park, Inholms Lane, Holmwood, RH5 4NX.

FACILITIES: No facilities on this walk.

➔ THE ROUTE

Holmwood's history dates back to medieval times. The land's association with royalty, from King Harold to William the Conqueror, adds a unique layer of intrigue. Over the centuries, the area has retained its charm, offering a blend of historical significance and natural beauty. At the heart of Holmwood lies the serene Holmwood Common, a treasured green space managed by the National Trust.

The National Trust has developed a family-friendly activity

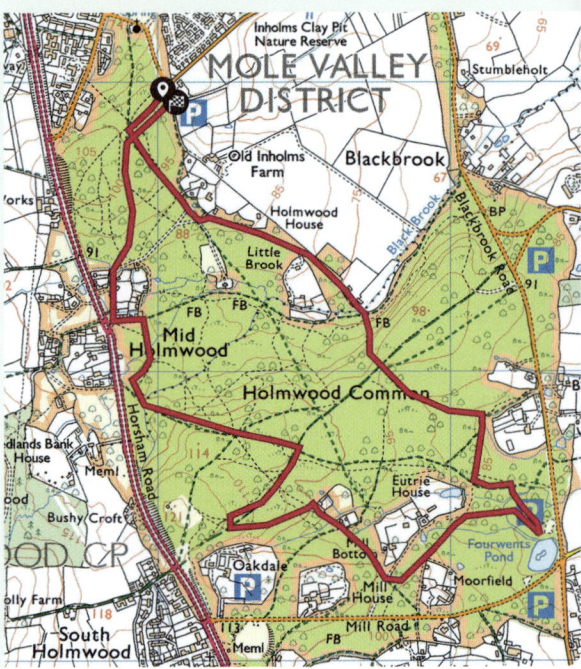

146 ■ ACCESS ADVENTURE

trail, which can easily be downloaded from their website, offering an interactive and educational experience for visitors of all ages. The beauty of this trail lies not only in its accessibility but also in the opportunity for spontaneity; it allows visitors to explore any of the numerous paths and discover hidden gems along the way, making each adventure unique.

The trail is designed to be accessible for mobility scooter users, as it is completely stile-free and gate-free across the entire common, ensuring that everyone can enjoy the natural beauty of the area. Additionally, there is a dedicated all-weather path that stretches from Scamells car park (RH5 4NX) around Fourwents Pond, providing a smooth route that is particularly suitable for wheelchair users, ensuring that these areas remain accessible regardless of the weather conditions. This thoughtful approach to accessibility ensures that the National Trust site is welcoming to a wide range of visitors, allowing families and individuals with varying mobility levels to enjoy the outdoors together.

NEED TO KNOW

A PLACE TO EAT: The Watermill Inn in Dorking (RH4 1NN) is a charming 1930s establishment, offering a welcoming atmosphere and disabled facilities for added convenience.

A PLACE TO DRINK: The Wotton Hatch (RH5 6QQ) is a charming country pub situated in the heart of the picturesque town of Wotton, and offers disabled facilities.

A PLACE TO SLEEP: The Denbies Vineyard Hotel, located in the heart of Denbies Wine Estate in Dorking (RH5 6AA) offers stunning views across the 265-acre estate and the surrounding rolling hills. The hotel is also wheelchair accessible.

IF YOU'RE LOOKING FOR SOMETHING ELSE...

Polesden Lacey is a stunning Edwardian house and estate located on the North Downs near Dorking. The estate offers breathtaking views of the Surrey Hills, beautiful gardens and rich history, including being a honeymoon retreat for Queen Elizabeth, the Queen Mother. The house is home to exquisite art, ceramics and historical treasures. Visitors can explore the accessible walled garden, enjoy a picnic on the South Lawn, or take part in activities like kite flying and ball games. With 567ha (1,400 acres) to explore, including ancient woodlands and working farms, Polesden Lacey is the perfect destination for nature lovers and history enthusiasts alike.

UFO TRAIL, RENDLESHAM FOREST
NR WOODBRIDGE, SUFFOLK

NATASHA SONES

Nestled in Suffolk, Rendlesham Forest exudes a serene beauty that captures the heart. The air carries the cool, damp scent of pine mixed with the musky aroma of decaying leaves, while beams of sunlight filter through the dense canopy, scattering warm, golden hues across the forest floor. For many, Rendlesham is a retreat for dog walkers, a playground for curious children and a sanctuary for nature lovers. But for Natasha Sones, it is far more than just a beautiful woodland – it is a place where the overwhelming weight of her chaotic, beautiful life feels a little lighter.

When I arranged to meet Natasha, she mentioned the UFO trail in Rendlesham Forest, a walk that promised a welcoming escape from the challenges of everyday life. As she spoke about it, I couldn't help but wonder: would little green men suddenly leap out from the trees, or was this just her way of injecting some adventure into her busy world?

    I met Natasha in the car park at the start of the trail, where the air smelled fresh and earthy after days of rain. The sky had finally granted us a reprieve, and though the grass was damp and muddy in places, the well-trodden path beneath our feet felt firm and inviting. As we stepped into the depths of the forest, towering pines and lush green ferns enveloped us, their fronds swaying gently in the breeze. Shadows danced between the trees, and an eerie stillness settled over the woods, as if nature itself was holding its breath, waiting for us to uncover whatever secrets lay ahead.

Natasha's connection to Suffolk runs deep. Born and raised in Ipswich, Natasha grew up surrounded by the county's gentle landscapes and close-knit communities. After studying Film, TV and Creative Writing in Derby, she moved back to Suffolk and built a family life.

Like for so many, the COVID-19 pandemic brought with it a whirlwind of challenges for Natasha and her family, testing their resilience in ways they could never have anticipated. Yet, amid the uncertainty and upheaval, it was a time to reassess what truly mattered. Seeking a fresh start and a sense of peace, the family of five relocated to Rendlesham. Here, surrounded by the tranquil beauty of the forest, Natasha discovered a place where she could find solace and reclaim moments of calm from her otherwise chaotic life.

Life for Natasha is anything but straightforward. She has three children, now aged 15, 13, and 10, all of whom have additional needs. But the process of securing diagnoses and support has been a long, exhausting battle – so far, only one child has received a formal diagnosis, while the other two remain in limbo, stuck on endless waiting lists and navigating a system riddled with bureaucracy.

As Natasha fought for her children's needs, she began to recognise pieces of herself in them – their quirks, their unique ways of processing the world and their struggles. Then, at the age of 44, she herself was diagnosed with autism, along with traits of ADHD. For Natasha, the diagnosis was life-changing.

THE ENTRANCE TO RENDLESHAM WOODS

NATASHA SONE AND DEBBIE EXPLORE THE UFO TRAIL

It offered her a lens through which to view her life's experiences – moments that had once felt overwhelming, inexplicable or isolating now made sense. Her neurodivergence had shaped her passion for storytelling, her deep connection to nature and even her struggles with the fast-paced demands of life.

Her diagnosis also became a source of connection within her family. When she shared the news with her son Lucas, who had by now been diagnosed autistic, she told him simply, 'Hey, Mum is autistic too.' Those words formed an unspoken bond, reassuring Lucas that he wasn't alone. It was a moment of mutual understanding that brought comfort to them both.

Natasha's husband also exhibits traits often associated with autism, adding another layer of shared understanding to their family dynamic. Together, they have built a home where neurodiversity is not just accepted but embraced, a tapestry of unique strengths and challenges woven together.

Walking through the forest was magical. In some areas, the trees grew so densely that peering through them felt like staring into the dead of night, their shadows casting an eerie stillness over the trail. It was easy to get lost in the mystery of the woods, letting my imagination wander, but for Natasha, reality was far from an escape. Just as she began making progress in supporting Lucas, her daughter Millie started to struggle, pulling her focus in yet another direction. The weight of it all was undeniable, yet here, among the whispering trees and hidden clearings, it felt as though she could briefly step away from the endless battle and simply breathe.

Millie was bright and curious but struggled with anxiety that began to spiral out of control. Unlike her brother, she was deeply introverted and exhibited perfectionistic traits that made her struggles less visible, but no less real. Natasha explained, 'Autism shows up differently in girls.'

The COVID-19 lockdowns proved to be a rare period of calm for Millie. Free from the pressures of the classroom, she thrived in the quieter environment of home schooling. However, when schools reopened, the thought of returning to school filled Millie with dread. By the time she was transitioning to secondary school, her anxiety had reached breaking point.

After wandering along the forest track, there suddenly appeared an opening into an obvious clearing, and as if to create an other-worldly experience, a break in the clouds sent beams of golden light cascading down. 'God Light' was piercing through. This was it. The spot where the spaceship had supposedly landed. At its centre stands a metallic replica of the craft, the size of a Mini, its triangular shape catching the light in an eerie glow. Scrawled across its surface in crude graffiti are the words: 'ET go home.' What a fantastic place to spark thoughts and theories about what really happened on a dark night in 1980 – when the aliens visited Earth!

As I took in the strange scene, Natasha's voice pulled me back to reality. She spoke about Millie, how her daughter had openly declared her hatred of school and refused to attend. What had started as frustration had spiralled into deep distress, her anxiety growing so severe that it began to take a toll on her health. While still locked in a battle for Lucas's support, Natasha had been thrown into another fight, this time, a relentless, year-long struggle to secure the mental health care that Millie so desperately needed. The weight of her words hung heavy in the air, contrasting sharply with the bizarre, almost surreal setting before us.

Just as Natasha was beginning to navigate the challenges with Lucas and Millie, her youngest child, Logan, began displaying clear signs of autism. Once again, Natasha found herself plunged into the system – facing long waiting lists, endless assessments and a frustrating lack of resources.

Over six years, Natasha's battle for her children's needs has been relentless. The process has been marked by moments of frustration, small victories and exhausting setbacks. The constant advocacy has taken a toll on Natasha's

ACCESSIBLE TRACKS THROUGH THE FOREST

mental and emotional health, yet she has persisted, driven by her unwavering love for her children and her determination to secure the support they deserve.

The struggle has not been without opposition. Natasha has often found herself at odds with schools and authorities who, she felt, rather than offering support, seemed quick to assign blame. She was accused of neglecting her children's education and was assigned an Education Welfare Officer, who monitored the family and issued threats of fines and imprisonment.

Rather than feeling supported, Natasha felt judged. Suggestions from officials were often unhelpful and even cruel. One official suggested she drive her ten-year-old son to school in his pyjamas to 'shame' him into attending – a proposal Natasha refused outright.

Arriving in an area where trees had once been felled, we stepped onto a ground now reclaimed by nature, a lush carpet of green and brown ferns stretching out before us. Above, the sky was vast and open, dotted with billowing white clouds, a stark contrast to the cool shadows of the dense woods we had just left behind. Just as the clearing had once borne the scars of destruction and now pulsed with new life, Natasha was carving out a space where her children could not only survive but truly flourish.

Recently, Natasha has found solace in wild swimming – a passion that offers her both a creative outlet and a way to recharge. She is currently writing a book featuring 100 swims across London and the South East, testing each one herself. From serene outdoor lidos to icy winter dips, Natasha's swims are not just a hobby but an essential lifeline, offering clarity and balance amid the demands of her busy life. Exploring locations like the Isle of Wight, and spots closer to home, Natasha's wild swimming adventures have become a way for her to reconnect with herself.

In 2023, Natasha took her love for the outdoors to new heights by applying for the Adventure Queens grant. This initiative supports women in undertaking creative, self-powered challenges. Natasha proposed a daring five-day paddleboarding expedition around the islands of Helsinki. The experience tested her limits, teaching her the intricacies of expedition planning while fostering personal growth. Supported by the Adventure Queens community, Natasha embraced the challenge.

Natasha's adventurous spirit has since become a part of her family's life. Her children and husband understand that she might be away for a challenge or out at dawn, watching the sunrise or taking a wild swim. This shared acceptance allows Natasha to fully embrace her passions while also finding moments of solitude and peace.

Through her adventures, Natasha has discovered a strength she didn't know she had. Whether navigating the challenges of parenting or embarking on a new wild swim, she approaches life with resilience, creativity and a deep connection to the natural world.

And as we finished our circular walk, I couldn't help but reflect on how much the journey through the forest mirrored Natasha's own story, from the dense, shadowy woods where light was hard to find, to the open clearing where the sun finally broke through. Just as the path shifted between darkness and light, so too had Natasha's journey – winding through struggles, uncertainty and moments of hope. In Rendlesham Forest, she had found more than just a walk; she had found a sanctuary, a place where she could reflect and reconnect. Here, beneath the vast sky and towering trees, she was reminded that even in life's thickest shadows, light always finds a way through.

THE UFO SPACECRAFT IN THE WOODS

THE WALK

IS IT FOR ME?

START/END POINT: Rendlesham Forest, Tangham, Woodbridge, Suffolk, IP12 3NF

GRID REFERENCE: TM352484

DISTANCE: 5.5km (3.4 miles) circular

MILES WITHOUT STILES GRADE: For Many

TERRAIN: Mainly solid tracks with areas of sandy soil and forest roads

ACCESSIBILITY: Forestry England has introduced a new easy-access trail of about 1 km with a smooth, wheelchair-friendly surface, and facilities such as accessible toilets and paths designed to support visitors of all abilities.

PARKING: Follow the B1084 Woodbridge to Orford Rd; fees apply.

FACILITIES: There are toilets near the car park, including one with disabled access. During the summer, a mobile café operates there providing takeaway refreshments. Visitors can make use of the numerous picnic benches, and trail leaflets are available at the visitor centre.

THE ROUTE

The Rendlesham Forest UFO Trail offers a fascinating mix of mystery, history and beautiful scenery, making it a perfect outing for families, dog walkers – and UFO enthusiasts!

While the sandy soil can be challenging for some mobility scooters, the trail is well signposted and begins at the Rendlesham Forest Centre, accessible via the B1084 between Woodbridge and Orford.

As the name suggests, the trail explores the world-famous UFO incident involving United States Air Force personnel stationed at RAF Woodbridge, who, in December 1980, reported strange lights and a glowing shape in the forest. Visitors can pick up a map from the information centre to guide them through key points of interest, including a sculpture depicting the reported UFO. The wide paths lead through a peaceful mix of coniferous and broadleaf trees with open heathland, ideal for birdwatching. Families will love the adventure play area, featuring climbing frames, log tunnels and a timber assault course. Facilities include parking (fees apply), accessible toilets and, in the summer, a food and drink hut near the car park.

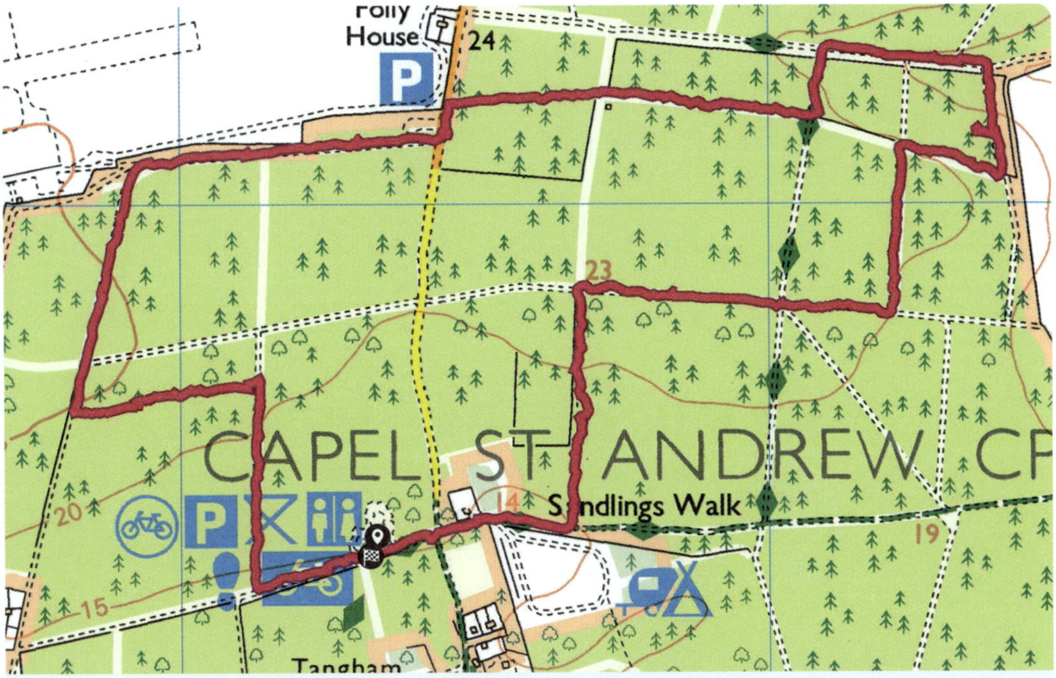

NEED TO KNOW

A PLACE TO EAT: The Unruly Pig in Bromeswell (IP12 2PU) offers a creative menu incorporating seasonal local produce.

A PLACE TO DRINK: The Coach & Horses in Melton (IP12 1PD) has shaded patio tables to enjoy a relaxing drink.

A PLACE TO SLEEP: Shottisham Campsite in Woodbridge (IP12 3HD) is situated in the Suffolk Coast and Heath AONB and offers accessible facilities.

IF YOU'RE LOOKING FOR SOMETHING ELSE…

Landguard Fort is one of England's best-preserved coastal defences, with a history spanning nearly 450 years. It was the site of England's last-opposed seaborne invasion in 1667 and the first land battle of the Royal Marines. The Grade I-listed fort, built in the 18th century, features additional 19th and 20th-century batteries.

While not fully accessible, efforts have been made to improve access, including wooden planks in corridors. Some areas have steps or uneven surfaces, but key areas remain viewable. Visitors can explore tunnels, enjoy panoramic views and engage with exhibits, tours and re-enactments. Entry is free for carers.

UFO TRAIL, RENDLESHAM FOREST | NR WOODBRIDGE, SUFFOLK

SUTTON HOO
WOODBRIDGE, SUFFOLK

OZZY AND VICTORIA RAYNOR

My next adventure to find stile-free walks brought me to Sutton Hoo in Suffolk, where I had the pleasure of meeting Ozzy and Victoria. Renowned for its Anglo-Saxon burial mounds and extraordinary archaeological significance, this iconic national treasure had long been on my list of places to explore. As we wandered through its sweeping landscapes, the site's deep sense of history provided a perfect setting for our conversation.

From the very start, I felt a deep admiration for my walking partner, Ozzy. His warmth, conversational ease and openness in discussing his experiences immediately struck me.

'I enjoy being in nature; it helps me feel calm, especially when I'm having a meltdown,' said 13-year-old Ozzy.

Whether it was his candid explanations about life with Prader-Willi syndrome (PWS) or his thoughtful engagement, Ozzy's sincerity was remarkable.

We stood on the gentle rise of Sutton Hoo, gazing out over the tidal estuary of the River Deben. The landscape stretched before us, where the shimmering waters of the river wound through the valley, reflecting the shifting sky. In the foreground, grassy burial mounds rose from the earth, weathered by time but still commanding attention. Once towering, these ancient barrows had softened into the undulating land, their presence a quiet reminder of the past. Beyond them, the river estuary glistened in the distance.

'It's beautiful here,' Ozzy remarked. And I couldn't help but agree, the landscape stretched endlessly before us, hauntingly beautiful.

As we walked away from the entrance to the site, Ozzy shared that he was diagnosed with PWS shortly after birth, when his mother noticed his muscle tone wasn't developing, describing himself as a 'floppy baby'. While PWS affects various aspects of physical and cognitive development, one of its most challenging and life-defining characteristics is its impact on appetite and eating behaviours. People with PWS experience an insatiable hunger that starts in early childhood and can become increasingly difficult to manage as they grow older. This extreme hunger is paired with a slower metabolism, making weight gain much easier and healthy weight maintenance very challenging. For someone with PWS, this isn't just a preference for eating but a physical and psychological drive that can feel impossible to control. As a result, they are at risk of severe overeating, which can lead to life-threatening obesity and other related health problems like type 2 diabetes, high blood pressure and sleep apnoea.

Managing this aspect of PWS requires a highly structured lifestyle. Ozzy's mum, Victoria, needs to control food access rigorously, sometimes by locking cupboards and the refrigerator, to prevent Ozzy from binge eating. She plans meals with strict portions to help Ozzy maintain a healthy weight. However, this constant restriction can be a source of frustration, anxiety and stress for both of them.

THE TIDAL ESTUARY OF THE RIVER DEBEN

OZZY AND DEBBIE AT SUTTON HOO

One of Ozzy's ongoing challenges is managing his appetite and his desire to snack.

'Mum makes sure there's nothing unhealthy in the house,' he says. 'At school, I have a packed lunch. I eat chicken and vegetables.' However, he admits to sometimes eating his packed lunch in the back of his taxi on the way to school, which then causes problems for the rest of the day as he battles his hunger pangs.

Victoria typically prepares meals that are high in protein and low in carbohydrates. Ozzy, who has a good understanding of nutrition, explains that he must make thoughtful choices about healthy foods.

'Sometimes I get to have an ice lolly if I've had a good day at school.'

Trips to the supermarket can be stressful, but as Victoria explains, as Ozzy grows older and becomes more independent, he must understand that it's an experience he needs to work through.

Walking along the tractor track that led us down towards Sutton Hoo farm, we took in the expansive view of Woodbridge, a historic port town known for its shipbuilding and sailmaking. The Suffolk Coast and Heaths National Landscape stretches beyond, a patchwork of fields, woodland and winding waterways. As we walked, Ozzy chatted endlessly, his imagination running wild with visions of the past. He spoke of Anglo-Saxon warriors, their ships gliding up the river, shields lining the sides, banners fluttering in the wind. His excitement was infectious, and together we pictured the estuary alive with the echoes of a time long gone. It was hard to believe that this young boy, so full of energy and curiosity, faced a daily battle living with his medical condition. Due to PWS, Ozzy often becomes extremely fatigued, and when he's tired he can experience 'meltdowns', where he struggles to control his temper. At times, these episodes can become intense and even violent, and on occasion Victoria has had to seek help from the police to calm the situation.

'In those moments, I feel like I can't control my behaviour,' Ozzy says, 'even though I know it isn't right.'

Victoria has developed a range of strategies to manage these episodes. Sometimes, she takes Ozzy for a calming drive to help him cool down, while

THE WALK

◉ IS IT FOR ME?

START/END POINT: National Trust Sutton Hoo, Tranmer House, Woodbridge, IP12 3DJ

GRID REFERENCE: TM287496

DISTANCE: 4.8km (3 miles) circular

MILES WITHOUT STILES GRADE: For Most

TERRAIN: Mix of grassy and tarmac paths and farm tracks

ACCESSIBILITY: The park is open year-round, though exhibition opening hours vary between summer and winter. For the most up-to-date opening times, it is recommended to check the National Trust website before your visit. Access to |the park is free, but there's a fee for exhibitions (free for National Trust Members).

PARKING: Fees apply (free for National Trust Members), though parking is free for Blue Badge holders.

FACILITIES: Accessible toilets are located in the visitor centre. The on-site café is wheelchair accessible.

THE ROUTE

Nestled in the tranquil landscape of Suffolk, Sutton Hoo's 103ha (255 acres) overlook the River Deben, near the town of Woodbridge. This peaceful site, now preserved by the National Trust, holds one of the most significant archaeological discoveries in British history. Here, in the summer of 1939, as the outbreak of the Second World War loomed, amateur archaeologist Basil Brown revealed a magnificent Anglo-Saxon burial ground. Commissioned by landowner Edith Pretty, Brown's dig unearthed a massive 27m (88.6ft)-long burial ship brimming with treasures that would forever change our understanding of early medieval England.

Visitors to Sutton Hoo can follow in the footsteps of this groundbreaking discovery on a self-guided walk that winds through the historic burial mounds, climbs a 17m (56ft) viewing tower, and offers spectacular views over the countryside and river. The walk takes you from the visitor centre to the Royal Burial Ground, where informational plaques recount the story of Brown's dig and reveal

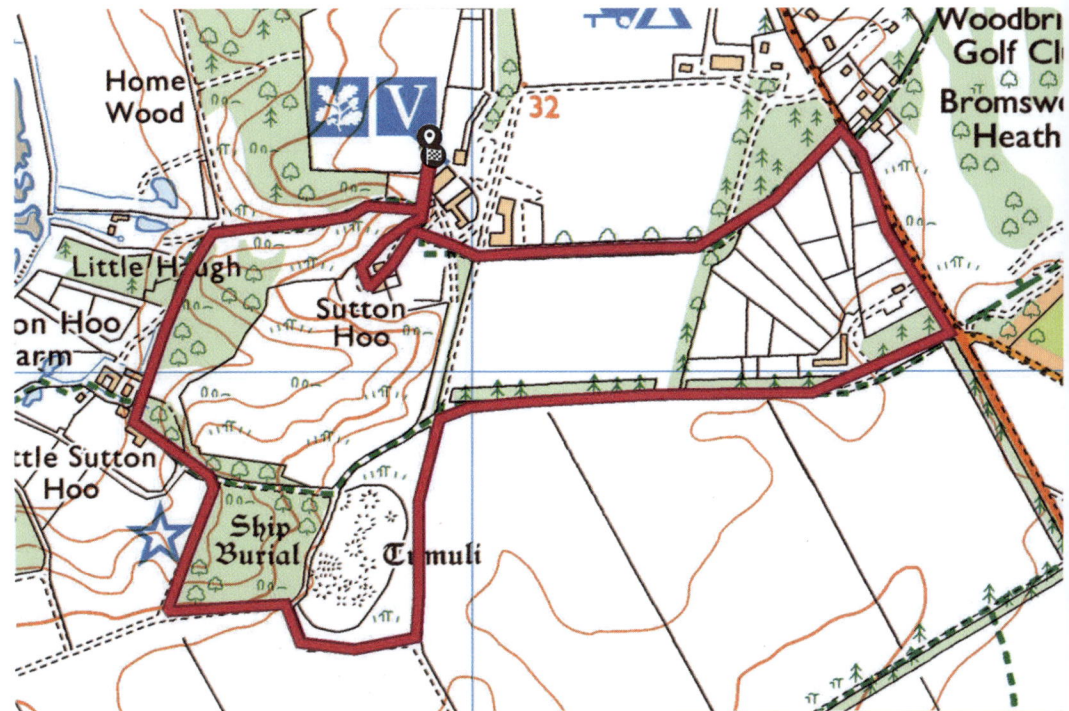

the significance of each mound. This immersive experience gives a glimpse into the life of the Anglo-Saxons, as well as into the meticulous process of archaeology itself.

At the heart of the Royal Burial Ground lies the site of the ship burial. Brown and his team of archaeologists carefully uncovered what initially appeared to be the mere outline of a ship beneath a mound. But as layers of soil were meticulously removed, the astonishing shape of a large ship began to emerge. Although the wood had decomposed, the placement of rivets in the sand preserved the ship's silhouette, allowing the archaeologists to reconstruct its shape. The discovery of this burial site, with such an enormous ship as its resting place, indicated that this was no ordinary grave – it was the final resting place of an individual of immense significance.

In addition to the ship itself, Brown's excavation revealed a wealth of objects buried alongside the deceased. These items, uncovered in what had once been the ship's central burial chamber, represented the height of Anglo-Saxon craftsmanship and international connections. One of the most famous artifacts found is the Sutton Hoo helmet, a beautiful piece decorated with a human face. Originally discovered in over a hundred fragments, the helmet took years to reconstruct and has since become an emblem of Anglo-Saxon England.

Sutton Hoo's treasures not only shed light on the wealth and power of Anglo-Saxon elites but also helped reframe historical perceptions of the so-called Dark

Ages. In the modern-day High Hall exhibition at Sutton Hoo, visitors can view both replicas and original artifacts, offering an up-close look at the craftsmanship that defined the Anglo-Saxon elite. Interactive displays allow you to dress up as an Anglo-Saxon warrior or king, engaging children and adults alike in the story of this ancient society.

Tranmer House, Edith Pretty's former residence, is another highlight of the site. Here, visitors can learn about the 1939 excavation through original photographs and personal accounts, deepening their understanding of the dig that forever changed British archaeology.

For those interested in outdoor activities, Sutton Hoo offers a wealth of options beyond the archaeological sites. Nature walks reveal the stunning landscape that frames the estate, with seasonal wildflowers and wildlife creating a rich natural tapestry. The site also features a sculpture trail, inspired by Anglo-Saxon myths, and an adventure playground for young explorers. Visitors can also enjoy refreshments at the King's River Café, or browse the gift shop for keepsakes of their visit.

NEED TO KNOW

A PLACE TO EAT: The Red Lion in Martlesham (IP12 4RN) is a great choice for classic country pub food and is wheelchair accessible.

A PLACE TO DRINK: Ye Olde Bell & Steelyard in Woodbridge (IP12 1DZ) is a lovely country pub, with accessible facilities.

A PLACE TO SLEEP: The cottage features a ground-floor double bedroom with an adjoining spacious accessible wet room and is set in the peaceful rural landscape of Butley in Suffolk, just a short drive from market towns and nature walks.

IF YOU'RE LOOKING FOR SOMETHING ELSE…

Suffolk offers several wheelchair-friendly beaches with accessible facilities.

Southwold has ramp access, an accessible pier, and a sandy stretch at Gun Hill. Its beaches hold Blue Flag and Seaside Awards for cleanliness and safety.

Lowestoft South Beach is ideal for wheelchair users, featuring a flat promenade, accessible toilets and a café.

Felixstowe has ramps to the beach, but the shingle may be challenging. However, a free beach wheelchair is available from the tourist information centre (01394 276770). The wide promenade is easily accessible via floodgates, making it perfect for a seaside stroll.

LADY CANNING'S PLANTATION

RINGINGLOW, NR SHEFFIELD, SOUTH YORKSHIRE

MAXWELL AYAMBA

I met Maxwell Ayamba on a windswept day at Lady Canning's Plantation, near Ringinglow, just outside Sheffield. As the wind howled across the exposed hills, the landscape seemed both serene and wild, with distant views of the city of Sheffield sitting in the valley. It was a typical day for this area, a combination of beauty and harshness, where nature can feel both welcoming and intimidating. Despite having been born and raised in Sheffield, I realised how much of the local landscape I had yet to discover, especially through the lens of someone like Maxwell Ayamba, who has dedicated his life to making the outdoors accessible to all.

Maxwell, a journalist, academic and environmentalist, has spent decades championing countryside access for ethnically diverse communities. As we talked and walked together along the old Roman road, I could sense his deep connection to the land and his passion for ensuring that everyone, regardless of their race, ethnicity or background, gets to share in the beauty and healing power of nature. For him, nature is a space where people can reconnect with their roots, find a sense of peace and bond with others.

   As we trudged along the dusty, uneven path, I was grateful for my TerrainHopper, its sturdy wheels tackling the rough, eroded ground with ease. 'I wonder how many trees are in the plantation,' I mused, my gaze sweeping across the endless stretch of woodland lining the rugged track. The sheer scale of it was mesmerising.

Maxwell glanced around, taking in the towering trees swaying gently in the breeze. 'It's such a contrast to the landscape back home,' he said, his voice tinged with admiration.

Originally from Ghana, Maxwell came to the UK in 1996 on a scholarship to study Journalism at Cardiff University. His move to the UK marked the beginning of a lifelong journey dedicated to activism and environmental advocacy. After completing his journalism studies, Maxwell pursued an MSc in Environmental Management from Sheffield Hallam University, where he eventually became an Associate Lecturer. Through his academic career, Maxwell deepened his understanding of environmental issues, but more importantly he developed a keen awareness of the barriers that marginalised communities face when accessing the natural world.

So, in 2004, Maxwell co-founded the walking group 100 Black Men Walking for Health, initially as a means of promoting healthier lifestyles for middle-aged Black men. What started as a small local initiative quickly grew into something much larger and more impactful than anyone could have anticipated. The group offered more than just physical exercise – it provided a space for fellowship, healing and reclaiming a sense of belonging in the British countryside, a place where people from diverse ethnic backgrounds often feel excluded. Through regular walks in and around the Peak District, the group created a powerful narrative of inclusion in spaces that are often associated with white, middle-class populations.

The success of the 100 Black Men Walking group eventually inspired a critically acclaimed play, Black Men Walking, which brought issues of representation in the countryside to national attention. The play, produced by Eclipse Theatre Company and Royal Exchange Theatre, toured across the UK in 2018/19 and received rave reviews for its portrayal of Black men's experiences in the British landscape. The story drew on real-life accounts of the walking group, weaving together themes of history, identity and belonging, while challenging audiences to reconsider who the countryside is for.

Soon, the trees on our right thinned out, their protective embrace fading as the grassy fields stretched into the vast, heather-clad moors. The moment we stepped beyond their shelter, the wind struck – brisk, invigorating and alive with untamed energy. The moors sprawled before us, an endless tapestry of russet and gold, wild and unbroken.

I couldn't help but marvel at what Maxwell had achieved, his passion for encouraging diversity in the outdoors shaping paths where few had ventured before.

'The story doesn't stop there, Debbie,' he declared, a spark of excitement in his voice. I turned to him, anticipation bubbling within me, eager to hear what came next.

Maxwell's work with the walking group and the play brought him widespread recognition, and he became a key figure in the movement to improve diversity and representation in environmental spaces. His dedication to this cause also led him to serve on the board of the Ramblers Association from 2005 to 2009, making history as the first Black person to hold that position. In addition, he was a member of the Peak District National Park Equality Comprehensive Audit Standards Committee, where he worked to promote greater inclusion within the National Park system.

Beyond these roles, Maxwell is also the founder and coordinator of the Sheffield Environmental Movement (SEM), a charity established in 2016 to

MAXWELL AND DEBBIE AT THE LADY CANNING PLANTATION

promote access to the natural environment for people from ethnically diverse communities. The SEM works closely with local groups to create opportunities for people to engage with the outdoors in meaningful ways. Whether through walking, nature-based activities or environmental education, the charity seeks to address the barriers – both physical and psychological – that often prevent marginalised groups from accessing green spaces. One of the key aspects of SEM's work is recognising that not all communities have the same relationship with nature. For instance, many first-generation migrants may have grown up with a deep connection to the outdoors in their countries of origin but now live in urban areas where access to nature is limited.

One of the most striking aspects of Maxwell's work is his emphasis on 'double jeopardy' – the compounded disadvantages faced by individuals who are both disabled and from minority ethnic backgrounds when it comes to accessing environmental spaces. Many of the people Maxwell works with face significant barriers, from a lack of physical access to natural spaces to deeper systemic issues of exclusion and discrimination. As he explained to me during our walk, 'People in these communities often lack the resources, equipment and advocacy needed to fully enjoy the benefits of green spaces, such as National Parks. This is particularly concerning given the mounting evidence that spending time in nature can have profound health and well-being benefits, especially for those in lower socio-economic groups.'

By working with communities that have been historically excluded from the British countryside, Maxwell and SEM are creating new narratives of belonging. They are helping to break down stereotypes about who the countryside is 'for', and challenging the idea that rural spaces are the domain of a privileged few.

The views stretched endlessly across Burbage Moors, a wild and untamed expanse where nature reigns supreme. In the distance, the rugged silhouette of Burbage Rocks jutted from the landscape, standing like ancient sentinels against the sky. The sheer remoteness was humbling, an open world of windswept heather and rolling land beneath a vast skyscape, where restless grey clouds raced overhead, casting shifting shadows across the moors. The earth track ahead, worn and winding, snaked its way toward Fox House, its golden hue reminiscent of the fabled Yellow Brick Road, only this one led not to Oz, but deeper into the heart of the wild.

For me, being out here in this vast space, it's hard to believe that there are entire communities of people who have no idea what a National Park is, or what their purpose should be. The work Maxwell is doing within the community is making real progress, but it also highlights just how elitist access to the countryside remains. The right for access should be for everyone, yet for so many these landscapes still feel distant, unfamiliar and unwelcoming.

Maxwell's academic research further compliments his practical work in the community. His research focuses on race, ecology and environmental justice in the UK, with a particular focus on the historical presence of Black people in Britain and their connections to nature. He has traced the genealogy of Black African ancestry in the natural environment, from Roman times through slavery, colonialism and post-colonialism. This research challenges the dominant narratives that often frame Black British history as beginning with transatlantic slavery or post-war migration. 'In fact,' Maxwell explained, 'there is evidence that Black people have been present in Britain since at least the 3rd century.' Maxwell's work highlights the contributions of Afro-Romans, such as the 'numerus of Aurelian Moors', a unit of North African men who served in the Roman army and were stationed in Britain. By exploring these overlooked aspects of history, Maxwell encourages a broader and more inclusive understanding of British identity.

Through his work, Maxwell is reshaping not only the way we think about the countryside but also the way we understand our own history. His message is clear: British history and the British countryside belongs to all of us. It is a shared heritage, one that we must work to make accessible to everyone, regardless of race, ethnicity or background. For those of us who have spent our lives thinking we know the land around us, Maxwell offers a powerful reminder that there is always more to discover, especially when we open our eyes to the stories of others.

Our walk came to an end as the rugged stone track gave way to the smooth, familiar stretch of tarmac road. The wildness of the moors faded behind us, replaced by the quiet hum of civilisation. With just a short distance of road walking, we finally reached our destination, the Fox House, where our efforts were rewarded with a well-earned pint of Black Sheep – golden, smooth and every bit as satisfying as we had hoped. As I took a grateful sip, I couldn't help but feel relieved that we had arranged transport back to the start of the walk. The thought of retracing our entire route on foot after such a ramble in the wind was one adventure I was happy to skip.

THE WALK

◉ IS IT FOR ME?

START/END POINT: From the Lady Canning's Plantation car park to Fox House

GRID REFERENCE: SK290834

DISTANCE: 3.7km (2.3 miles) one way

MILES WITHOUT STILES GRADE: For Some (challenging terrain)

TERRAIN: Rough, even ground, often rutted in places

ACCESSIBILITY: The old Roman road from Lady Canning's Plantation to Fox House walking route has some uneven sections. It is accessible by bus to Fox House and has parking at both ends.

PARKING: Off-road parking at Lady Canning's Plantation car park (S11 7TU).

FACILITIES: The Norfolk Arms and Fox House pubs serve hot food and drink all day.

➤ THE ROUTE

The journey along the Roman road from Lady Canning's Plantation to Fox House combines natural beauty with rich history. Starting in the plantation, you're surrounded by tall trees, peaceful woodland sounds and a calm, green atmosphere. While the area is popular with mountain bikers, its forest trails also offer a tranquil start to your walk.

Leaving the plantation, you join Long Causeway, an ancient Roman road once linking forts and settlements across the Peak District. Though time has worn its stones, walking this route still evokes the footsteps of Roman soldiers and travellers from centuries past.

The trail rolls across open moorland,

framed by vast skies and the calls of curlews and lapwings. In summer, purple heather blankets the hillsides, contrasting with the greens and browns of the rugged landscape. Expansive views stretch across the Peak District, where gritstone edges and distant hills define the horizon.

As you approach Burbage Moor, dramatic rock formations rise from the heather, adding to the wild beauty. The moor's history spans over 4,000 years – from prehistoric hillforts and burial cairns to medieval trade routes and later millstone quarries. During World War II, the area even served as a training ground and aircraft decoy site.

The route concludes at Fox House, a historic inn marking the edge of the moors – the perfect spot to rest and reflect on your journey through time and landscape.

Parts of the trail are uneven and deeply rutted, so a sturdy all-terrain wheelchair like a TerrainHopper is ideal. Standard mobility scooters may struggle with the rough terrain, but, for those prepared for a challenge, the rewards are truly remarkable.

NEED TO KNOW

A PLACE TO EAT: The Bird Café in Hathersage, Hope Valley, S32 1EG, has accessible facilities.

A PLACE TO DRINK: The Fox House Country Inn at Longshaw (S11 7TY) has accessible facilities.

A PLACE TO SLEEP: Hope Cross Cottage at Tideswell (SK17 8JA) offers accessible facilities, including a profile bed.

IF YOU'RE LOOKING FOR SOMETHING ELSE…

Eyam, a historic village in the Peak District National Park, Derbyshire, is forever marked by the Black Death of 1665/66. When villagers contracted the plague from cloth delivered from London, they made the brave decision to isolate themselves to contain the disease, saving surrounding communities but losing many of their own. The name 'Eyam', meaning 'village by the water', dates back to Anglo-Saxon times, with remnants of a 1588 water system still visible in the form of stone troughs. The village also has a rich industrial past, with mines dating back to Roman times and mills from the 18th and 19th centuries. Eyam's oldest building, Laburnum Cottage, dates to 1550.

CULLEN TO PORTKNOCKIE
MORAY

GEORGINA JACKSON

The waves roll steadily against the shore, releasing a refreshing mist into the cool air. The crisp autumn breeze adds a sharpness, perfect for a tranquil walk by the sea. Tip, my faithful collie, eagerly chases the retreating surf, barking happily as it vanishes into the rugged shoreline of the Moray Firth.

This peaceful scene unfolds in the quiet fishing village of Cullen, where life moves at a slower, calmer pace – starkly different, as I found out, from the stormy path Georgina Jackson has walked. It was the perfect setting to meet up with Georgina: a place that holds special meaning in her heart.

Our walk began on the seafront at Cullen, where we followed a path that wound behind the golf club and up to the top of the cliffs. Below us, the beach stretched out in a golden expanse, the village harbour nestled in the distance, its colourful houses clustered along the shore. I could see why Georgina loved this place.

Georgina, an advocate for outdoor adventure and a beacon of resilience, was born in the coastal city of Brighton. Yet her early life was far from the peace and beauty typically associated with the seaside. Her father, a Major in the Signals Corps, was a figure of strict discipline and authority, but behind closed doors their family life was unstable. Her mother, a survivor of rape before meeting Georgina's father, carried deep emotional wounds. Their relationship, as Georgina would later describe it, was forged through a 'trauma bond'.

GEORGINA AND DEBBIE ON THE CLIFFTOP AT PORTKNOCKIE

From a young age, Georgina was exposed to life's darker sides, with alcohol and wild parties defining her parents' lifestyle. At just five, she and her brother were forced into self-sufficiency, often cooking meals and preparing for school while their hungover parents remained incapacitated. This turbulent upbringing instilled resilience and independence but left deep scars. One vivid memory is of her father threatening her mother while she was cradled in her arms, a moment that shattered their fragile family.

Shortly after, her father left for the Middle East, severing all ties with his children. Georgina's mother, grappling with unresolved trauma and the breakdown of her marriage, suffered a mental health crisis resulting in yet more loss for the children. Her mental health and agoraphobia deepened, leaving Georgina and her brother to fend for themselves.

The coastal path we were following traced the route of a long-disused railway line, its tracks now replaced by gravel. At times, the sea disappeared from view, hidden by steep embankments rising on either side. The way ahead was clear, well-marked and predictable, so unlike the life journey Georgina had faced from such an early age. While our route offered stability underfoot, hers had been anything but steady. Life had thrown sharp turns and sudden drops her way, yet she pressed on, forging resilience with each difficult step. The path behind her was lined not with guideposts but with moments of survival, instinct and strength carved from uncertainty.

At seven, the move to Cardiff with her mother's new partner initially seemed hopeful but soon revealed new horrors. The partner, an alcoholic, became abusive, and at 13, Georgina witnessed him strangling her mother. Intervening, Georgina faced his rage but was met with eerie calm as he released his grip and pretended nothing had happened.

The volatile relationship escalated, leading to both her mother and her partner attempting suicide, a traumatic event Georgina and her brother witnessed. When her brother left for university, Georgina felt utterly alone. Her mother's health continued to decline, and she was frequently in and out of the hospital. Despite the turmoil at home, Georgina was determined to pursue her education. She excelled in school and earned the grades necessary to attend university, where she studied Physics. But even as she tried to build a life of her own, the responsibilities at home followed her. Her mother's health deteriorated further, and Georgina chose to transfer to universities to be closer to her.

On her 19th birthday, her mother was admitted to the hospital for liver failure. A month later, she passed away. Her death left Georgina emotionally conflicted. Though she had cared for her mum until the end, she struggled with the realisation that she didn't truly like the woman she had spent her life trying to support.

Adding to the complexity of her grief, her mum's second husband inherited everything, leaving Georgina and her brother with nothing. She was forced to fight for financial support as an independent student, knowing that education was her only way out of the life she had been trapped in since childhood.

Despite her struggles, Georgina's determination paid off. She graduated with first-class honours, but the cost to her mental and physical health was high. She was left utterly exhausted, often too tired even to walk.

During her final year at university, Georgina had met a man who would become her partner. Together, they converted a campervan and set off on a six-week adventure around Europe. But even this brief escape from her turbulent life wasn't the fresh start she had hoped for. Her new partner soon revealed his own abusive tendencies, lashing out in violent temper tantrums and controlling her emotionally.

The cycle of abuse, which had defined so much of Georgina's early life, had returned. She struggled to reconcile her reality with the promises she had made to herself, promises that she would never again allow herself to be part of an abusive relationship. Yet here she was.

Our conversation flowed easily, and before long we were emerging from the old railway path into the village of Portknockie. Rows of low-rise fishing cottages lined the narrow streets, weathered by salt and time. I felt a flicker of excitement; we were heading back toward the clifftops, and Georgina had promised me an unforgettable view of Bow Fiddle Rock.

As we walked, she spoke candidly. The COVID-19 pandemic had marked a turning point in her life, forcing her to confront a painful truth. When her partner drove away in their campervan with another woman, Georgina was left with the stark realisation that once again she had to start over.

But this time was different. Instead of retreating inward, Georgina turned to the natural world for strength. She found solace in the outdoors, a space where her mind could reset and her spirit could begin to mend. She challenged herself in ways that pushed both her body and resolve: cycling the Coast to Coast route in a single day, hiking the full length of Hadrian's Wall in just three days, and paddleboarding across England in five days. These adventures became so much more than achieving physical feats: they were affirmations of resilience, moments where she discovered a sense of accomplishment that had eluded her for much of her life.

There we were now, sitting on the clifftop, gazing out over the sea to the dramatic silhouette of Bow Fiddle Rock. Time was to be enjoyed, not rushed, so we stayed for a while, letting the moment settle around us, amid the cries of seabirds wheeling overhead, the salt tang of the air and the rhythmic crash of waves far below. After the hushed solitude of the old railway track, the clifftop felt vibrant, almost celebratory, as if the elements themselves were acknowledging that Georgina's life was finally turning a corner.

As she began to rebuild, Georgina sold her house and moved into a rental property close to her brother – now happily married with two children. This new chapter brought unexpected joy in the form of Jack, her brother's best friend, and soon, a new love. With renewed excitement for the future, Georgina began planning a long-dreamed-of move to Scotland, drawn by the sea and the wild beauty of the land.

And just as her plans began to take shape, life offered her something extraordinary: an invitation to join a leg of the Clipper Round the World Yacht Race, sailing from Australia to Vietnam – despite having no prior sailing experience. It was a bold challenge, but one that echoed everything Georgina had come to embody: courage, renewal and an unshakable belief in starting again.

By January 2024, Georgina began a new chapter in Scotland, settling near the Moray Firth with renewed hope. Reflecting on her journey, she called it 'the craziest year' – one where past burdens lifted and happiness finally took hold after years of struggle, marking the start of true peace and possibility.

THE WALK

IS IT FOR ME?

START/END POINT: The car park at Cullen Links Golf Club, Buckie, AB56 4WB

GRID REFERENCE: NJ511670

DISTANCE: 2.4km (1.5 miles) one way

MILES WITHOUT STILES GRADING: For All

TERRAIN: Solid tracks throughout

ACCESSIBILITY: With its level surface, the path is ideal for wheelchairs and buggies, making it accessible for all.

PARKING: Beach front car park (AB56 4WB)

FACILITIES: Accessible toilets are available at the beach car park in Cullen (AB56 4WB). Refreshments can be purchased at the Cullen Links Golf Club (see above).

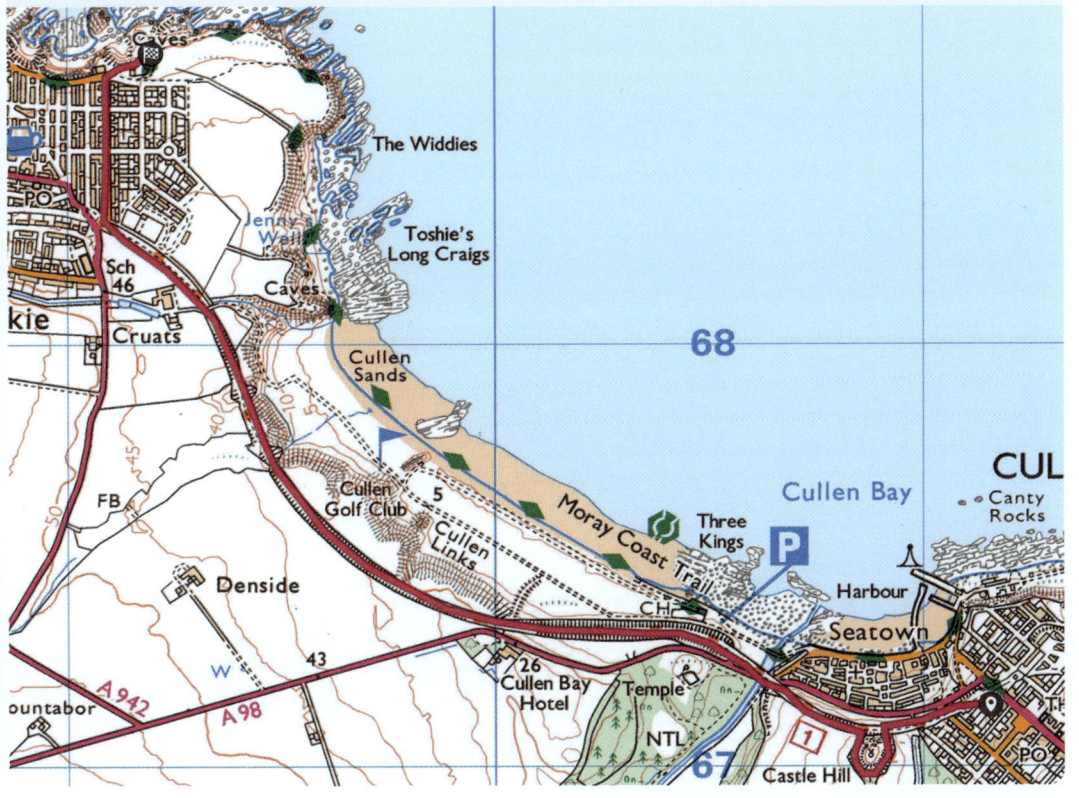

THE ROUTE

This one-way walk begins at the Cullen Links Golf Club car park, following the national cycle path that connects Portknockie to Cullen via the historic Cullen Viaduct, which was once part of the old railway line.

At Portknockie, the route turns right down the quiet road. Just past the garages is a short path which leads to Bow Fiddle Rock, a dramatic geological formation shaped by the elements. Thanks to the crystal-clear air of the Moray Firth, you'll be treated to panoramic views stretching north, east and west. The coastline also hosts a variety of seabirds, making it a haven for birdwatchers.

The route returns to the main path. From here, follow the road to the right along the waterfront. A sharp left turn brings you to a spot overlooking the harbour. From here, you can choose to continue to explore the coast path or turn around and retrace your steps.

NEED TO KNOW

A PLACE TO EAT: The Cullen Bay Hotel (AB56 4XA) offers wheelchair access and comes highly recommended for its Cullen skink – a traditional Scottish fish soup that's rich, comforting and full of flavour.

A PLACE TO DRINK: The Seafield Arms in Cullen (AB56 4SG) has a wheelchair-accessible bar area and serves fresh local produce.

A PLACE TO SLEEP: The Red Lion Tavern situated in Fochabers (IV32 7DU)is a locally run pub and hotel with accessible facilities.

IF YOU'RE LOOKING FOR SOMETHING ELSE...

Located just 40km (25 miles) from Cullen, the **WDC Scottish Dolphin Centre** at Spey Bay is a welcoming and accessible destination where visitors can enjoy both wildlife and heritage. The centre offers level access throughout its indoor exhibition spaces, gift shop and café, along with accessible toilets and dedicated parking. From the raised, grassy viewing area near the historic Tugnet Icehouse – perfect for wheelchair users – you can look out across the Moray Firth and spot bottlenose dolphins, grey and harbour seals, and a variety of seabirds. The best time to visit for dolphin sightings is between April and October, when these playful marine mammals are most active along the coast. Whether you're browsing the exhibits, enjoying a coffee or simply taking in the sea air, the centre offers a peaceful and engaging day out for all.

THE KELPIES TO THE FALKIRK WHEEL

CHRIS BUTTERFIELD

On a cold, wet December morning, with wind howling and rain driving sideways, I sensed my meeting with Chris Butterfield would be anything but ordinary. His broad smile and warm, easy manner immediately put me at ease, drawing me into the story behind his passion.

We found brief shelter in a café at the start of our walk, where Chris spoke with infectious enthusiasm about the towering horse-head sculptures known as *The Kelpies*, and the peaceful canal path that winds towards the engineering marvel that is the Falkirk Wheel. It was a striking contrast to the rugged hills of the South Pennines, where he once roamed as a young man growing up in Bradford. Now settled in Edinburgh with his wife, Priscilla, Chris has embraced the beauty of his adopted home, a reminder that sometimes the most extraordinary sights are closer than we think.

Before heading out on our walk, we had a wander around *The Kelpies*, a pair of monumental steel horse-heads. The 35m (115 foot) equine sculptures, designed by Andy Scott, pay homage to Scotland's industrial past and its reliance on horsepower. Inspired by real-life Clydesdale horses, Duke and Baron, the sculptures are also deeply rooted in Scottish folklore about mythical water horses.

As we embarked on our walk, I began learning about Chris's love for the outdoors, which was sparked at an early age, nurtured by his time in the Cubs and Pathfinders, where he was introduced to the Yorkshire Dales. His first glimpse of Malham Cove at just ten years old left an indelible impression, igniting a passion for the vastness and beauty of rolling limestone hills.

For a boy growing up on a council estate with a hardworking, single-parent mother who didn't drive, the outdoors felt like another world – far removed from the constraints of home life with his two sisters and brother.

By the early 1990s, Chris had moved to Mytholmroyd, where he fully embraced the rugged charm of the South Pennines. His favourite walk around Stoodley Pike became a cherished escape, cementing his deep connection to the natural world.

However, at 18, Chris almost gave up walking. Under pressure from his fellow students at university, he found himself ridiculed for enjoying such a simple pleasure. His friends, eager to fit in and uphold the prevailing trends of college life, laughed at him, mocking his choice of leisure activity, saying that walking was for 'old people', or 'pensioners who wore anoraks'. They called him a 'trainspotter', a label that stung. In a society where appearances and social status were so heavily influenced by what was 'cool', the peer pressure was overwhelming. Chris felt the weight of their judgements and began to question whether his love for walking was something he should continue to cherish. Despite this, he secretly slipped away to the hills, calling his passion for walking his 'dirty little secret'. The cruel teasing made him doubt himself, yet deep down he knew that his quiet walks brought him peace – something that kind of noise could never offer.

Chris met Priscilla in a chance encounter at Victoria coach station in London, a meeting that would eventually shape both their lives. Originally from Northern Ireland, Priscilla had moved to Portsmouth in 1991 to attend university. It wasn't until 2009 that they exchanged numbers, sparking a relationship spanning two years of long-distance challenges. Priscilla applied for a job in Edinburgh and, determined to be together, the couple decided to take a leap of faith when she got it, relocating to the Scottish capital. Chris found work in engineering, and for the last 11 years they have built a life together in Edinburgh, embracing the city and its surrounding beauty as their home.

It was as a student studying engineering in Halifax that Chris first learned about the Pennine Way, a legendary long-distance walking route stretching 431km (268 miles) from Derbyshire to the Scottish Borders. For years, walking the trail remained a pipe dream, an ambition that always seemed just out of reach. However, inspired by Alfred Wainwright's *Pennine Way Companion* (1968), in 2013, to mark his 40th birthday, Chris and Priscilla decided to turn his teenage dream into reality. Setting off together, they embarked on an adventure that would prove transformative, deepening Chris's love for the outdoors and leaving an enduring mark on his life.

As we walked along the towpath, the rain lashed against our faces. In parts of the canal, the water levels were alarmingly high, with some barges being tossed around by the gusty wind. Through his laughter at the water dripping from my hood and landing on my face, Chris grinned and quoted, 'Alfred Wainwright would have said, "There's no such thing as bad weather, only unsuitable clothing,"' a line often attributed to him in his 1973 book *Coast to Coast*.

In fact, the book became the catalyst for another big adventure, and the pair laced up their hiking boots once more and embarked on the 312km (194 mile) journey from St Bees to Robin Hood's Bay. Guided by Wainwright's words and illustrations, they traversed the mountains of the Lake District, the rolling hills of the Yorkshire Dales, and the rugged expanse of the North York Moors, ultimately arriving at the windswept shores of the East Coast. The experience deepened Chris's appreciation for Wainwright's craft. In 2016, Priscilla bought him the box set of Wainwright's *Pictorial Guides to the Lakeland Fells*, a treasure trove of meticulous line drawings and lyrical prose that captured the soul of the fells. Chris's thirst for knowledge about Wainwright burned brighter than ever – he delved into the life and work of this extraordinary writer and illustrator, hooked on the brilliance of Wainwright's timeless artistry.

For Chris, reading Wainwright's guides felt like a deeply personal, one-on-one experience with the man himself.

'Wainwright had an extraordinary ability to connect readers to the landscape through his words and illustrations, making the terrain come alive in a way few others could,' Chris explained.

Driven by admiration, Chris began collecting every book Wainwright had ever produced, immersing himself in the works of the legendary fellwalker. But simply owning the books wasn't enough – Chris wanted to delve deeper. He resolved to meet people who had known Wainwright personally, knowing that time was against him, as many of those who had been a part of Wainwright's life were no longer around. His quest took him to Kendal, where Wainwright had lived from 1949, and there he knocked on doors and began piecing together stories from friends, family and colleagues.

Over the years, Chris unearthed insights and anecdotes that had never been shared publicly, uncovering a more intimate portrait of the man behind the guides. One of the pivotal figures in his journey was Andrew Nichol, a friend of Wainwright and a publisher at the *Westmorland Gazette*. Nichol, instrumental in preserving Wainwright's legacy, became a key ally, offering invaluable insights. Meeting Andrew for the first time was a transformative moment for Chris; not only did he become a true friend and mentor, but he also opened countless doors for Chris, helping him to deepen his understanding of Wainwright's life and work.

As we reached one of the locks, we stopped to admire the incredible engineering that went into their design. Canal locks use a system of gates and chambers to raise and lower boats between stretches of water at different levels. The principle, dating back to the early 15th century, relies on gravity and controlled water flow to make waterways navigable, and it revolutionised transportation during the Industrial Revolution. As an engineer himself, Chris could fully appreciate the precision and craftsmanship behind these mechanisms, the intricate balance of forces, the careful construction of sluices and the robust materials ensuring their longevity.

Returning to Wainwright's influence, Chris says, 'What began as a passion for finding out more about Wainwright's life snowballed into something much greater.' Soon, his knowledge about the author and fellwalker put him in

CHRIS BUTTERFIELD AND DEBBIE AT THE KELPIES

increasing demand. Over four years, he balanced his full-time engineering job with writing for various publications, giving talks and participating in interviews about Wainwright. It became clear that his admiration for Wainwright was evolving into something more: a calling.

At 48, Chris found himself at a crossroads in his life. Having followed the traditional path into adulthood – university, career, a steady job – the structured routine that had once provided stability now felt like a constraint. His research into Wainwright wasn't just feeding his own curiosity; it was resonating with others, sparking conversations and inspiring new generations of walkers and adventurers. With Priscilla's unwavering support, Chris began building a strong presence on social media, sharing his insights and passion with a growing audience. What had once been a side project was transforming into a new way of life. In 2018, he made the bold decision to step away from his engineering career, leaving behind the security of the familiar to fully dedicate himself to his newfound vocation. It was a leap into the unknown, but one that felt as exhilarating as a long walk through the fells, guided by passion, purpose and the spirit of exploration.

Chris's passion and fire for his new career as an expert and collector of Wainwright's works has propelled him to remarkable heights. His ambition burns brightly: one day he hopes to establish a permanent exhibition dedicated to his extensive collection of Wainwright memorabilia, ensuring the fellwalker's legacy endures for future generations.

Arriving at the Falkirk Wheel, the sight is staggering, a masterpiece of modern engineering standing proudly against the Scottish landscape. We arrived just in time to see a boat being gently lifted, the massive structure rotating with slow and steady precision. As the world's first and only rotating boat lift, the Falkirk Wheel seamlessly connects the Forth and Clyde Canal to the Union Canal. Watching the wheel in motion, Chris couldn't help but reflect on his own journey – one driven by passion, persistence and a deep love for exploration. Filled with gratitude and fulfilment, he saw how his dedication to walking, despite the challenges of his youth, had shaped his life's purpose. With the support of friends and family, he had stayed true to himself, turning his fascination into a vocation. No longer just an admirer, Chris had become a published author, a recognised journalist and a respected authority on Wainwright and his legacy. His transformation from enthusiast to expert is proof that following one's heart can lead to something extraordinary, just like the wheel, lifting dreams as effortlessly as it raises boats into the sky.

THE WALK

⊙ IS IT FOR ME?

START/END POINT: *The Kelpies* finishing at the Falkirk Wheel.

GRID REFERENCE: NS907819

DISTANCE: 6.3km (3.9 miles) one way

MILES WITHOUT STILES GRADE: For All

TERRAIN: Compacted soil and tarmac tracks

ACCESSIBILITY: The walk is suitable for manual wheelchair users.

PARKING: There are large car parks at both *The Kelpies* in Helix Park and the Falkirk Wheel; fees apply.

FACILITIES: Both Helix Park and the Falkirk Wheel have visitor centres equipped with accessible toilets and cafés. Each location offers a great café experience, making them ideal spots to relax and enjoy a meal or refreshment during your visit.

➡ THE ROUTE

Enjoy a historic walk along the canal path that connects two of Scotland's most iconic landmarks: *The Kelpies* and the Falkirk Wheel. Starting at Helix Park, home of *The Kelpies*, follow the tranquil Forth and Clyde Canal on a well-maintained, stile-free path, which is perfect for walking, wheeling or cycling. While there are two sections with steps along the towpath, these can be easily avoided with a short diversion onto the road, ensuring accessibility for all.

For added flexibility, it's possible to walk one way and take a canal trip back to the start of the walk – check with the boat operators for opening times and prices. Both boats are wheelchair accessible, making this a great option for everyone. Along the route, enjoy serene waters, glimpses of local wildlife and historical reminders of Scotland's industrial heritage, such as locks and aqueducts.

Your journey culminates at the incredible Falkirk Wheel, the world's first and only rotating boat lift, which connects the Forth and Clyde Canal to the Union Canal. Standing at 35m (115ft), this engineering marvel uses minimal energy – equivalent to eight domestic kettles – yet lifts boats with stunning efficiency. Beyond its functionality, the Wheel is a masterpiece of design, attracting over 500,000 visitors annually.

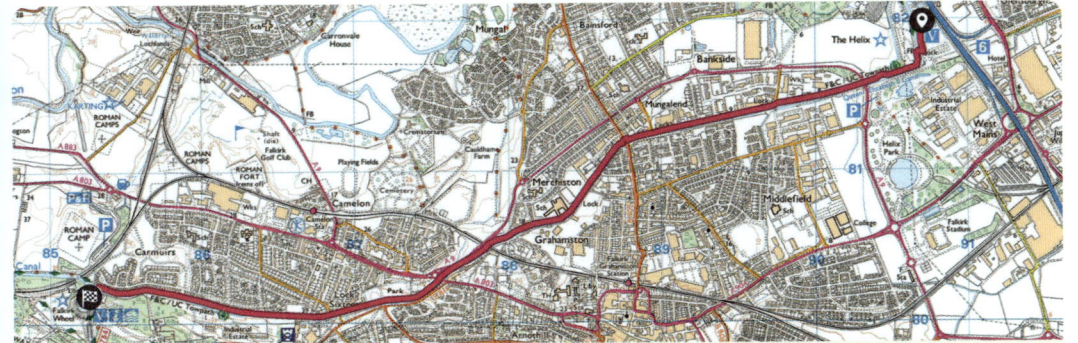

The attraction also offers something for everyone, with boat trips, a café, a gift shop, water play areas, canoeing and woodland walks. Whether walking, cycling or combining your walk with a canal cruise, this 8km (5 mile) route provides a breathtaking blend of art, engineering and history, making for an unforgettable day out in central Scotland.

NEED TO KNOW

A PLACE TO EAT: Bob & Berts in Falkirk (FK1 1NR) is a vibrant and welcoming café known for its relaxed atmosphere, hearty breakfasts and artisan coffee. The café offers wheelchair access.

A PLACE TO DRINK: Johnston's Bar Bistro in Falkirk (FK1 1DG) is a stylish and modern spot known for its great food, cocktails and relaxed atmosphere. The venue is wheelchair accessible.

A PLACE TO SLEEP: The Leapark Hotel in Grangemouth (FK3 9BX) offers a limited number of accessible rooms but does not have a lift. If you require a ground-floor or wheelchair-accessible room, it's best to contact the hotel directly to confirm availability.

♣ IF YOU'RE LOOKING FOR SOMETHING ELSE...

Next to the Mariner Leisure Centre in Camelon, near Falkirk, the Forth Valley Sensory Centre offers a peaceful garden designed for people with sensory impairments. Free to visit, it includes outdoor seating and a picnic bench – perfect for sunny days – and supports accessibility through the Neatebox Welcome app. Visitors can also meet the friendly Tin Man, now a PokéStop for Pokémon GO players. Inside, there's a fully accessible café and a child-friendly sensory room. The centre's mission is to help people with sensory loss live confident, inclusive lives.

EDINBANE
ISLE OF SKYE

SARAH LISTER

Up on the Isle of Skye in September, the signs of autumn were just around the corner. The mist swirled hauntingly around the peaks of the Cuillin Hills, creating an atmosphere that felt both ghostly and serene. Yet down in Portree, the streets were a bustling hive of activity, with holidaymakers still flocking to the island's capital. The narrow roads were packed with motorhomes, and it seemed nearly impossible to escape the crowds.

It was therefore such a relief that my walking partner for the day was Sarah Lister, a local from Portree who knows the island like the back of her hand. She had the perfect solution for guiding me away from the crowded streets to a hidden gem that only a true local could know. As we ventured further away from Portree, the noise of the town faded into the background, replaced by the gentle sound of the wind and the rustle of leaves. Skye's true beauty lies in these quiet, untouched places, and thanks to Sarah, I found exactly what I was looking for – an escape from the hustle and bustle, where nature wraps you in its calm embrace.

    The walk Sarah had planned for us holds a special place in her heart, as it was one she regularly did when she first moved to the island. She was eager to show me the miles of stile-free tracks that were created during the construction of Edinbane Wind Farm, which began in early 2008. Sarah was slowly recovering from ill health and though she can now manage about a mile using her walker, she was excited to use the TerrainHopper, an all-terrain wheelchair, which allowed us to explore farther into the wind farm than she'd ever been able to before.

SARAH LISTER USES THE TERRAINHOPPER FOR THE FIRST TIME

After reading Sarah's book, *The Good Thing About Having a Brain Tumour*, I was eager to meet her in person. The first line of her memoir had me in stitches: 'The best thing about having a brain tumour was that my husband left me!' Sarah's dry humour instantly appealed to me.

Originally from Norfolk, she and her husband had moved to Skye in search of the idyllic country life they'd always dreamed of. Everything seemed perfect: they had their dream house, fulfilling jobs and a peaceful life in the Scottish countryside.

Though the sun was shining in Portree when we reached the start of our walk, a low mist clung to the landscape, obscuring everything in sight. It was as if the world had quietly withdrawn behind a veil, a fitting backdrop, I would soon realise, for the sudden darkness Sarah's story was about to unveil.

'I started having really bad headaches, dizziness and sickness,' she told me. Despite her worsening symptoms, her GP dismissed her concerns, brushing her off as overly dramatic. But Sarah knew something wasn't right and demanded a brain scan.

Oddly, on the day of the scan, Sarah wasn't consumed by nerves or anxiety of what might be diagnosed. Instead, she was more excited about the chance to leave the island and head to Aberdeen. The scan felt like a mere inconvenience, during what she saw as a much-needed city shopping trip. Little did she know that the routine check would alter the course of her life.

After the scan, Sarah was called into a small consultation room, where she received news that would forever change her life. The consultant's words are something she will never forget: 'You have a brain tumour, but it's not cancer.' In the whirlwind of events that followed, Sarah was immediately transferred to Aberdeen Royal Infirmary for a night of observation and further tests. The tumour, shockingly the size of a small orange, required urgent intervention.

It was hard to believe that this woman, so full of life and energy, had faced such traumatic news. As we walked, the path began to climb steadily. At first, it was rocky and uneven, jolting us with every step – a fitting reflection of the turmoil Sarah had suddenly found herself navigating during that period of her life. We were still shrouded in fog.

Back in Aberdeen, the first step was to fit a shunt into the tumour to drain the excess fluid. But that was only the beginning. Over the next few years, Sarah endured a total of six brain surgeries, each one a monumental challenge. Between operations, she would return to Skye, in an attempt to maintain some semblance of a normal life despite the ongoing turmoil.

However, just as Sarah began to adjust to this new reality, she was dealt another devastating blow. Her husband, overwhelmed by the gravity of her illness, told her he could no longer cope. He left her, and by 2011 Sarah found herself alone – recovering not only from a series of gruelling surgeries but also from the end of her marriage.

Determined not to let these setbacks define her, Sarah started over. She found a new home in Portree and began to rebuild herself, accompanied by her two loyal dogs.

During her fourth brain surgery, Sarah suffered nerve damage that led to Bell's palsy on the right side of her face. This caused her eyelid to stop closing properly, which resulted in corneal damage. On top of that, tinnitus set in, severely reducing the hearing in her right ear. She vividly remembers the heartbreak in her father's eyes the first time he saw her disfigurement. Adjusting to her new appearance was incredibly challenging, but Sarah's determination to move forward remained unshaken.

Despite her vulnerabilities, things took an unexpected turn while she was out walking one day. She bumped into an old school friend, and what began as a chance encounter blossomed into a relationship. Though it wasn't easy for Sarah to let someone in, given the physical and emotional toll of her journey, she embraced the opportunity for love and companionship.

Shortly after, Sarah experienced another setback when she suffered a seizure and was diagnosed with epilepsy. This new condition was yet another obstacle in her path, but through medication she was able to control it. After 12 months of being together, Sarah moved in with her boyfriend.

Despite everything she had endured – multiple surgeries, the loss of her marriage and ongoing health challenges – Sarah once again believed she had found her 'happily ever after'.

However, Sarah's journey wasn't over – she still had to face two more surgeries. Before her fifth operation, Sarah and her partner decided to marry. It was a simple, intimate affair, a moment of hope amid the uncertainty. Her 40th birthday came shortly after, but it was spent in the hospital. 'Not many people can say they had "Happy Birthday" sung to them by a group of neurosurgeons,'

Sarah said with her characteristic humour. It wasn't the last birthday she would spend in a hospital, but she remembers it as the best one.

After her sixth operation, Sarah woke up knowing something wasn't quite right. Clouded by morphine, she struggled to understand what had happened. When the fog of medication lifted, she learned the devastating news – she had suffered a stroke during the surgery that had affected the left side of her body. Suddenly, Sarah had lost the ability to speak, swallow and perform the simplest tasks, such as picking something up.

The road to recovery was long and slow. Physiotherapy began with the basics, teaching her to stand and walk again with the aid of a Zimmer frame. Yet she was determined to get out of her wheelchair, and gradually she regained some independence.

But the challenges weren't over. Despite all her surgeries, a small portion of the tumour remained, and Sarah had to undergo radiotherapy to address it. Meanwhile, her marriage, which had once seemed like a beacon of hope, began to unravel. Her husband became controlling, limiting her from doing the things she loved because of her disability. Recognising that she needed to take control of her life again, Sarah made the brave decision to leave. She packed a bag and headed to a hotel in Portree, seeking a fresh start.

The low fog that had enveloped us had obscured everything beyond the track right ahead. According to the OS map, we were right next to a wind turbine, but visibility was so limited that we couldn't see it. Then, as if the curtain at a theatre was being lifted, the fog began to dissipate. Majestic and looming against the landscape, the wind turbines emerged from the mist – a quiet metaphor for how even in the murkiest moments, strength and clarity may slowly come into view.

For Sarah, that moment mirrored her own path. Moving forward from the darkest period of her life, she now has a little house in Portree and is surrounded by a strong support network of friends and loved ones. With the help of her friend Mel, she co-founded the website Skye for All, which offers valuable information on accessible, stile-free walks across the island. Despite the challenges she's faced, Sarah is thriving. She can now walk up to 1.6km (1 mile) using a wheeled walking frame, and with the help of the island's bus network, she's out exploring new places and embracing the freedom that comes with rediscovering her love for adventure.

Sarah's story is one of remarkable resilience. Her determination to reclaim her life, continues to inspire all who know her.

Beyond the Edinbane wind turbines, tracks stretch into the distance, linking each one. It's easy to imagine Sarah here, charting her course and discovering new ground. Like those paths, her journey moves forward – open-ended and full of possibility.

THE WALK

◉ IS IT FOR ME?

START/END POINT: Through the gate at the start of the Edinbane track, just after the Greshornish turn off

GRID REFERENCE: NG3476851319

DISTANCE: 25km (16 miles) there and back

MILES WITHOUT STILES GRADE: For Many

TERRAIN: A mixture of grassy tracks and compounded aggregate

ACCESSIBILITY: The first section of the trail is rocky and would require an all-terrain wheelchair.

PARKING: There is free off road parking at the start of the walk, off the A850 west of Edinbane just after the Greshornish turn off. Please park with care and courtesy, taking care not to block any farm driveways.

FACILITIES: There are none available on the walk.

➜ THE ROUTE

Nestled on the sloping heather moorland around Edinbane in the north-west of Skye, the Edinbane Wind Farm is a fascinating place to visit. Construction of the wind farm began in early 2008 and it is now home to 18 Enercon 2.3 MW turbines, each reaching a towering height of up to 100m (328ft).

Our route passed through the gate and followed a steep and bumpy track leading towards the turbines. We were both grateful that we each had an all-terrain powered wheelchair to use, as the track is unsuitable for a manual chair. Once on the track, exploring the area became much easier.

Though our route didn't take us all the way to the summit of Cruachan-Glen Vic Askill, which stands at 295m (968ft), we were fortunate enough to skim around its foothills and it gave us the opportunity to say that we had, in fact, climbed a small section of a Scottish 'Marilyn'. These hills, with their distinct prominence of at least 150m (492ft), are celebrated among walkers and hikers, and while we didn't make it to the top, we still enjoyed the challenge of exploring part of this unique Scottish peak. After soaking in the beauty of the surroundings, we retraced our steps back to the car,

reflecting on the unforgettable experience of walking amid the towering turbines.

What about the crowds of tourists on the island? Well, we didn't see a single person on this walk and had this breathtaking landscape entirely to ourselves.

NEED TO KNOW

A PLACE TO EAT: The Granary, Portree (IV51 9EH) is a small café serving a selection of hot and cold snacks.

A PLACE TO DRINK: The Isles Inn, Portree (IV51 9EH) is one of the most centrally located dining spots in the village, offering a cosy traditional Highland pub atmosphere. You'll find it tucked away at the corner of Somerled Square, conveniently close to the disabled parking area.

A PLACE TO SLEEP: Air Leth B&B, Portree (IV51 9LR) offers a warm Highland welcome in a peaceful setting just a short walk from central Portree. The universally designed B&B rooms provide comfort and accessibility for all.

IF YOU'RE LOOKING FOR SOMETHING ELSE…

Join **Stardust Boat Trips** for an unforgettable wildlife watching adventure along the beautiful west coast of Scotland, exploring the stunning scenery of Portree Bay, the Sound of Raasay and the wider Isle of Skye. With boats departing daily from Portree Harbour, their experienced and fully qualified skippers prioritise your safety and comfort, allowing you to relax and fully enjoy the journey.

On board their wheelchair-accessible vessels – *MV Stardust II*, *Wavedancer* and *Saorsa na Mara* – you'll have the chance to get up close with incredible wildlife, including the majestic white-tailed eagle, the largest bird of prey in the UK.

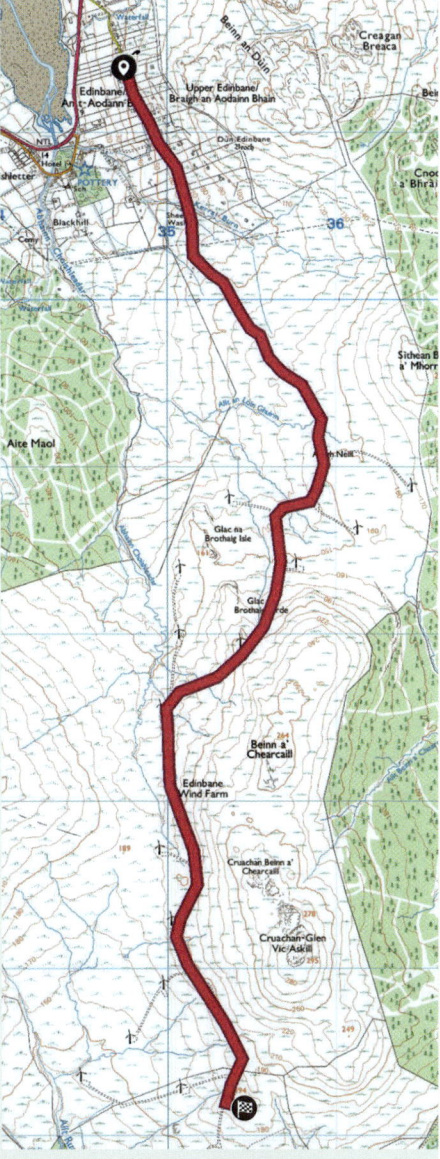

BEACON FELL
GOOSNARGH, LANCASHIRE

SARAH DORNAN

My quest to uncover accessible, stile-free walks led me northward once again, this time to the Forest of Bowland National Landscape. There, I was to meet Sarah Dornan, the area's Countryside Access Officer. I'd never set foot in this part of Lancashire before, and the promise of new paths – and a chance to touch a trig point – was more than enough to stir my curiosity. How could I possibly resist?

The drive alone felt like the beginning of an adventure. A ribbon of narrow country road twisted and climbed through dense woodland, each bend unveiling more of the rolling hills beyond. Then, at last, a sign emerged from the trees: Beacon Fell Country Park. I had arrived.

Waiting at the entrance was Sarah, ready with a warm smile and an unmistakable Sheffield lilt that instantly put me at ease. A fellow Steel City native – I liked her already.

The landscape was immediately captivating. A steep, cobbled path unfurled before us, disappearing into the embrace of ancient woodland. Not a challenge for my all-terrain wheelchair, which took to the rugged incline with ease. The air was cool and rich with the scent of pine and moss, and every crackle of twig beneath the wheels seemed to echo with anticipation. With Sarah as my guide and the forest path beckoning, I had a feeling this was going to be a walk to remember.

As we meandered up the hillside, Sarah's memories flowed as freely as the breeze rustling through the bracken. She spoke fondly of her childhood in Whirlow, a leafy suburb of Sheffield, where weekends were sacred adventures – her family roaming the woodlands of Longshaw Estate, or wandering through the landscaped serenity of Whirlow Brook Park. With only 15 months between her and her older brother, William, the two had been inseparable: companions in curiosity, co-conspirators in mischief.

'William was the intellectual one, and I was the troublemaker,' Sarah said with a grin, her eyes twinkling with the recollection. 'He got blamed for everything I did – but he always forgave me.'

Reaching the summit of the hill offered Sarah a chance to catch her breath and me an opportunity to soak in the towering presence of the Scots pines, their dark green needles stark against the pale sky.

'They're remarkable,' Sarah said, awe woven into her voice. 'It's the UK's only native pine species – brilliant for biodiversity and one of the most important timber producers. Strong, resilient, rooted in our landscape.'

We paused on a bench beneath their shade, the hush of the forest folding around us. As the breeze stirred, Sarah continued painting scenes from her childhood. She spoke of her cocker spaniel, Prince, and of how she grumbled at the mention of going for a walk with the dog but loving the adventure once she

SARAH DORNAN AT BEACON FELL

hit the trail, of days spent lying in sunlit meadows, gazing up at the clouds as they drifted lazily across the sky. 'I was a proper daydreamer,' she said with a nostalgic laugh.

Yet beneath her easy laughter lay quieter truths. Sarah described herself as a shy, uncertain girl in school. 'I didn't really know where I fit in,' she admitted. 'I had a small circle of friends … never very confident, never one to speak out.'

But then came a spark – the Duke of Edinburgh Award. Encouraged by her parents, Sarah reluctantly signed up.

'I was a misfit at first. Totally unsure of myself. But a few weeks in, my dad said he saw a change. I stood a little taller, spoke a little louder.'

Though pushed beyond her comfort zone, she felt supported – by the leaders, by her group, and eventually by her own growing sense of self-belief. It was, she told me, a turning point.

Further along the track from the quarry towards the tarn, Sarah slowed, pointing to a cluster of delicate trees with slender trunks and fluttering leaves. 'Rowan trees,' she said, almost reverently. 'We had to study them at school in Environmental Studies. I was fascinated; these trees are steeped in folklore, but they also support so much wildlife. That was the start of it for me.'

The rowan sparked more than just academic interest, it opened a doorway into a deeper understanding of the landscape – how it breathes, how it connects with human life and how it suffers from our impact.

'I wanted to know it all,' Sarah said. 'Acid rain, global warming, river systems … I just kept asking questions.'

Her passion for the environment had begun to take root, and soon she was dreaming of a career that would let her live and breathe the outdoors, ideally one that involved long walks, horseback rides or, as she confessed, grinning, 'maybe even tearing across the hills on a quad bike!'

We both laughed at the image, but beneath it was a clear truth: Sarah had found her path, one forged in the fields of childhood, strengthened by challenge and lit by an ever-burning curiosity for the natural world.

Continuing her education with quiet determination, Sarah went on to achieve a BSc Honours degree in Environmental Management at the University of Central Lancashire. It was a personal triumph – especially given the sting of a comment once made by her secondary-school Biology teacher: 'You'll never achieve anything, and you certainly won't make it to university.' Sarah smiled wryly as she recounted it, her eyes shining with quiet pride. How wrong she was.

We sat together by the edge of the tarn, the water dappled with drifting ducks and dancing dragonflies. The sunlight glimmered on the surface as Sarah shared more of her journey. At university, she had met her best friend – a bond that still holds strong to this day. And it was during a field trip to Beacon Fell that Sarah first fell in love with this landscape. 'I remember standing right here and saying, "One day, I'd love to work in this place,"' she recalled, a dreamy smile tugging at her lips.

But life had other adventures in store first. After university, Sarah was offered an extraordinary opportunity to work at the Montserrat Volcano Observatory in the Caribbean.

'I flew in by helicopter from Antigua,' she said, her voice hushed with wonder, as if she still didn't believe it years later. 'I had to literally pinch myself. It didn't feel real.'

As fate would have it, the volcano erupted on the very day she arrived.

'It was 4am back home in England, but I had to call my parents. I needed them to know I was safe.' Sarah laughed. 'They were tucked up in bed – completely unaware their daughter had landed in the middle of a volcanic eruption on the other side of the world!'

As we continued along the path, a sign pointed us towards the trig point – standing 266m (873ft) above sea level, it offers sweeping views over Morecambe Bay and far beyond to the Lake District. The wind tugged at our clothes as we reached it, the air sharp and clear with the scent of pine and open sky. I took a quiet moment to savour the thrill of being there, while Sarah stood beside me, her face full of belonging.

After returning to England, Sarah began to lay down new roots in Nottingham. She volunteered with the British Trust for Conservation Volunteers, eager to gain hands-on experience, and it wasn't long before opportunity knocked again. Her line manager fell ill and Sarah was offered a temporary paid position.

'It was the boost I needed,' she recounts. 'He looked at me and said, "You've got what it takes to make change."' It was a world apart from the negative words of her Biology teacher – this time, someone believed in her.

From there, Sarah flourished. Her days were filled with hedge-laying, dry stone walling, stock fencing – she even learned to use a chainsaw.

'I loved it,' she said, laughing. 'Proper countryside graft. I felt like I was doing something that mattered.'

But then, life shifted once more. As the wind blew gently across the trig point, Sarah's voice softened and her eyes welled. 'It was after a short illness … my mum passed away,' she said quietly. 'It shattered us. I had to move back to Nottingham to be near my dad. He needed me. We needed each other.'

Those were painful years, heavy with grief – but still, Sarah held to her purpose. She continued her work in environmental management and, always thinking ahead, began to champion the link between nature and mental health.

'We were ahead of the curve,' she said, eyes alight again. 'We started an allotment programme for people struggling with their mental health. Watching how time outside could heal, how digging a patch of soil or watching something grow could bring people back to life – it changed me.'

Then, one day, out of the blue, the phone rang.

It was her best friend from university – now a ranger at Beacon Fell. 'Come and work with me,' she said.

Sarah didn't hesitate. Returning to the landscape she had once fallen in love with, she brought with her a bucketload of experience, passion and vision.

'We were instrumental in setting up access opportunities for Beacon Fell,' she beamed. 'We made it possible for people to explore the park in all-terrain wheelchairs. That's what this place is all about – belonging, for everyone.'

As we descended from the trig point, we stopped to admire the woodland sculptures dotted along the path. A massive stone snake coiled down the hillside, its tail winding playfully through the ferns – a delight for children and grown-ups alike.

Then, as sunlight filtered through the canopy, Sarah grew quieter. 'I began to get a strange sensation in my legs,' she said slowly. 'My foot dropped. I felt weaker by the day.' Her voice caught.

Like many in the modern world, she turned to Google. Typing in her symptoms, one result leapt off the screen: multiple sclerosis.

'I slammed the laptop shut,' she admitted. 'I wasn't ready. I couldn't face it.'

For weeks, she tried to ignore the signs. But eventually, she confided in her partner – and with a father who was a doctor, she was soon in hospital undergoing tests. 'When I was discharged, I had a diagnosis: MS. It was real, and I couldn't ignore it anymore.'

But even with her dream job under her belt and the pine-scented air of Beacon Fell all around, Sarah was now facing her most difficult challenge yet – a battle not just with her physical health but with her mental well-being, too. The diagnosis had shaken her to her core. But at first it was the psychological toll that hit hardest. Her mind began racing to worst-case scenarios, spiralling into dark thoughts. Would she ever feel her legs again? Would sensation ever return? The very idea of losing her independence haunted her. Walking, once a joy, became an uphill struggle. She was absent from work for three months, her life narrowed to hospital appointments and managing each day as it came.

Still, Sarah was determined. With a quiet grit that had already carried her through so many of life's bends and brambles, she returned to work – but her body wasn't ready. Within the first month, she experienced a relapse, and once again found herself off the trail she loved so much.

This time, however, her medical team began a targeted plan of disease-modifying therapy. The treatment wasn't a cure, but it was a turning point – it began to sharpen her focus, improve her memory, aid fine motor skills, and offer some relief from the heavy fog of fatigue that had enveloped her.

At her next annual review, she was handed a prescription. She glanced at the paper. 'What's that for?' she asked.

The doctor replied, 'Epilepsy.'

Another blow. MS, it seemed, had yet more shadows to cast. Losing her ability to drive for 12 months was just one more piece of freedom taken – but her husband stepped in, driving her to work each day without complaint. Sarah never missed a shift. She might have been slowed, but she would not be stopped.

Slowly, day by day, she rebuilt her strength. Another course of therapy followed, and regular infusions gave her body a fighting chance. And she fought – with a quiet, enduring strength that left me in awe.

'MS has an unknown path,' she told me as we looked out across the hills. 'It's like canoeing down a river; you never know what's coming. It might be a gentle meander, or it might be white-water rapids.' She paused, then added with quiet conviction, 'The therapy doesn't stop it completely. But it helps hold it back.'

Years have now passed without a relapse, a remarkable stretch that speaks volumes of her courage, discipline and belief in the healing power of nature.

'The outdoors has always been a part of me,' she said softly. 'Without it … I think I'd be lost.'

It was clear that her parents had laid the first stepping stones on this path, encouraging her to love the land, to seek adventure, to be brave even when she didn't feel brave. And now, with every accessible gate she installs, every stile-free path she maps, Sarah is honouring them by helping others find their way into the countryside.

Here at Beacon Fell, with its woodland sculptures, gentle trails and sweeping views, it's easy to see why this place is carved into her heart. It isn't just where she works, it's where she healed. It's where her story continues to unfold. The ranger service became another family for her, and it's with their support that she carried on growing and learning.

As we sat quietly beneath the shifting sky, the clouds moved gently above us, their shapes ever-changing. I couldn't help but imagine her mum sitting on one, looking down with pride at the daughter who, despite every storm she's weathered, continues to build a world others can walk through – freely, joyfully, together.

And I know her dad is proud. And so, I think, are all of us who have the privilege of walking beside her, if only for a while.

THE WALK

IS IT FOR ME?

START/END POINT: Beacon Fell Country Park, Goosnargh, Preston, Lancashire, PR3 2NL

GRID REFERENCE: SD564427

DISTANCE: 3.3km (2.08 miles) circular

MILES WITHOUT STILES GRADE: For Many

TERRAIN: Woodland trails, compounded soil and steep incline in some sections but mostly level

ACCESSIBILITY: Paths are accessible for powered mobility scooters. Certain woodland paths can be uneven, with tree roots making the ground uneven in places.

PARKING: Available on site; fees apply

FACILITIES: There's a visitor centre on site, offering helpful information and a welcoming place to start (or end) your walk. A café is also available, though it's recommended to check the website for current opening times before your visit. The site includes accessible toilets and a large car park with ample space, ensuring a comfortable experience for all visitors.

THE ROUTE

Starting from the visitor centre, head up the steep, cobbled path towards the Orme Sight, a 2.4m (7.9ft) stone head perched overlooking the forest, originally designed so visitors can peer through its eye toward Great Orme in Wales. The path veers off to the left and continues upwards through the forest. The circular woodland trail around Beacon Fell offers a scenic and accessible way to explore the park's diverse landscape. This route gently weaves through a series of enchanting woodlands – Larch Avenue, Shield Wood, Tarn Wood, and Middle Wood – before leading you towards the summit. Along the way, you'll pass a variety of tree species and habitats, making it a haven for wildlife watchers and nature lovers. There are plenty of peaceful spots ideal for a picnic, as well as a children's play area to keep younger visitors entertained. To reach the trig point it is recommended to follow the up-and-down route from the play area, which is the most suitable for all-terrain wheelchairs; other paths can be more challenging. All routes are colour-coded, and trail maps are available from the visitor centre to help guide your adventure.

NEED TO KNOW

A PLACE TO EAT: The visitor centre has a café, with a good range of hot food and snacks.

A PLACE TO DRINK: The Sun Inn in Chipping (PR3 2GD) has step-free, wheelchair-accessible entry and facilities. Staff are welcoming and happy to assist. Dog-friendly and full of local charm, it's a cosy 17th-century inn with open fires, hearty food and a warm village atmosphere.

A PLACE TO SLEEP: Tucked into the rolling countryside near Beacon Fell, the Gibbon Bridge Hotel (PR3 2TQ) offers an elegant and tranquil place to stay with views across the Ribble Valley. The hotel provides fully accessible rooms that combine comfort with thoughtful design, including level access, walk-in showers and grab rails.

IF YOU'RE LOOKING FOR SOMETHING ELSE…

Cobble Hey Farm, on the edge of the Forest of Bowland, spans 100 ha (247 acres) of farmland, woodlands, ponds, and meadows. Family-owned for generations, it's a working farm with cattle, rare-breed sheep, goats, pigs and chickens, blending agriculture with conservation and education.

Part of Access the Dales, Cobble Hey offers accessible parking, toilets, and an off-road mobility scooter. Borrow the scooter to explore farm trails and reach the bird hide, enjoying meadows, woods, and stunning views. Book at www.access-the-dales.com

GISBURN FOREST
RIBBLE VALLEY, LANCASHIRE

DECLAN FRASER-HIGGINS

Meeting my walking partner for the day, Declan Fraser-Higgins, in Gisburn Forest was an absolute delight. The gentle walk along the accessible trail was the perfect setting for him to share his story, during which he openly discussed the challenges he's faced, particularly during his transition and struggles with depression. Despite these hardships, Declan now feels a renewed sense of hope and positivity as he embraces the changes in both his life and body.

We started our walk from the car park, the crisp air filling our lungs as we followed the main driveway until it gave way to the dense forest. The wide, light-filled track contrasted sharply with the shadows beneath the towering pine trees. The forest floor was a thick carpet of pine needles, soft underfoot but heavy with the weight of quiet secrets. As we moved deeper into the woods, Declan's voice broke the stillness as he began to unfold his story.

Born in Harrogate in 1980, Declan was the middle child of three siblings in a close-knit family with hardworking parents. But though his early years were filled with love and laughter, Declan harboured a deep, unspoken truth that would shape his future. From as early as he can remember, Declan knew he was different. Assigned female at birth, he felt a deep disconnect between his gender and the identity he felt inside.

As a child, Declan was more at home playing football with the local boys than anywhere else. Football wasn't just a game; it was an escape, where he could be himself without judgement.

At home, Declan's parents were supportive, though they didn't fully grasp the depth of his feelings. They would jokingly comment on his short hair, his preference for baggy clothes and his refusal to wear dresses. 'When will you bring your first girlfriend home?' they would tease, not realising the pain those words sometimes caused. To them, Declan was 'just one of the lads', a 'tomboy' going through a phase. But for Declan, it was much more than that. Even then, he knew deep down that he wanted to be a boy.

Declan grew up in the 1980s and 90s, when transgender identities were still taboo, leaving him to navigate his feelings alone. At secondary school, he struggled even more as he tried to conform to the expectations of being a girl, but it never felt right. The boys accepted him, but he still felt like he was living a lie. Without the support or language to express his feelings, Declan struggled in silence and didn't do well in school.

The forest at Gisburn stretched out before us, vast and orderly, its pine trees planted in rigid formation like soldiers on parade. Their tall, straight trunks carved narrow corridors of shadow, where dim light struggled to reach the forest floor. An eerie stillness hung in the air, the kind of silence that sharpens your thoughts and invites reflection. As we walked between those towering ranks, the scent of resin and damp earth thick around us, Declan's voice broke through. In a place so structured and controlled, it felt strangely fitting when he revealed that, at just 17 years old, he had turned to the army,

DECLAN FRASER-HIGGINS AT GISBURN FOREST

desperate for change, hoping that its rigid discipline and overt masculinity might bring his inner world into line with the one the world expected of him.

But at that time the army was an unforgiving place to those who didn't conform. When Declan entered into a relationship with a woman, they were discovered, and Declan was locked in a cell, then dismissed from the army. This marked the beginning of a dark period in Declan's life, where depression took hold. Desperate for help, he finally reached out to his GP, who introduced him to the possibility of gender transition. This gave Declan his first glimpse of hope, setting him on the path to becoming the man he always knew he was.

After leaving the army, Declan felt lost, carrying the burden of shame and rejection. At 21, he attended Manchester Pride, where he met the woman who would become his wife. They started a family together, making them one of the first same-sex couples to have a child through embryo implantation. Declan was the egg donor, but due to legal restrictions, he wasn't recognised as a parent on the birth certificate. This exclusion was a painful reminder of his denied identity.

When their daughter was nine months old, Declan and his partner separated, which was emotionally devastating. The legal and social systems did not adequately protect parents like Declan, making it difficult for him to maintain a relationship with his child.

Declan sought to rebuild his life, entering the caring profession. He trained as a lifeguard and later became a first aid trainer, marking the first time since his military discharge that he felt on the right track. A turning point came when someone he had trained in first aid used those skills to help his mother during a stroke. This motivated Declan to become a paramedic, providing him with renewed purpose.

In the paramedic service, Declan met Nicole, a fellow paramedic, and they fell in love. However, Declan was still presenting as a woman while hiding his true identity. After having a child together, Declan finally confronted the truth, revealing to Nicole his desire to transition. This was one of the darkest periods of his life, as the weight of his hidden identity led to a suicide attempt. But Nicole stood by him and, with her support, Declan decided to undergo medical transition, including hormone therapy and gender-affirming surgeries. Debbie was no more. He emerged through the darkness as Declan.

During this time, Declan turned to the outdoors for solace, finding peace while hiking the hills of Lancashire. The time spent in nature helped him calm his mind and find the strength to continue his transition. He also worked on building a relationship with his eldest daughter. As we strolled through the forest that day, Declan expressed that, for the first time in his life, he was genuinely happy. He had a wife, children and a promising career, and while

DEBBIE USES THE ALL-TERRAIN WHEELCHAIR AT GISBURN FOREST

his journey to full transition isn't complete, he feels strong enough to face the challenges ahead.

The forest tracks led us onwards, the soft crunch of pine needles underfoot our only company. The dense canopy above began to loosen its grip on the light, and gradually, the trees thinned out. Through the gaps we caught fleeting glimpses of the reservoir, its surface catching the pale afternoon sun in flashes of silver. As we moved nearer, the forest gave way to open space, and the distant sound of water lapping against the shore began to replace the hush of the woods. The air felt fresher here, tinged with the cool breath of the lake.

In 2023, Declan's life came full circle in a way he never imagined. An independent inquiry led by Lord Etherton began to uncover the experiences of LGBTQ+ individuals who served in the armed forces during the period when it was illegal to do so as a LGBTQ+ person. This inquiry acknowledged the prejudice and mistreatment Declan, and others like him, endured. In February 2024, Declan and others were formally honoured for their service in a moment of profound healing and reconciliation. The ceremony, where Declan was presented with his beret and cap badge, symbolised the restoration of his military service, which had been abruptly cut short. It wasn't just about restoring honour; it was about validating his journey and recognising the man he had become.

As we sat at the picnic table beside the water, the flask of tea between us offered more than warmth; it became a quiet toast to Declan. His story, steeped in courage and resilience, lingered in the stillness around us. From a fearful young adult grappling with identity, to a man who now walks in truth and self-acceptance, Declan's journey is one of profound transformation. His choice to live authentically not only brought him peace but deepened the bonds with those who matter most. As he reflects on the path he's walked, he does so with pride, knowing he faced the darkness and came through it, not just surviving, but thriving.

THE WALK

⊙ IS IT FOR ME?

START/END POINT: Stephen Park car park ending, at Stocks Reservior

GRID REFERENCE: SD745558

DISTANCE: 5.8km (3.6 miles) one way

MILES WITHOUT STILES GRADE: For Many

TERRAIN: Surfaced paths of tarmac and gravel

ACCESSIBILITY: Gisburn Forest is easily accessible, with well-maintained trails and a designated car park, making it a welcoming spot for walkers, cyclists and nature lovers alike.

PARKING: There is parking available at Stephen Park, in Gisburn Forest; fees apply.

FACILITIES: Accessible toilets are located in the car park.

➡ THE ROUTE

Gisburn Forest offers a fantastic experience for the entire family, with a wide variety of trails, including many designed for biking. Children will especially enjoy the Gruffalo Trail, but what sets Gisburn apart is its accessibility for visitors with disabilities. The forest provides two all-terrain wheelchairs for use and has a designated accessible trail that leads to Stocks Reservoir.

The walk starts at the café at Stephen Park, where you head down the forest road towards the Gisburn Hub car park entrance. Take the first right, pass the barrier and follow the forest track, which eventually leads to a road. Cross the road and take the opposite track, which will bring you back onto the road. Continue along this quiet stretch, rounding the corner past Dalehead Church.

Cross the causeway, then take the left track, which leads to the car park at Stocks Reservoir. Continue along the stone track for a short distance, passing a picnic area on the left. At this point, the trail veers right, but if you take a left turn around a dry stone wall, you'll find a 70m (230ft) path that leads to the reservoir's edge, with a wheelchair-accessible bird hide.

The trail narrows and gently ascends. The views open up across the reservoir to Saddle Hill, Bloe Greet and Catlow Fell. Turn right at the junction and follow the

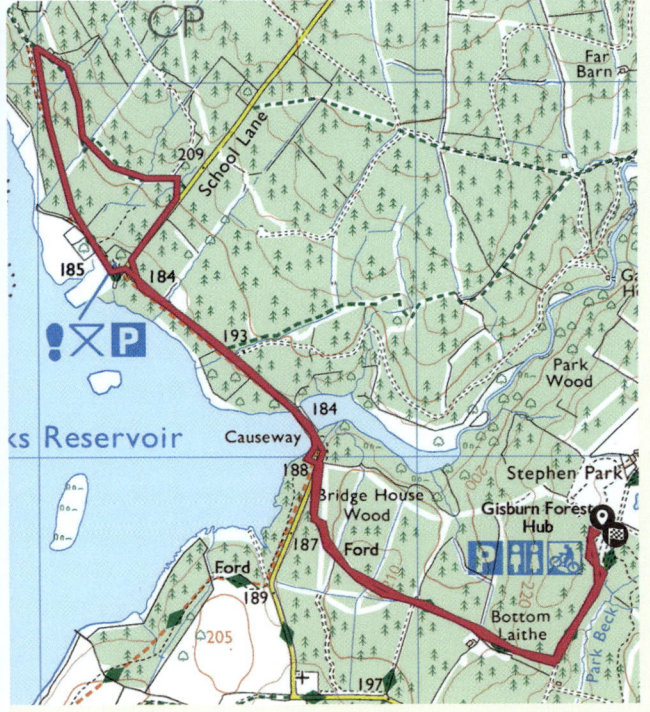

streamside path uphill into the woods. As the gradient steepens, continue past a stone gatepost and an old farm compound leading to another forest. Turn right onto the forest road, which offers a gradual descent over a surface of pine needles and tree roots.

Cross a small bridge and follow the path to re-join the original trail near the car park gate on your left. From here, retrace your steps back to the car park at Stephen Park. Maps of the route are available at the café.

NEED TO KNOW

A PLACE TO EAT: The Spread Eagle Inn in Sawley (BB7 4NH) offers wheelchair-accessible facilities, including accessible parking and dining areas.

A PLACE TO DRINK: There is a small café at Gisburn Forest that offers takeaway refreshments.

A PLACE TO SLEEP: The Spinning Block Hotel at Holmes Mill in Clitheroe (BB7 1EB) offers accessible accommodation with two specially designed rooms featuring wet rooms and wheelchair access throughout the property.

IF YOU'RE LOOKING FOR SOMETHING ELSE…

The Ingleborough Estate Nature Trail in Clapham, Yorkshire Dales, is a 3km (1.3 mile) woodland walk for all ages and abilities. The tarmac, gently sloping path passes a lake, river valley, and ends at Ingleborough Cave, which is wheelchair accessible. A powered mobility scooter is available by pre-booking.

The trail features exotic plants introduced by Reginald Farrer and seasonal highlights like spring rhododendrons and bluebells.

SPROTBROUGH

DONCASTER, SOUTH YORKSHIRE

ANDI WHITE

Heading to Doncaster for a stile-free walk might not sound like the start of a grand adventure, but as I pulled into the village of Sprotbrough on a golden June afternoon, I felt that unmistakable flutter of anticipation. I'd been promised something extraordinary: a viaduct longer and higher than the iconic Ribblehead in the Yorkshire Dales. A towering feat of engineering, hidden away in plain sight. Few knew about it. Fewer still had walked beneath its shadow.

My guide for the day was Andi White, filmmaker, presenter, author and devoted train enthusiast, who greeted me outside The Boat Inn with an infectious grin and the energy of someone about to reveal a well-kept secret. Around us, the South Yorkshire Navigation Canal buzzed with early summer life. Narrowboats gently nudged the lock gates, ducks pattered across the water and voices echoed from the towpath.

What struck me instantly was the sheer greenness of it all. Trees arched overhead, thick and vibrant, filtering sunlight into soft patterns across the path. We were barely a couple of miles from Doncaster town centre, yet it felt like we'd stumbled into a pocket of countryside which time had quietly preserved.

Somewhere up ahead, behind the trees and turns of the trail, the great viaduct waited. Andi promised it would stop me in my tracks.

'Welcome to my part of the world,' Andi declared with a wide sweep of her arm.

Born and bred in Doncaster, Andi radiated pride as she spoke about the walk she'd planned. Her filmmaking career had since taken her all over the UK

– even as far afield as the Falklands and the Scilly Isles – yet no matter where she travelled, Doncaster always called her home.

'It's a gentle stroll,' she announced, already settling into a rhythm. 'Walking doesn't always have to mean climbing mountains or chasing trig points. For me, it's about being outdoors, in beautiful places like this. This stretch of canal has been my sanctuary for years. I never grow tired of it.'

Andi had studied filmmaking at Wolverhampton University, and soon after graduation she landed a dream role in Rome as a filming assistant. It was there, amid the bustle of Italy's capital, that she first discovered her appreciation for stillness. 'I'd sit for hours,' she said, 'just watching the world go by, tourists racing from one landmark to the next like they were collecting stamps. That's when I realised: the outdoors aren't there to be rushed.'

We meandered along the wide, purpose-built multi-use track that flanked the early stretch of the canal. The water shimmered beside us, birdsong trickled from the trees and the scent of early summer hung in the air like a promise. This was no adrenaline-charged hike, but something deeper: a slow immersion into place, memory and hidden wonder.

We paused at a raised platform overlooking the river, a quiet spot where the River Don split in two, one half continuing its natural course, the other diverted

ANDI WHITE AT SPROTBOROUGH

into the canal. Below us, the water lay calm, disturbed only by a few gentle ripples stirred by the breeze. Trees leaned over the banks as if listening to the quiet murmur of the current.

'This walk tells a story,' Andi said, gazing out over the scene. 'It has a beginning, a middle and an end.'

Storytelling, it seemed, had always been in her blood. She credits her parents for planting the seed. As a child, she'd been captivated by television, not just cartoons or glossy shows but classic cinema. She spoke fondly of watching Harold Lloyd, the legendary American silent film star, whose comedies relied not on dialogue but on visual wit and clever effects, especially impressive for their time.

'That's when I first started wondering how things were made,' she said. 'Back then, film was magic.'

Her dad recognised that spark early on and gave her a cine camera – a bulky, whirring device that became her prized possession. She started filming mock game shows in the sixth form common room, roping in fellow students as contestants. From those early reels, a filmmaker was born.

While studying in Wolverhampton, Andi began to explore short walks through the Black Country – known to locals as 'Little Venice' for its intricate network of canals, even more extensive than those in Venice itself. It was there that her love of walking merged with her love of film. The landscapes, the characters, the quiet details of everyday life – they all became material for her lens.

'Whether I'm making something for TV or just out filming on my own,' she explained, 'my goal is always the same: entertain, inform and educate.'

She said it simply, but with conviction. And as we stood there, surrounded by water and sky and the soft hush of nature, it was easy to see how storytelling, whether in film or in footsteps, had become the guiding theme of Andi's life.

A little further along the track, we passed beneath a railway bridge, the ironwork above us weathered and echoing with stories of countless journeys. This was no abandoned relic – it carried the main Liverpool to Cleethorpes line, and right on cue, we heard the distant rattle of a train approaching.

As it thundered overhead, Andi looked up with unmistakable enthusiasm. 'That was a 185 DMU,' she announced.

I gave her a sideways glance, eyebrows raised.

'Diesel Multiple Unit,' she explained with a grin, 'basically a self-powered train, no need for a separate locomotive.'

I had to admit, I was impressed. This was no casual interest; this was genuine knowledge, spoken with the kind of affection usually reserved for old friends.

'The love of trains,' she said, 'definitely runs in the family.'

Andi told me about her grandfather, who had worked as a shunter at Rotherham Masborough Station, a role long since vanished but vital in its time. Her dad, too, had inherited the railway bug, and Andi, as a young child, would often tag along on days out around Doncaster, watching and waiting for the big engines to roar by – *The Mallard*, *The Flying Scotsman*, names that carried the same weight and wonder as mythical beasts.

But it was during family holidays in Wales that her fascination truly took root.

'We'd be in the mountains or by the coast, but I was always scanning the horizon for trains,' she said. 'I started jotting down engine numbers, making notes – proper old-school trainspotting.'

A trainspotter, she explained, wasn't just someone who liked trains. It was a hobby of precision and patience, identifying locomotive numbers, types, classes and histories. A kind of railway archaeology for the enthusiastically curious.

'And for me,' Andi added, 'it's not just about the trains; it's the stories they carry, the places they connect. Every train has a purpose. A past.'

We walked on to the rhythmic turn of my wheels on the path, the lingering hum of the train now long gone. It struck me then how deeply personal this walk was for Andi. Every path, every sight and sound seemed to connect to a memory, each one quietly shaping the story we were unfolding with every step.

With a deep-rooted passion for transport, Andi naturally turned her camera to railways, buses, trams and the now-lost trolleybuses. Long before the rise of YouTube, she and lifelong friend Gareth Atherton began producing transport documentaries on VHS. Their first release, *Buses of the South Yorkshire PTE: 1974–1986*, came out in 1997, and was driven by nostalgia, curiosity and their love of everyday transport.

'This was always more than a hobby,' Andi said as we strolled on.

The path gently curved around us, following the river's easy rhythm. This stretch of the Trans Pennine Trail had come alive with weekend walkers, families, dog owners and a few cyclists gliding past with polite nods. The mood was unhurried; this was the kind of place where conversations unfolded naturally between strangers.

'This is what's so lovely about this walk,' Andi said, motioning to the people around us. 'There's a real social side to walking – especially when you're away from the honey-pot places. Here, people relax. You see real lives, real moments.'

It was during a walk like this, she told me, that an idea first took root – there was clearly an untapped market for accessible, gentle walks. Not treks up snowy peaks or ten-hour slogs, but realistic outings with scenery, stories, and a pace that welcomed families and first-timers.

And so, Walks Around Britain, which focused on short walks between 2 and 8 miles (or 3.2km 13km) was born, which soon became a successful TV series.

But storytelling was never confined to documentaries alone. In February 2022, Andi took a new step publishing her first novel, *A New World*, the opening title in *The Walker Mysteries*. Fiction allowed her to explore new terrain, blending her knowledge of landscapes with suspenseful storytelling.

And now, here we were, walking one of her favourite routes, retracing the quiet roots of her journey, both as a filmmaker and as a person who had turned her passion into her life's work.

Andi married in 2001. The relationship brought two daughters into the world, Alannah and Olivia, and for a time, life carried a surface-level sense of stability. But beneath it all, something vital was missing.

Andi described the relationship as 'more of a partnership than a marriage'. As a stay-at-home parent, Andi struggled with the day-to-day routines, tasks started but never finished, trails of mess left behind, and a growing tension that hung in the air like a storm cloud. Arguments were common. Confidence, once present, began to unravel thread by thread.

The threat of divorce was a constant drumbeat.

When Alannah was diagnosed with ADHD, Andi saw mirrored patterns – restlessness, distraction, flashes of brilliance and confusion all at once. It prompted a long-overdue self-reflection, and in 2023, Andi underwent an assessment that changed everything. The diagnosis confirmed what she had quietly suspected for years: she also had ADHD.

And with that understanding came a profound shift.

'I realised I wasn't a "shit adult",' she said. 'I just didn't know I was wired differently.'

But that wasn't the only truth waiting to be unearthed. The clarity sparked by the diagnosis gave Andi the courage to examine something even deeper. There was a quiet truth, buried for decades, that now rose to the surface with undeniable force: Andi, known as Andrew at the time, was not a man pretending to cope. Andi was a woman waiting to live.

'I was trapped,' Andi said. 'Trapped in an unhappy marriage and trapped in a man's body.'

As part of her gender expression, Andrew announced she was now using the name Andi. She spoke about having experienced significant gender dysphoria throughout her life. For her, it's the journey that matters most, the process of becoming whole.

It began with quiet admissions to close friends, confessions that weren't met with shock but with understanding. On New Year's Day 2024, Andi came out to her wife. It was, inevitably, the end of their turbulent marriage. The pain of that ending was real, but so too was the relief of stepping into truth.

Throughout this storm of change, green space remained her sanctuary. Time outdoors, on familiar paths and quiet trails, offered space to think, to grieve, to breathe.

Moving out of the family home marked the beginning of a new chapter. Slowly, tentatively, Andi began to rebuild, not into someone new, but into the person she had always known herself to be. The first bold expression came in the form of a pair of pink Dr. Martens, followed by the courage to walk into the world in a flowing denim skirt, a bright blouse and the weight of a lifetime lifted from her shoulders.

'My daughters have been amazing. And my close friends. Their support has meant everything.'

Eventually, she hopes to have gender-affirming surgery. Her goal, quietly and confidently, is to blossom fully into Andrea.

As we walked, Andi pointed out subtle signs of past industry and regeneration. And then, rising suddenly and dramatically into view, the Conisbrough Viaduct appeared, a truly unforgettable sight. As we finally arrived beneath its soaring arches it was impossible not to feel the symbolism. This towering, quiet giant, hidden in plain sight, was the perfect reflection of Andi's strength: solid, patient, enduring.

We stood under the shadow of its grandeur, the air still around us, until the sudden, almost comic burst of music from a passing canal cruiser shattered the quiet. A hen party was on board, the laughter unmistakable, the anthem unmistakable too: Gloria Gaynor's 'I Am What I Am.'

Andi laughed, a bright, full sound that echoed under the arch.

'Perfect timing,' she said.

And in that moment, as the music echoed down the canal and the viaduct stood tall behind us, it was clear: Andi's walk wasn't just about where she'd come from or what she'd seen. It was about who she'd become, step by step, truth by truth.

And she was still walking, still unfolding. As we approached, the viaduct grew ever larger, each arch framing the landscape in a different way. It felt like walking towards a cathedral of brick and iron, standing not for worship but for wonder. It was a fitting climax to our gentle walk, and a powerful metaphor for Andi's own journey which was built on endurance, shaped by history and open now to a new path ahead.

THE WALK

◎ IS IT FOR ME?

START/END POINT: The Boat Inn Sprotbrough, Doncaster, DN5 7NB, turning point at the Conisbrough Viaduct

GRID REFERENCE: SE549024

DISTANCE: 5.4km (3.4 miles) there and back to Conisbrough Viaduct

MILES WITHOUT STILES GRADE: For All

TERRAIN: Tarmac track, with gentle slopes

ACCESSIBILITY: Paths are accessible for manual wheelchairs.

PARKING: The pub car park is for guests only but there are some roadside parking spaces available.

FACILITIES: The pub at the start of the walk has accessible toilet facilities.

➤ THE ROUTE

Facing the River Don, we turned right along the smooth tarmac track – a path that gently winds its way along the water's edge. This is an easy-going 'there and back' route, giving you the freedom to turn back whenever you feel ready. But we had a clear destination in mind: the Conisbrough Viaduct, just over 2.7km (1.7 miles) away.

This section forms part of the Trans Pennine Trail – a coast-to-coast route across northern England, between Southport on the west coast and Hornsea on the east coast. Following former railways and canal paths, it's designed for walkers, cyclists and horse riders. Here, the trail traces the South Yorkshire Navigation Canal, offering a peaceful, history-rich alternative to busier countryside paths.

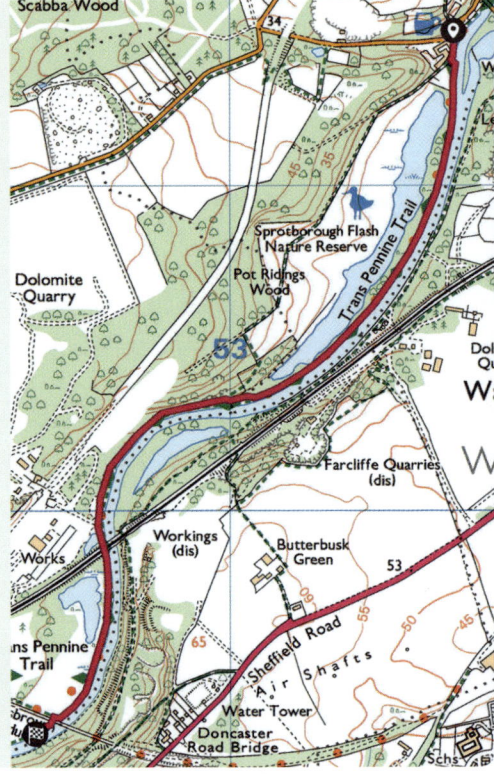

ACCESS ADVENTURE

At 465m (1,527ft)-long, with 21 arches and a 46m (150ft) lattice iron girder span over the River Don, the Conisbrough Viaduct is a striking feat of early 20th-century engineering. Opened in 1909, it linked the Hull and Barnsley line with the Great Northern and Great Eastern railways. After its closure in 1965, it was rescued by Railway Paths in 2001 and, along with the charity Sustrans, transformed into a formal cycleway by 2010.

NEED TO KNOW

A PLACE TO EAT AND DRINK: The Boat Inn, a charming 17th-century riverside pub right next to Sprotbrough Lock, has served the local community since around 1652 (one story even credits Sir Walter Scott with penning part of *Ivanhoe* during a visit). Having survived floods, it was lovingly restored in recent years to retain its characterful old style interior, making it the perfect spot to gather before or after your canalside walk.

A PLACE TO SLEEP: The Hex Wildlife Hotel at Yorkshire Wildlife Park (DN9 3QY) offers a thoughtful selection of accessible rooms, complete with roll-in showers, grab rails, lowered towel rails and wider doorways.

IF YOU'RE LOOKING FOR SOMETHING ELSE...

Yorkshire Wildlife Park, located just outside Doncaster, is home to around 475 animals. It is wheelchair accessible, with Blue Badge parking bays and Changing Places facilities. The park is widely praised for its commitment to inclusivity. Most pathways are level, paved and gently graded, making them suitable for wheelchair users and pushchairs. Mobility scooters can be hired on site.

THE YORKSHIRE WILDLIFE PARK

NATEBY FELL

YORKSHIRE DALES NATIONAL PARK

ADAM MEDLOCK

Tucked away at the northern edge of the Yorkshire Dales National Park, the small village of Nateby sits quietly in the Cumbrian landscape, where rolling fields give way to the rugged beauty of the fells beyond. Though officially part of Cumbria, Nateby shares the distinctive character of the Dales – dry stone walls, winding lanes and a deep-rooted connection to the land. From its doorstep rise the wild, open fells that reach southward, offering sweeping views, solitude and a gateway to some of the most unspoiled countryside in England. It was here that I would meet with Adam Medlock.

Adam, born in Cleckheaton and now living in Halifax with his wife, Amy-Rose, spoke with quiet passion about the landscape.

'This place holds such a special spot in my heart,' he said, and as we stood looking out across the stillness of the fells, it was easy to understand why. Ahead of us, the narrow road to Swaledale wound through the open access land like a dark thread, inviting the eye, and the mind, to wander. Sheep grazed undisturbed on either side, scattered across the rough grass, while the fells rose gently beyond, their soft contours etched against the pale sky.

Adam still feels the pull of this place, though he visits far less often than he once did. His mum and stepdad had lived on a farm just above the village, and he and Amy-Rose were regular visitors there. Long, free days were spent exploring the hills and learning the shape of the land. But now, life is busier, the visits fewer, and the journey to Nateby has become something more personal. Now, he returns mostly on special days to experience moments of quiet remembrance for his stepdad, whose presence lingers in every familiar curve of the landscape. The road towards Swaledale seemed to carry those memories with it, winding gently through a place that to Adam still feels, unmistakably, like home.

'When my mum and stepdad first showed me their new home, I instantly knew this place was going to be a part of me' Adam recalled. 'They had first seen the house years ago while hiking the Coast to Coast Walk, and it felt destined to become a cherished retreat.'

We paused to catch our breath beside a weathered wooden fingerpost, one of those familiar markers where countless Coast to Coast walkers have paused before, leaning on it briefly to gather strength or simply take in the view. The quiet of the fells surrounded us, the only sounds the soft rustle of wind through the grass and the distant bleating of sheep. It was there, in that stillness, that Adam began to speak quietly about the challenges he had faced over the past few years. These were stories he rarely shared outside of the safe circle of his immediate family and his closest friend, Kane.

As his words came, a tear welled in his eye, an unspoken testament to the weight he carried and, without hesitation, we hugged. The hug was a silent exchange of support and understanding, a fragile but powerful connection amid the vast openness of the landscape. The fells, with their timeless presence, seemed to hold the space for his grief, absorbing it without judgement.

VIEWS ACROSS NATEBY FELLS

DEBBIE AND ADAM AT THE SUMMIT OF INGLEBOROUGH

When we eventually moved on, Adam's story emerged gradually, each word weighted with hardship yet underscored by a quiet, steady resilience. It was the kind of honesty that feels rare and deeply human, something that only rises to the surface when the world slows down, when the landscape around you falls silent enough to listen, offering its own wordless kind of comfort.

Growing up, Adam had both a birth father and a stepdad after his mum remarried. Both men were very different, and both were called Andy, which was quite convenient for his mum! His birth father was extremely organised and operated with military precision, while his stepdad was the complete opposite – untidy, laid-back, and almost horizontal in his relaxed demeanour.

'I am told that I came from a broken home,' he says with a laugh. 'But I don't see it like that, 'cos I've had the best of both worlds. I learned practical skills from my dad, and my stepdad taught me to follow my dreams and just go for it.'

Life as a teenager was good for Adam. Having graduated from Leeds College of Music, he qualified as a special needs teacher and started on a career that would lead him to becoming headteacher at a special school in Halifax. He fell in love with a beautiful lady, marrying Amy-Rose in the summer of 2016.

'It was a wonderful day. My family unit is small – just my mum, stepdad, dad and stepmum – and it was lovely to see all four parents come together to share and celebrate our special day.'

However, shortly after the wedding, his father's health began to deteriorate after a long battle with cancer. The newly married couple spent countless hours at his father's bedside in the hospice in Halifax.

'It was murder watching my father fade away. Each day he grew weaker, and every visit brought fresh heartache.'

Adam found solace in the countryside, where the vast open spaces gave him room to process his thoughts and emotions. Visits to his mum and stepdad in Cumbria became a refuge, the wide, rolling fells offering him a chance to breathe deeply and lift the weight of his grief, even if only for a little while. His dad, Andrew Medlock, passed away in early 2017.

While Adam was dealing with his dad's illness, there was a dramatic change in his mum's health, too, and eventually she would undergo a 12-hour operation.

'My stepdad and I spent the day walking the streets around the hospital, both of us avoiding mentioning how we were fretting over whether his wife and my mum would get through the operation. But she did. She is made of strong stuff!'

By now, we had reached the brow of the hill, where the landscape unfurled before us in a breathtaking panorama. A sharp intake of breath came almost instinctively as we turned to take in the full 360-degree view. Straight ahead, the imposing bulk of Wild Boar Fell commanded the skyline, its rugged flanks etched sharply against the pale sky. Further on, the gentle contours of the Howgills emerged through the haze, their soft, rounded peaks rising like waves in the distance. To our right, beyond a quilt of green fields and dry stone walls, the Lake District revealed itself, Blencathra's flat, unmistakable summit anchoring the far horizon. Behind us, the rolling outlines of the Northern Pennines faded into layers of blue and grey.

It was a place that invited stillness. We sat for a while in quiet awe, letting the beauty settle around us, soaking in the vastness and silence of the hills.

Adam, six-foot-four with an athletic build, had always valued fitness. In recent years, he'd taken up Brazilian jiu-jitsu, committing to training at least twice a week. But it wasn't just martial arts that had captured his imagination. He and Amy found a new passion: wild swimming. 'The cold water is exhilarating,' he remarked with a smile. The couple spent many happy weekends exploring hidden streams, secret pools and remote tarns, eagerly plunging into the chilly waters.

Amy, who had struggled with ill health in her younger years, found strength and joy in this shared adventure. Alongside Adam's mum and stepdad, they'd begun taking on new challenges, climbing mountains across the Lake District and the Yorkshire Dales, pushing their limits while embracing the stunning countryside around them. Life had demanded a significant adjustment for Adam's mum when she became a wheelchair user, but that had never stopped the family from seeking out days of laughter and discovery in the outdoors. Together, they carved out new ways to experience the wild beauty that had always drawn them back to these hills.

'We have a secret tarn up there, beyond that hill,' Adam said, nodding towards the cairn that marked the skyline. 'We've spent many a happy hour swimming in it.' His eyes lit up at the memory, a quiet joy carried in his voice. As we made our way across the road and up onto Nateby Common, he smiled and added, 'The views up there are even more incredible. But the best time to go swimming is at sunset when the light begins to shift and everything turns golden.' He paused for a moment, lost in thought. 'There was one time, it felt almost sacred. The clouds had gathered, dark and heavy, but then the sky opened just enough, and those beams – "God Light" – streamed down through the gap. It lit up the tarn like something out of a dream. We just stood there, soaking wet and shivering, but completely still. It felt like the world was holding its breath.'

It was clear that this place, with all its weather and wildness, had offered not just adventure but moments of quiet wonder – memories held close and returned to often.

In 2021, Adam received more devastating news: his stepdad was diagnosed with an aggressive form of cancer that was untreatable. Within just eight weeks of the diagnosis, he passed away. During these dark times, Adam turned to the countryside for peace and reflection. Dealing with the grief of losing two fathers was incredibly challenging, but he found comfort in being surrounded by nature.

The climb up to the cairn at Tailbridge, across open access land, was challenging – even for me, an experienced user of an all-terrain wheelchair. The terrain was rough and uneven, clumps of stubborn grass and steep inclines demanding every bit of concentration and effort. But there was something exhilarating about going off-piste, pushing beyond the usual tracks and taking on the wildness of the land head-on. Reaching the cairn felt like a real accomplishment, a moment of quiet triumph earned with grit and determination.

ADAM WITH HIS SON MICHAEL

From the top, the views opened up in all directions, and they were nothing short of spectacular. To one side lay the sweeping emptiness of Dukerdale, a hidden valley wrapped in silence and solitude. In front of us rose High Seat, its broad shoulders rising gently into the sky. This was no ordinary hill; it was a place of deep personal meaning. 'That's where Andy rests,' he said quietly. His stepdad's ashes were scattered there, at the cairn, forever part of the landscape he had loved so much.

We saw no one else all afternoon, no walkers, no distant figures on the ridgelines, just the two of us alone in the wide silence of the fells. This place invites reflection, the wind seeming to carry memories and the earth holding on to stories. In that stillness, there was peace.

Adam has shown immense resilience and inner strength in coping with everything life has thrown his way. But through it all, he has held on to what matters most: life, in all its messiness and beauty, goes on. I see the pride in his eyes when he talks about Amy-Rose, and the quiet admiration he carries for her strength and spirit. I see it too when he speaks about his role as a headteacher – how hard he has worked, how far he's come.

But it was when he became a father that something shifted in him. Holding his newborn son, Michael Andrew, who was born in May 2024, Adam finally allowed himself to exhale.

'My son will grow up with a love of the outdoors,' he said, standing beside me, gazing across the hills. 'Life is good. I love my wife. I love my son. And I love you, Mum.'

I smiled through tears, quietly taking in the view and the moment.

Because I am his mum.

I am Debbie North.

THE WALK

IS IT FOR ME?

START/END POINT: Rakehead Farm, Nateby (CA17 4JR)
GRID REFERENCE: NY776068
DISTANCE: 9.2km (5.7 miles) circular
MILES WITHOUT STILES GRADE: For Some
TERRAIN: Grassy slopes on open access land
ACCESSIBILITY: Much of this walk crosses open access land, where the terrain is uneven and can be demanding underfoot. For those using an all-terrain wheelchair, I recommend the shorter route to the lime kiln as a rewarding yet suitably challenging option. A TerrainHopper – a robust, 4x4 all-terrain wheelchair – is available to borrow from Rakehead Farm in Nateby. This offers a fantastic opportunity for people with reduced mobility to experience the wild beauty of the fells with added confidence and stability.
PARKING: Off-road parking is available next to the farm.
FACILITIES: Accessible toilets available in nearby Kirkby Stephen.

THE ROUTE

From Rakehead Farm, follow the road as it climbs gently towards Swaledale. On dry days, when the ground is firm, it's possible to head up through Middleber Sike. Just beyond the quarry on your left, take the track on the right that leads you out onto open access land. This rough path skirts alongside a wall before guiding you towards an old lime kiln, a striking reminder of the area's industrial past. Since this is open access land, take the chance to wander freely. Climb to the top of the kiln for sweeping 360-degree views across the fells – a perfect spot to pause and take it all in.

To continue, return to the road, picking your way carefully until a clear track branches off to the left, cutting beneath the craggy outline of Great Edge. Follow this to the boundary fence, then make your ascent toward the cairn. The return leg takes you back along the quiet road, descending steeply via Tailbridge. With very little traffic along this stretch, it offers a peaceful and safe end to the journey.

There's no need to rush – this is a walk to savour. In spring, curlews call out across the fells, and the air is alive with the bubbling song of skylarks overhead.

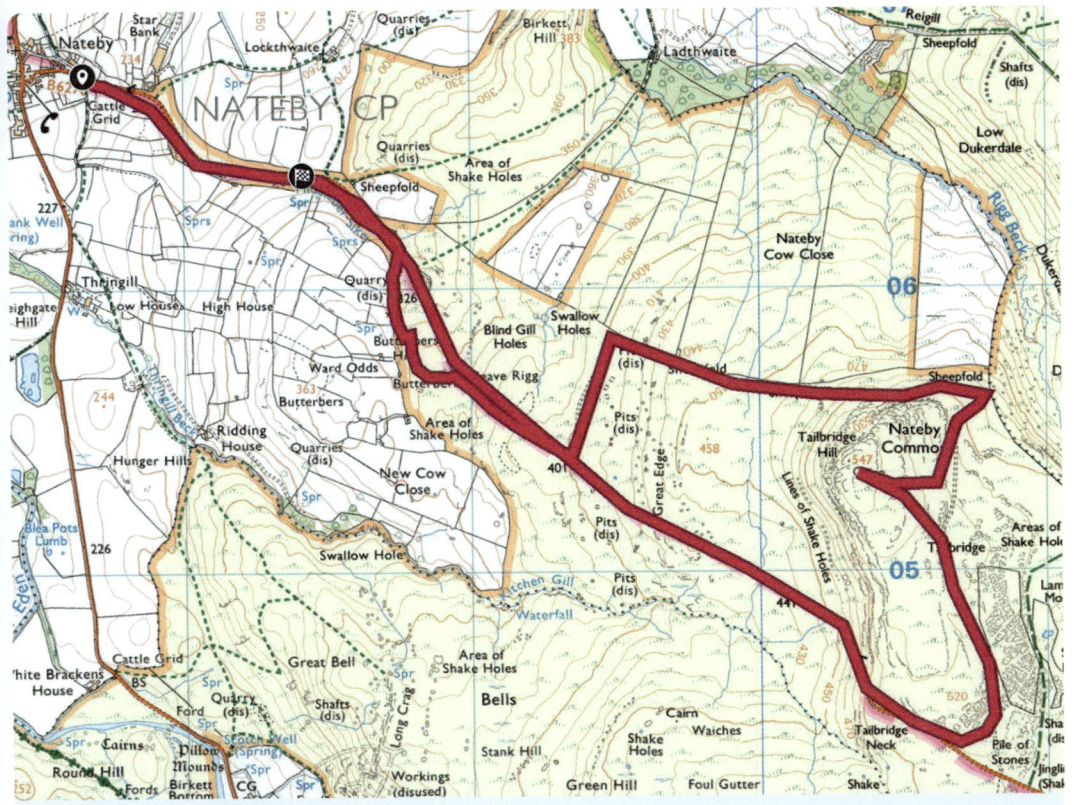

🏠 NEED TO KNOW

A PLACE TO EAT: Pennine View Caravan & Camping Park (CA17 4SZ), just outside Nateby, is home to The Engine Shed, a quirky and welcoming venue for food and drink.

A PLACE TO DRINK: The Berry Grain & Grape in Kirkby Stephen (CA17 4QW) is a charming café and deli offering a curated selection of wines and a tempting deli counter.

A PLACE TO SLEEP: The Pennine View Caravan & Camping Park (CA17 4SZ) offers accessible facilities, making it a convenient and inclusive base for exploration.

♣ IF YOU'RE LOOKING FOR SOMETHING ELSE…

The **wheelchair hub** at Eden Ewe Nique Lonnin, Tebay (CA10 3XZ), supported by Access the Dales, offers the Tramper – a rugged all-terrain wheelchair for exploring the peaceful Howgills foothills. Perfect for solitude and stunning views. More info: *www.access-the-dales.com*

USEFUL WEBSITES

The following websites were all correct at time of writing.

www.debbienorth.org

www.access-the-dales.com

www.lakedistrict.gov.uk/visiting/things-to-do/walking/mileswithoutstiles

www.peakdistrict.gov.uk/visiting/miles-without-stiles

www.yorkshiredales.org.uk/plan-your-visit/essential-information/access-for-all/miles-without-stiles

https://www.southdowns.gov.uk/get-active/south-downs-walks/miles-without-stiles

https://www.northyorkmoors.org.uk/access-for-all/miles-without-stiles

https://www.dartmoor.gov.uk/enjoy-dartmoor/outdoor-activities/accessible-dartmoor/miles-without-stiles

https://www.exmoor-nationalpark.gov.uk/exmoor-for-everyone/walking/miles-without-stiles

https://countrysidemobility.org

https://www.outdoormobility.org

centrepoint.org.uk

forestryandland.gov.scot

www.forestryengland.uk

www.mind.org.uk

www.mindovermountains.org.uk

www.nationaltrust.org.uk

naturalresources.wales

www.papyrus-uk.org

www.semcharity.org.uk

www.sustrans.org.uk

www.walkingpace.uk

www.wwt.org.uk

www.woodlandtrust.org.uk

https://www.cotswolds-nl.org.uk/exploring/self-guided-route/stow-on-the-wold-miles-without-stiles

INDEX

100 Black Men Walking group 165

Abbots Leigh, Somerset 70–6
Adventure Queens grants and community 152–3
Anglesey 42–9
Ashdown Forest, East Sussex 90–5
Ayamba, Maxwell 164–8

Balding, Claire 13
Bannau Brycheiniog (Brecon Beacons) National Park, South 50–7
beaches, Suffolk
Beacon Fell Country Park, Lancashire 190–7
Brown, Genny 142–5
Budleigh Salterton, Devon 84–9
Bush family 134–9
Butterfield, Chris 177–81

castles and forts
    Beaumaris Castle, Anglesey 49
    Dover Castle, Kent 141
    Helmsley Castle, North York Moors 23
    Landguard Fort, Suffolk 155
    Martello Towers, Folkestone 134, 139
    Sandgate Castle, Folkestone 135
Clipper Round the World Yacht Race 174
Coast to Coast Walk 12–13, 174, 213
Coniston to Tarn Hows, Lake District 36
Cornwall 77–83
Craig-y-nos Country Park, South Wales 50–7
Crute, Dee 70–5
Cullen to Portknockie, Moray, Scotland 171–6
Cumbria 10–15, 24–9, 30–9, 212–19

Devon 84–9
Doncaster, South Yorkshire 204–9
Dorking, Surrey 142–7
Dornan, Sarah 190–5

Edinbane, Isle of Skye 184–9
environmental activism and advocacy 80–1, 165, 166–7, 192–4
Eyam village, Derbyshire 170

Felixstowe Beach, Suffolk 163
Folkestone Coastal Path, Kent 134–41
Folkestone Warren, Kent 120–5
Forest of Bowland National Landscape 190–7
fossil hunting 85
Fraser-Higgins, Declan 198–201

gardens and parks
    Eden Project, Cornwall 83
    Forth Valley Sensory Centre, Scotland 183
    Hergest Croft Gardens, Herefordshire 69
    Polesden Lacey, North Downs 147
Generation Green programme 92
geocaching 31–2
Gisburn Forest, Ribble Valley, Lancashire 198–203
Gloucestershire 58–63

Hampshire 126–33
Handley, Bethany 58–61
Harris, Darren 104–9
Harris, Karen 50–5
Harrison, Emma 96–101
Hart, Aarron 24–9
Heartwood Forest, Hertfordshire 96–103
Helmsley, North York Moors 23
Herefordshire Trail 66
Hergest Ridge, Herefordshire 64–9
Hertfordshire 96–103
Holmwood Common, Dorking, Surrey 142–5
horse-riding 112–16

Ingleborough Estate Nature Trail, Clapham, Yorkshire Dales 203
Isle of Skye, Scotland 184–9

Jackson, Georgina 171–4

Kelpies to the Falkirk Wheel, Scotland 177–81
Kent Heritage Coast 120–5
Kenyon, Isaac 84–7
Kerwin-Nye, Anita 90–3
King Charles III England Coast Path 134–41
Kings Wood, St Austell, Cornwall 77–83
Kovacs, Marika 64–9

Lady Canning's Plantation, Ringinglow, South Yorkshire 164–70
Lake District National Park
   Coniston to Tarn Hows 36–9
   Orrest Head 30–5
   Threlkeld to Keswick 24–9
Lancashire 190–7
landmarks and attractions
   animal sculptures, Heartwood Forest 96–7
   Castlerigg Stone Circle, Keswick 29
   Clearwell Caves, Forest of Dean 63
   Cobble Hill Farm, Forest of Bowland 197
   Donkey Farm, Sidmouth 89
   Kelpies and the Falkirk Wheel, Scotland 177, 181
   Polesden Lacy, North Downs 147
   Ribblehead Viaduct, Cumbria 17
   Sutton Hoo Anglo-Saxon burials, Suffolk 156
   Talybont Reservoir, Bannau Brycheiniog (Brecon Beacons) National Park 57
   The *Watercut*, Mallerstang Valley 10–13
   WDC Scottish Dolphin Centre, Moray 176
   White Cliffs of Dover, Kent 125
   White Horse, Cleveland Way 16, 19
   Yorkshire Wildlife Park 211
   see also castles and forts; gardens and parks; museums and heritage centres
Leigh Woods, Abbots Leigh, Somerset 70–6
Lowestoft South Beach, Suffolk

Mallerstang Valley, Cumbria 10–15
Medlock, 212–17
Miles Without Styles grades 9
Millennium Quay, Portsmouth, Hampshire 126–33
Mind Over Mountains charity 38–9
Mitchell, Gini 120–3
Moray, Scotland 171–6
museums and heritage centres
   Big Pit National Coal Museum, South Wales 57
   Dorking Museum & Heritage Centre, Hertfordshire 103
   Mary Rose Museum, Portsmouth 133
   Pencil Museum, Keswick 29
   Ruskin Museum, Coniston 41
   see also castles and forts

Nateby Fell, Yorkshire Dales National Park 212–19
nature and wildlife reserves
   British Wildlife Centre, Lingfield 95
   Budleigh Salterton Nature Reserve 84–9
   Lake District Wildlife Park, Keswick 29
   Leigh Woods National Nature Reserve 70–6
   Newborough National Nature Reserve and Forest, Anglesey 42–9
Newborough National Nature Reserve and Forest, Anglesey 42–9
Nixon, Pauline 126–33
North, Debbie 7, 10–15, 217
North York Moors National Park 16–23

Offa's Dyke Path 64
'One Mile Walks' programme, Walking Pace 93
Orrest Head, Lake District 30–5

Palmer, Mike 42–7
Peak District National Park 164–70
'Penfold Adventures' project 134, 139
Pennine Way 178
Portsmouth, Hampshire 126–33

Quintrell, Stephanie Jane 112–16

railways 10, 17, 206–7
'Ramblings' BBC Radio 4 show 13
Raynor, Ozzy and Victoria 156–60
Redbrook, Wye Valley, Gloucestershire 58–63
Rendlesham UFO Forest, Nr Woodbridge, Suffolk 148–55
Ribble Valley, Lancashire 198–203
'Ride to Freedom' challenge, FWC 116
River Otter Estuary, Devon 84–9

Saint Austell, Cornwall 77–83
Settle–Carlisle railway 10, 17
Sheffield Environmental Movement (SEM) 166–7
Smith, Pat 77–81
Somerset 70–6
Sone, Natasha 148–53
South Downs National Park 112–19
South West Coast Path 73–4, 80
Southwold Beach, Suffolk 163
Sprotbrough, Doncaster, South Yorkshire 204–9
Staniforth, Alex 36–9
Stanstead Park, Stoughton, West Sussex 112–18
Suffolk 148–62
Surrey 142–7
Sussex
    East 90–5
    West 112–18
Sutton Bank, North York Moors 16–23
Sutton Hoo, Woodbridge, Suffolk 156–62
Sutton Park, West Midlands 104–11

Threlkeld to Keswick, Lake District 24–9
Towart family 30–3
Towers, Sara 16–21

Wainwright, Alfred 12, 30, 178, 179, 180–1
Walking Pace project 93
watersports and boating
    Baltic Wharf, Bristol 76
    Coniston Launch, Lake District 41
    Lake District 35
    Stardust Boat Trips, Isle of Skye 189

Sutton Sailing Club 111
    Wetwheels Solent, Portsmouth 119
West Highland Way 137–8
West Windermere Way, Lake District 33
wheelchair hub, Tebay, Yorkshire Dales 219
White, Andi 204–9
wild swimming 152, 215–16
Wild with Wheels project 122–3
Wye Valley, Gloucestershire 58–63

Yorkshire
    Dales National Park 203, 212–19
    North York Moors National Park 16–23
    South 164–70, 204–11

PHOTO CREDITS

Billy Richards Photography / Getty (p3)
Farm Images / Getty (p6)
Loop Images / Getty (p8, p15, p59, p63)
Eddie Hyde / 500px / Getty (p11)
Chris McLoughlin / Getty (p17, p18)
Andrew Turner / Getty (p21)
Andrea Pucci / Getty (p23)
Ashley Cooper / Getty (p35)
Lancashire Images / Alamy (p53)
Mike Kemp / Alamy (p67)
Thomas Faull / Getty (p81)
David Cayless / Getty (p83)
David Warren / Alamy (p105)
Graham Prentice / Alamy (p113)
Wetwheels Solent (p119)
Patrick Donovan / Alamy (p137)
Stephen French / Alamy (p138)
Medioimages / Photodisc / Getty (p141)
Jason Jones / Getty (p152)
ImageryBT / Getty (p211)

All other photographs by Debbie North